Masala Chai

Masala Chai

Spiced Tea

Vinod Luthra

Library of Congress Control Number: 2009911004
ISBN: Hardcover   978-1-4415-9055-8
                         Softcover   978-1-4415-9054-1

To order additional copies of this book, contact:
Xlibris Corporation
1-888-795-4274
www.Xlibris.com
Orders@Xlibris.com
68559

INTRODUCTION

I NDIA, THE LARGEST democracy in the world, has a political system similar to Britain, only it has a president as the figurehead rather than the queen. Politics can be a dirty game in India. Some politicians support and shelter criminal gangs and use them to intimidate the poor to secure votes. Often, slums are breeding grounds for crime and, at the same time, are recruiting grounds for terrorist organizations and criminal gangs.

Masala Chai (Spiced Tea) is a fictional romance-cum-social thesis and is intertwined with many heartfelt stories which revolve around a slum. It illuminates the plight of the three hundred million indigents who live in slums without proper sanitation and other facilities, which we in the Western world take for granted. *Masala Chai* also brings to life the close relationships, family values, and cultural traditions that enrich the lives of the people there despite their hardships. They always find time in their busy day to have a cup or two of *masala chai*!

India's mind-boggling growth rate stands at 11 percent, the middle class is getting bigger, the rich are getting richer, but the indigents are still there caught in a vicious circle of poverty. As a result, India is sitting on a pile of *barood* (dynamite) waiting to be ignited. The pundits (priests) of politics and politicians do not understand that you can only push the poor so far and, when their backs are against the wall, they will fight back or turn into terrorists. India is aflame with terrorist attacks. Poverty and jealousy abet terrorism, and it is propagated by corruption. The terrorist attacks on Mumbai were only possible as the terrorists were able to buy their way through the corrupt coast guards. Corruption must be eradicated to remove vulnerability and to secure India.

I have written this book to help the poor of India and that of the world at large; I will try to help them financially with the royalties received from the sale of this book.

CHAPTER 1

August 2010

A DELEGATION OF talented and jubilant British students was to represent their country at a youth festival at Talkatora Gardens in Delhi, India. Delegation members were chosen because of their talent in music, dance, and drama. As a doctor, Bharti was chosen to go with the contingent, but above all, she was a talented semiclassical Hindi singer and an outstanding Kathak (a form of Indian dance) dancer. Lucky to be chosen as most of them had never been to India, the students were so ecstatic at the thought of visiting mystic India that they were partying all night before catching the flight to Delhi in the morning.

At that time, Bharti was sharing a flat with her friend Heather in the heart of the fashion district of Chelsea in London. This expensive small centrally located flat was bought by Bharti's father, Mr. Kapoor, to make it more convenient for Bharti to go to medical school, especially when he was away on business so that he didn't have to leave her alone in a big house in a posh residential area of Hampstead Heath. Coming from a relatively poor background, Heather, a studious type, was more interested in becoming a doctor so she could start earning and was not interested in the extracurricular activities. Heather, one day, suddenly found herself on the street after being kicked out of her stepfather's house and was taken in by her true friend Bharti.

At the crack of dawn, while Bharti was packing, Heather remarked, "You're so lucky to be going to India. I hope you find a nice handsome prince, get married, and live happily ever after."

"No chance of that, Heather, as I'm not ready for that yet. Anyway, I'm not sure if I want to get married to an Indian in India. From what I hear, they are mostly male chauvinists, and I cannot stand a male chauvinist. Anyway, I have to finish my specialization, which won't be for another three years."

"Keep an open mind, missy."

"I believe in fate and destiny. I'll let you know if somebody blows me away, but I doubt it."

"Don't be so negative, love."

"I'm all packed. The cab must be on its way to take me to the airport."

Bharti and Heather hugged each other. "Have a good time, now that you'll be all alone in the flat," Bharti remarked.

"You too, and don't do anything I wouldn't do!"

"That leaves my options wide-open knowing you, love."

"Now, that's being nasty."

"You know I didn't mean it that way," Bharti whispered and then hugged Heather again.

The student council of Delhi University was the organizer of the youth festival and was also responsible for providing accommodation and looking after the welfare of all the students coming from all over the world to take part in the festival for ten days. Accommodation was arranged all over Delhi, but the one close to the venue was given to the contingents taking part in the variety program of music, dance, and drama to be held at the Talkatora Gardens.

Lush green gardens with intermittent water masses and vibrant flowers epitomize the beauty of the gardens. Built according to Mogul style, Talkatora Gardens is a delight to the discerning tourists. Swimming pools, three colossal gateways, and a centrally placed indoor stadium are some of the special features of this architectural monument. The soft-scented breeze at the gardens rejuvenates the tired soul and invigorates the body; Talkatora Gardens has the magical charm of Mogul design. The gardens boast of exquisite restaurants and an international cuisine food bazaar to quench your thirst and tantalize your appetite.

Coming out of the arrival lounge in the hustle and bustle of the passengers where everybody was trying to get ahead of the others, hundreds of relatives and other people were standing around with name placards to receive their loved ones. Bharti was grabbed by a man from behind, and in anger, she turned around with the intention of hitting the person grabbing her, but was totally stunned to see her father. The anger through the catalyst of surprise turned into love as she grabbed and kissed him on the cheek several times and, at the same time, questioned, "How are you here, you are supposed to be in America?"

"To surprise you, I cut my trip short. Anyway, most of my work was done in America, but most importantly, I wanted to make you feel comfortable in India. You're the only person in my life that matters, and I want to make sure that your trip to India is a pleasant one that you have been looking forward to for such a long time."

"Thank you very much, Papa." And she hugged him again. "But I'm planning to stay with the rest of the students as I have to be their doctor, but that doesn't mean I won't spend any time with you as it is always a pleasure to see you. By the way, have the contractors finished the renovations of the Golf Links house?"

"Yes, my dear. It is all ready and equipped with a chef and one maid waiting for you to arrive."

"I might want to have a get-together with my friends a couple of times and, for sure, will stay for a little while after the festivities are over, especially now that you're here. I'll have an opportunity to spend some time with you, which I've not had in the last three months as I was busy with my pediatrics program and you were busy with your business expansion."

"How are you going to your assigned accommodation, and what's your program here?"

"The student council in Delhi sent us an e-mail and told us the location of the culture programs and accommodation. There should be a couple of liaison students who will arrange the transportation et cetera for us. Yes, I see a couple of girls holding a placard for the English contingent. Okay, Papa, bye for now, and I'll call you on your cell phone as soon as we have things settled." And she hugged and kissed her father.

The English delegation was given accommodation in a youth hostel within walking distance from Talkatora Gardens. They sat down with the host students Rita and Meena and gave them a list of all the performers in the contingent; in turn, they were informed that lists of selected and not selected performances would be placed on the notice board outside the auditorium for three days at a time. All the performances were scheduled for the evening only, and in the morning, the performers rehearsed for the evening performances. They were also given relevant informative tourist maps including material for the Talkatora Gardens and the surrounding area.

Next morning, excitement took over their fatigue from travelling; Bharti and her friends were up early and met their hosts at the prearranged meeting place and walked around the garden buzzing with activities, with a handicraft-and-jewelry bazaar on one side and games, fun and frolic, and the international food bazaar on the other side. After walking, shopping, and sampling various appetizing delights, finally they arrived at the auditorium where the lists of performances selected and not selected were placed. To her utter surprise and dismay, her name was on the "not selected" list of the dance performers. Rita told her the name of the person in charge for all the scheduling of performances was Vijay Shastri and she could probably see him watching the rehearsals tomorrow morning at the auditorium.

Bharti was looking forward to her dance performance in India as she had never performed in India and wanted to get feedback from the Indian audiences. Next morning, bright and early, she reached the auditorium; and after asking around, she found Vijay talking to some students on the stage. Vijay felt he was being approached by a person, and as he turned around, he couldn't believe his eyes that he was looking at the *devi* (diva) of his dreams – a fair-complexioned five-and-half-foot-tall slim maiden with long silky hair charging toward him in a rage.

Bharti, visibly livid and upset, went over to Vijay and introduced herself with a straight face, "I'm Bharti from the British delegation, and I would like to know why my performance was not selected?"

Vijay took a good look at her again and replied in a very gentle but formal manner, "Can you please give me ten minutes to finish what I'm doing and I will see you right after that?"

Bharti sat in the auditorium, watching Vijay direct a play rehearsal. She suddenly went into a trance; and in a vision, she saw herself wearing a wedding dress and standing with Vijay – a resolute-looking six-foot-tall guy with long black hair to his neck with middle parting – performing the garland ceremony surrounded by all their relatives and friends applauding and throwing flower petals. Bharti thought it was bizarre to imagine this, and she started thinking to herself that she must be going crazy. Just at that time, Vijay tapped her on the shoulder and whispered, "You wanted to see me?"

"Oh yes," Bharti whispered back and continued very gently as if she had forgotten the anger she had earlier. "Why was I not scheduled for a dance performance?"

Vijay, going through his notes on the laptop, replied, "We had too many Kathak performers before you put your name forward. I'm sorry, but I scheduled on a first-come-first-served basis and did not want to have the whole show consisting of merely Kathak dances. We need more English or Hindi singers. If you have any in your contingent, I'll be glad to schedule them."

"I'm a semiclassical Hindi singer."

"Would you like to give a performance in Hindi?"

"Yes, I would like that very much."

"Would you mind giving a little audition?"

"But I don't have my harmonium, and there's nobody to play tabla."

"I will arrange that for you." And Vijay called for one of the boys to bring a harmonium and a tabla along with a tabla player.

While waiting, they were getting to know each other, and a tabla player brought a tabla and a harmonium. Bharti sang a song; Vijay really appreciated it and scheduled a performance for her intentionally on the day he was performing. Earlier in the conversation, Vijay invited Bharti for coffee after the performance, but Bharti did not answer. She liked Vijay and was infatuated with him, and without thinking, she asked, "Do you still want to go for a coffee?"

Touched to the quick, Vijay replied, "Sure, I would love to."

While walking to one of the cafés in the garden, Bharti remarked, "You look a bit young to be doing this job."

He replied, "I'm not as young as I look! I'm twenty-six years old and have been doing this for the last six years."

"I apologize for being presumptuous."

After reaching the café, Bharti requested, "Could I have a cup of tea, please?"

Vijay brought two teas and sat down. Getting to know each other, Vijay asked, "Obviously, you're a student, so what's your field of study?"

"Actually, I am a doctor pursuing my specialization in pediatrics, and are you a student or a professional in the field of dramatics?"

"No, dramatics is my hobby. I'm a student of law in the final year completing my combined law and MBA degree. So you are a singer, a dancer, and a doctor. Is there anything you haven't done?"

"I'm not an actor," Bharti remarked jokingly and smiled.

"Are you trying to be sarcastic?"

"No, I'm merely saying that we do things we like."

"I'm sorry, my remark was not to needle you, but I really believe you are very talented. In fact, I scheduled you the same day I'm singing a song, and would you like to sing a duet with me?"

"I would love to."

"In that case, come for a rehearsal the morning of the day of your performance, which is scheduled for the evening."

Bharti thanked Vijay for the tea and quickly left to get back to her group as they had planned to go out on a tour of the city in the afternoon.

Bharti and Vijay practiced in the morning and gave a superb performance while Vijay's sister, Pooja, and Bharti's father, Mr. Kapoor, were in the audience. Pooja thought Vijay and Bharti had hit a chord, so after the performance, she invited Bharti to visit their home one evening after the youth festival was over.

That same night, Bharti called her father. "Hi, Papa, sorry I couldn't talk to you after the performance as Vijay and I were just mobbed and in the melee. I couldn't find you."

"I understand. Your performance with Vijay was outstanding. The love duet you sang seemed so real that it seemed to be coming from the heart. If I may add that you and Vijay make a fine couple."

"You know, Papa, when I first met him, I was angry at him. And as soon as he talked to me, my anger had vanished into thin air, and in a vision, I saw that I was getting married to him. That was preposterous, but I do agree that I kind of like him. In fact, I am infatuated with him, but nothing more."

"*Beta* [son or daughter], you have been getting premonitions from your childhood days, but I know you will not rush into anything as you have three years before you finish your specialization."

"Yes, Papa. I got the hint, and I can assure you I am not in any hurry to get into that kind of a relationship. Okay, bye for now, love you and will call you tomorrow."

Time passes quickly when you're enjoying it. For Bharti and Vijay, ten days passed in a flash. The students in the contingent made their own way to see India, and Bharti moved in to her Golf Links house to be with her father for few days.

Ultimately, Bharti went back with a hollow feeling that she had left something precious in India. Looking at each other through the Webcam, Bharti and Vijay kept in close contact. Over the next three years, Bharti and Vijay visited each other, and the distance made their love grow fonder. Finally, after finishing her specialization in pediatrics, Bharti got a job in India in the new hospital designed the same as a sick kids' high-tech hospital in Canada. Bharti's father also decided to move back to India to be with his daughter and to open his corporate head office in New Delhi, India.

CHAPTER 2

August 02, 2013

ANXIOUS MOMENTS WERE over when finally that long-awaited day came for Vijay when Bharti was moving lock, stock, and barrel to India. He went to receive her at the airport, and so did Bharti's father. She arrived past midnight, and after exchanging pleasantries, Mr. Kapoor took Bharti home.

Vijay lay awake all night, thinking about what was wrong because she did not pay much attention to him at the airport. Morning took a long time to come; but to his sheer delight, early in the morning, Bharti called on Vijay's cell. "Sorry, sweetheart. I was too tired at night, and when are we meeting?"

He breathed a sigh of relief and replied, "Whenever you want, I am free as I'm not working today being a Saturday."

Her yearning of love had overtaken the tiredness. "Let's meet at eleven in the morning and be together all day and evening. Can you pick me up from the beauty salon at Khan Market?"

"Of course, I'll be there."

Bharti and Vijay couldn't wait to be in each other's arms. Last time they met was at Christmas when Bharti had come to India. Bharti planned to stay the night with Vijay as she desperately wanted to make love to him. So was Vijay burning with a desire to make love to her?

Vijay met her at the beauty salon; they hugged and kissed each other as if they were meeting after aeons. They got into the car, and Vijay headed straight on the highway to Agra.

In absolute surprise, Bharti asked, "Where are we going?"

"We're going to the Taj Mahal."

"But why?"

"Because it's the greatest monument of love." He paused for a few seconds and then continued, "I hope you remember we started our relationship here with a kiss three years ago, and if you don't mind, I'd like to start our relationship now by paying homage to that greatest icon of love."

"I remember, sweetheart, you were so scared just to kiss me. Anyway, when will we be back?"

"Whenever you want, tonight or tomorrow, it is for you to decide."

"This is unbelievable, but I like it. At least, we'll get a chance to talk and catch up."

Verdant stretches with rows of water fountains and beautiful flowers exemplify the gardens of the Taj Mahal. Walking around admiring the marvel of architecture and monument of love, tired Bharti sat down, enjoying the pleasant mild breeze with the overcast sky of the monsoon season. Usually, it was very hot at this time of the year, but heavy rain falls week before and the lack of sunshine made it very pleasant.

Vijay took out a diamond ring from his pocket and bent down, showing the ring to her, and whispered, "Will you marry me, be my soul mate and a friend for life?"

Surprised and dumbfounded, Bharti realized after a couple of minutes that she was being proposed to, hugged and kissed Vijay, then lovingly whispered, "Absolutely yes, I'll be your partner and soul mate, and I love you very much."

For five minutes, they went into oblivion, kissing and hugging each other without knowing that a group of foreign tourists passing by saw the whole charade and started clapping and cheering. Vijay and Bharti suddenly came to reality, thanked everybody around them, and walked away holding each other.

"So do you want to stay here for the night, or do you want to go home and spend the night in my little condo?" Vijay asked.

"I would like to go to your condo if possible as it is not dark yet, but dark low clouds are upon us, so let's get out of here as we have three hours of journey ahead of us."

"Yes, let's go."

"They say it is a must to see the Taj Mahal by moonlight, but being overcast, we won't be able to see the Taj in the moonlight as there will be no moon. We'll do that another day."

"Yes, definitely we will come another time for a whole weekend."

"Tell me what is new in India as I have a lot to catch up on!"

Vijay, painting a financial picture of India and showing concern for poor people, remarked, "The growth rate is 11 percent, malls are popping up everywhere like mushrooms, the metro is expanding, the middle class is getting bigger, people have more money, the rich are getting richer, but the indigents are still there caught in a vicious circle of poverty. India is sitting on a pile of *barood* [gunpowder] waiting to be ignited. The pundits of politics and the politicians do not understand that you can only push the poor so far and, when their backs are against the wall, they will fight back."

"People in India are so peace loving. Can something like that happen in India?" Bharti inquired.

"Yes, I know what you mean. People are so peace loving in this country of Buddha and Gandhi, and yet in the same land, we fought the struggle for independence," said emotionally charged Vijay. And he continued, "You don't know what happened in 1984, at the time of Indira Gandhi's assassination. My father told me that not only were people taking revenge against the Sikhs, but also most of the fights were between the haves and have-nots and most of the looting was done by the poor people living in small colonies. The army was called in, and a curfew was imposed for weeks on end!"

"So where were you living at the time?"

"At that time, we were living in a colony called Lajpat Nagar, where we had a small house built on a one-hundred-yard lot. I was just a little baby, a few months old. My grandfather was a schoolteacher and was involved in the struggle for independence. He lost two brothers and my grandmother during the riots in 1947. In lieu of their ancestral property in an area now in Pakistan, he was given a small plot of land in Lajpat Nagar, Delhi, where he built a house."

"You said that you used to live in this colony next to your friend Ajay and that you grew up together."

"When the prices of real estate soared up in the '90s, my father sold his house and moved to an unauthorized colony, which was later named Anand Enclave, bought two plots of land to build a house on one and a school on the other plot. At that time, this colony had no sewers water or electricity."

"I know the story after that: your father was getting old and your mother was not keeping well, so he got a good teacher to run the school and sold his house so that he could move to an area where he did not have to worry about electricity and water," Bharti said.

"You know, my father is a visionary. He planned for his old age twenty years ago. He became a member of the housing society where he has a house now. Land prices are so high that it is difficult for a poor person to afford a house nowadays. What worries me is that the economy is moving at such a fast pace, and with the construction boom and the countryside shrinking, I wonder what will happen to the farmers! And see what is happening to the labor class. They cannot make ends meet. What a poor laborer would spend in the whole year the rich people spend in one night!" Vijay stated in an emotionally charged manner.

"We're getting close to Delhi, so I would like to call my father and inform him that I am staying with you."

Bharti called her father. "I have fantastic news to tell you, Papa. Vijay proposed to me today and gave me a diamond ring."

"Congratulations, beta! This is really good news on your first day back, and where are you?"

"I'm with Vijay. He took me to see the Taj Mahal and proposed there. It's kind of late now, so I'm going to stay with Vijay at his condo, if it's okay with you?"

"Well. I can come and get you if you want. After all, it is your first day back."

"No, Papa. I would like to stay with Vijay as we have a lot to talk about."

"Okay, beta. As you wish, but call me tomorrow."

Bharti was dreaming of being together and making love to Vijay whereas he was all charged up about the problems of the country.

"We are almost home. I don't want you to think of the problems. I got permission from my father to stay at your house tonight, but he didn't seem very happy at the idea of my staying away on my first day back."

"Your father gave me the impression that he's very liberal minded, with British values and businesslike."

"Even though my father has mostly stayed abroad, he is still very Indian minded, and that's the reason he always wanted to come back to India. He gave me education in Indian music and culture, and he always said that culture comes through language, which is why I had to go to Hindi classes."

"Well, we are home now. You go up to the condo, and I'll park the car in the underground garage."

"No, I will wait in the lobby for you," sang Bharti in a loving tone.

The front door opened into the foyer, and straight ahead was the combined dining-cum-drawing area with hallways on both sides leading to the bedrooms with attached bathrooms. In front, at the end through the sliding doors, was the balcony. Carved furniture, Persian carpets on white-and-crimson marble flooring, and satin linen on the beds made the condo look beautifully furnished.

"It is nice that your building is fully air-conditioned and the condo is beautiful," Bharti remarked.

"Yes, it's certainly not bad, and definitely it's nice that it has air-conditioning. I still remember those days when we used to sleep on the roof, in the old colony, to get away from the heat. Anyway, do you want something to drink?"

"What do you have, Vijay?"

"I can offer you tea, coffee, milk, or juice."

"Don't you have anything hard to forget the rest of the world and bring on the loving mood, like wine for example?" Bharti asked with a mischievous smile.

"For a nice hug and kiss, I might manage a bottle of wine!"

"I never expected that from you since you don't really like to drink."

"I had a feeling that it was going to be a very special night, so I went and bought a couple of bottles of wine."

"I like beer and wine both. Why did you choose wine?" Bharti asked.

"Actually, I bought beer and wine both, but I know you like to drink wine after dinner."

"Well done, now I want to wash my hair and take a shower."

"Go ahead. In the meantime, I will watch the news and also take a shower, and then we will enjoy the wine and the evening."

Vijay put the wine in the fridge and decided to take a shower first.

"I am out of the bathroom," Bharti announced.

He walked to the bedroom where Bharti was and said, "You were quick, sweetheart."

"I'm speedy when it comes to dressing up as this is part of my profession and I thought you were watching the news. You have already changed into *kurta pyjama*!"

"You look stunningly beautiful in that negligee. Where did you get that?" And Vijay came close to her, kissed her passionately, and stood there holding her.

"When I was in England last year, I bought it and saved it for a special occasion," Bharti whispered in between kissing him.

"How did you bring it? I didn't see you carrying a case?"

"Yes, you did. Do you see this big handbag I'm carrying? It has my negligee and one top."

"So you had planned to stay the night anyway!"

"I just thought in case you want to cuddle up with me I might as well be prepared."

"What is the special occasion today?"

"Well, today you gave me a ring and proposed to get married to me, didn't you?"

They stood whispering to each other while kissing, and then Vijay went and opened the cork with a pop.

"Don't tell me, you got champagne!"

"You wanted to make a special night tonight, so I got this Indian champagne, which was on a display with two free champagne glasses. I just could not pass up the deal. I don't have a champagne bucket to chill it, so I put it in the fridge."

"I'm not fussy about the drink, but I am fussy about who I drink with," Bharti whispered.

He poured two glasses of wine, handed one over to Bharti, kissed her on the lips, and whispered, "Cheers, here's to us."

"It is getting very late. Do you want to get into bed with me, or do you want to sleep in a separate room?" Vijay questioned.

"Sleeping in a separate room doesn't make a special night. Of course, I want to sleep with you. I've been thinking about this, waiting for this night, and you're giving me an option?" disappointed Bharti whispered.

"I didn't mean that. I didn't want to be forward and did not want to impose myself on you. I was brought up in India, and you're the first woman I have ever been intimate with. Please don't get upset. I love you very much. You know you are my life." He started crying as he hugged and kissed her.

Bharti, in turn, hugged and kissed him passionately. Vijay picked her up and put her down on the king-size royal blue satin-covered bed. After dimming the light, he took off his pajamas and stood there admiring her body shimmering through her near-transparent negligee.

"Oh my god, look at you! You're looking so handsome and, I should say, ready to give me the time of my life," Bharti whispered.

Vijay bent down and kissed her all over her body and then lay next to her, loving her passionately.

While going to sleep, Bharti said, "Do wake me up early if you are up before me."

"Are you up?" Bharti asked when she woke up in the morning.

"Yes, I am very much up and am just finishing yoga."

"I'll be out in a few minutes."

Vijay went to the kitchen and made a couple of cups of tea.

Bharti came out and said in a very loving manner, "Good morning." She hugged and kissed Vijay. "I'll be like a perfect Indian wife and make masala chai for you."

"Sorry, I made the masala chai already. You can make the breakfast, honey!"

"Oh, but I wanted to practice making masala chai."

They sat down to drink the cup of chai, and then Bharti walked out to the balcony.

"The view from this flat is breathtaking in the morning. The golden rays of sun are making the surroundings glitter as gold, and the park below is picture-perfect and lush green at this time of the year especially after the monsoons."

Bharti was standing against the sunlight; to Vijay, it seemed as if she was standing nude without her negligee.

"I can see the whole shape of your body, and you're looking stunningly beautiful."

"Oh my god! And I thought you're looking at the view."

"Yes, my dear, I am looking at the view in the background and a beautiful goddess standing in front of it. How could I ignore it?"

He grabbed her from the back, kissed her neck, and said, "I love you, honey. Let us hope every morning of our life starts like this."

"Now tell me, what do you want for breakfast besides me?"

Vijay thought for a while and said, "I don't want to eat you, but want to make love to you before or after breakfast. The choice is yours."

Quickly, Bharti answered, "Both!"

Vijay hugged and kissed her, picked her up, and carried her to the bedroom.

They made love. Bharti and Vijay went in for a shower, and after the shower, Bharti said, "I'm starving. What you have in the fridge?"

"Juice, eggs, and toast, everything you want."

"All of that."

While having breakfast, Vijay said, "I may have to go to Mumbai on Thursday morning."

"When will you know for sure?"

"On Monday."

After finishing breakfast, Bharti said, "Honey, can you please take me home? I would like to spend some time with my father."

On the way, Bharti started off, "Call me as soon as you know as I may want to go to Mumbai with you."

"What will you do there? I'm going to be so busy."

"I have a friend from England. We were in school and college together, and when I went to medical school, she got married to this guy who was the son of a very rich man and is settled in Mumbai. She has been chatting with me online every two to three days and inviting me to visit Mumbai."

"We won't stay with her as it will compromise our independence. We will stay in a hotel."

Outside her house, they held each other, feeling sad having to end the short interlude. Vijay whispered, "Okay, I will call you as soon as I know. I love you, and I must go now as I have to prepare a report for tomorrow morning's meeting."

"Okay, honey. Love you and bye for now," Bharti whispered with a teardrop down her cheek.

CHAPTER 3

O N WEDNESDAY AFTERNOON, Vijay called Bharti. "I'm leaving tomorrow at seven a.m. by Indian Airlines flight. My company has made all the arrangements, and I told them to book me in a double room as my fiancée may be staying with me, and it is all taken care of."

"Okay, I will tell Raju to book me on the same flight."

"Do you need any help in that?"

"No, Raju, my cousin, knows everybody, and he can get anything done."

"Well then, I will leave it in your good hands, and now I have to go."

"Bye, sweetheart. See you on the flight."

"No, I will call you in the evening from home."

"Okay, that's nice."

Vijay came home in the evening and saw two missed calls from Bharti. He called Bharti right away. "You called, honey?"

"Yes, I wanted to tell you that all my flights are booked for going and coming. I'm leaving tomorrow morning with you and coming back Sunday noontime. What time is your flight, Vijay?"

"My secretary booked me on the flight in the morning and coming back Saturday."

"Why do you work here on Saturday?"

"No, the Sunday flight was very busy, and she couldn't book it for me."

"If you want Raju to help, he would gladly do that. You know he is very resourceful. He's the main driver of my father's engine. He can get anything done anywhere, may it be a government department, bank, police, or an airline. He has friends all over the place. He schmoozes them, gives parties at five-star hotels, and is a very friendly person."

"Okay, I will let you know if my secretary cannot change the flight."

"You cannot disturb your secretary at this time in the evening before the flight. I will just tell Raju to get me another seat for my Sunday flight."

"Okay, if you insist, I will call you back soon, sweetheart."

She hung up the phone and called Raju. "Can you do me a favor?"

"Of course, Bharti Didi [elder sister], anything for you!"

"Can you book another seat for the flight on Sunday?"

"Yes, of course. Now you want two seats for Sunday noon flight?"

"Yes, because Vijay's secretary had booked a Saturday flight."

"So do you want me to cancel the Saturday flight?"

"No, I will let Vijay call his secretary from Mumbai tomorrow."

In about half an hour, Raju called Bharti. "It's all done, Bharti Didi."

"How did you do it so fast?"

"My travel agent is available twenty-four hours a day, and he's online with the airlines. He's a man of influence."

"Thanks, Raju, and bye for now."

"Have a good time in Mumbai, and call me from there if you need anything."

"Okay, bye."

Next morning, Bharti and Vijay met on the flight. They had adjoining seats in first class.

Vijay asked, "How did that happen that we are sitting next to each other?"

"It is all Raju's doing."

"Wow! He thinks of everything, doesn't he? And how did you take so much time off from your work?"

"Most Saturdays are off, and every Sunday is off. I do not have a clinic on Friday. Most Fridays I go to the hospital and make rounds on the inpatients. Anyway, that's why I was thinking of holding the clinic in the slum on Tuesdays and Fridays."

"This has worked out just wonderful for us."

"So did you talk to your friend last night, and does she know that you are coming?"

"Oh yes, she offered to pick me up from the airport, but I wasn't sure whether you wanted to go straight to the office or check in to the hotel. If so, where do we have the reservation?"

"It's at the Taj Mahal Hotel, and my office is not very far from there. There will be somebody to pick me up. What I can do is drop you off with the baggage at the hotel. You can check in and call up your friend."

"Yes, that is fine."

The air hostess brought the morning breakfast. "How would you like your eggs, madam? And you, sir?"

"I would like a scrambled egg."

Vijay said, "I would like the same too."

They had some juice, yogurt, toast, and scrambled eggs. They finished it off with fruit and tea.

"Please fasten your seat belts as the plane is ready to land in Mumbai," announced the captain.

The plane landed, and they picked up their baggage and went out.

There was a pretty girl with a placard with the name Mr. Vijay Shastri.

Vijay approached the girl and said, "I am Vijay Shastri."

The girl said, "I am Shilpa, and I will be your hostess while you are in Mumbai."

"This is my fiancée Bharti."

"Pleased to meet you, madam."

She used her cell phone to call the car chauffeur and told him to bring the car. "Sir, you have a meeting at the office and people waiting for you."

"Do you work at the office?"

"Yes, I am the public relations officer."

"Very well, can we drop Bharti and the baggage on the way to the office?"

"Yes, of course."

Bharti checked in to the hotel and went to her room. She freshened up and called her friend. "Sonya, I'm here."

"I've been waiting for you to call. What's the plan?" asked Sonya.

"I'm at your disposal till Vijay calls me."

"Which hotel are you in?"

"I am at the Taj Mahal Hotel, room number 520."

"I will be there in about half an hour."

"I will have something to eat, and I will see you in the lobby, and should I wear anything special?"

"No, just your regular pants and top."

"Okay, see you."

Sonya arrived in half an hour. She went to the hotel lobby and told the driver to wait outside.

"Look at you, Bharti! You are looking as pretty as ever, and looking slim as ever too."

"You're looking the same."

"No, I'm not! I have gained weight."

"Are you pregnant?"

"Yes, I am."

"Congratulations!"

"I have the whole day planned for you. First, we will have breakfast, and then I will show you around Mumbai. Mumbai is very green and beautiful this time of the year just after the monsoons, and at lunchtime, we will go home and you can meet my husband. I told him to be home for lunch to meet you."

"How is your husband?"

"He's fine now. We had a few problems at first, but now that I'm pregnant, he's been behaving like an angel."

"What does he do for a living?"

"He's the manager in one of the foreign banks. He spent a few years in New York, and from there, he was transferred to Mumbai. He asked for this transfer as his family is in Mumbai. Tell me about yourself and Vijay."

"I met Vijay about three years ago and fell madly in love with him at that time. I spent about two months in India and went back to England to finish my specialization. We kept in touch, chatting online and via e-mail. I came for a short visit last Christmas, and then finally came back for good to India in July this year as I got a job working in a new state-of-the-art pediatrics hospital."

"So when did you get engaged?"

"I'm not officially engaged, but he proposed to me a few days back and gave me a ring."

The driver opened the door, and they sat in the car.

"My driver is very good. He used to be a tour guide in Mumbai. He will show us around and will give us the history behind it too."

"So what is your name?" Bharti asked the driver.

"My name is Chhotu [small]."

"You're pretty big for Chhotu."

"Yes, ma'am, but I was the youngest in my family."

"Oh, I see, very interesting!"

Sonya said, "Show us all the places you want, but make sure we get home at one because Deepak Sahib [sir] is coming home at one p.m."

"Okay, madam. We have less than two hours to get home, and I will try to show you as much as I can while sitting in the car. You see in front of us is the Gateway of India. The English king George V landed in India in 1911 at this very spot. The citizens of Bombay pooled money to build this grand memorial for him and called it the Gateway of India. After Indian independence, the last British soldiers departed through this arch. The most important thing about the Gateway is that beyond this, the sea is deep, calm, and safe. That's the first thing that attracted the Portuguese, who called it Bom Bahia – Good Bay [that's where the city's name comes from]. The Portuguese later gave away the island to the English as part of the dowry of the Portuguese princess Catherine of Braganza. The English East India Company developed Bombay into major shipping and trading harbor."

Bharti asked, "You are such a good tourist guide, so how come you left that job?"

"The management changed, and they wanted an educated person who could interact with the foreigners. It was difficult for me to do that, but they gave me a good recommendation . . . To your left, starting at the Art Deco Regal Cinema is Colaba Causeway. This road is linked to Mumbai's physical history. It was built by the British to connect Colaba Island to Mumbai as a part of the city's expansion drive. Lots of neat stuff can be bought here – jewelry, footwear, leather, and gifts – but remember to bargain, and it is going to be about ten minutes to get to the next place of interest."

Sonya asked Bharti, "Have you ever been to Mumbai before?"

"Yes, when I was very little with my mother and father. I remember we had a really good time, at Chowpatty, eating *chat papri* and *pow bhaji.*"

"What do you want to do this evening?"

"I don't know yet. Vijay is going to call me, and I'll know the program then. What is your plan anyway?"

"My husband was saying that he has something planned, but he said he can cancel it to be with you guys."

"Madam, next is Cama Road that goes to Nariman Point, past the Institute of Science. This road leads to Mumbai's modern business district and reminds you that Mumbai is the commercial capital of India. Next, past the National Gallery of Modern Art, is the road to the art district of Mumbai and into the heart of the old British fort area. The Prince of Wales Museum is to your right on this road. You can spend a couple of hours there if you're interested in history, sculpture, painting, and art. Exploring the areas around Regal Cinema can take you up to two hours if you exclude the museum. And, madam, shall I take you to Koli fishing village? It is about twenty-minute drive."

"If you think you can make it home by one."

He took them to Koli fishing village and said, "A trip to Mumbai is not complete without taking a look at the city's original inhabitants – the Koli fisherfolk. On the way to your right, you will see colorful fishing boats. This is a little Koli village that has kept its traditional occupation and culture. You'll see salted Bombay duck hanging by the dozen, drying in the sun. You'll see fishermen mending nets. Walk into the village and you'll see the women selling fish at the markets. You'll see little kids flying kites and playing cricket. There's a village temple, a barbershop, a goldsmith, a grocer, a tailor, a small jewelry store – all in a little ten-minute walk. The fishing community has a clear division of labor. The men go to fish while the women take the fish to the markets. So the fisherwomen – the Kolins – hold the economic reins of the household. Nobody messes with them! So don't leave Mumbai without seeing a Kolin! Now I will take you to Victoria Terminus – a magnificent building. Now we are on our way back to home."

Bharti said, "Don't cancel any programs for me till the time I find out from Vijay what his program is. Anyway, I can spend the afternoon with you and rest because I got up early to catch the flight."

"Even I want to rest. I told you I am pregnant, and I get tired very quickly."

"Madam, we are about to go on the flyover, and I will stop at the spot on the flyover from where you'll see your first panoramic view of Marine Drive and the sea. The new business district of Nariman Point is at one end of Marine Drive, and Chowpatty Beach at the other end. And if you see the view in the evening, you'll see glorious views of the sunset on the Arabian Sea. In the late evenings, the streetlights come on, lighting up the curve of Marine Drive in what locals call the Queen's Necklace."

He stopped on the flyover, and they admired the view.

Bharti said, "The view is breathtaking, and I think it'll be really interesting to see it in the evening."

"If you want, we can bring you both in the evening again."

"Let us see what Deepak and Vijay say."

"And on our way back home, we will look at the Hanging Gardens, the Jain Temple, and the Parsi Towers of silence as madam lives in Malabar Hill."

Chhotu said, "I hope you enjoyed the tour, and we will be back at home in about fifteen minutes, right at one p.m."

Bharti said, "That was very good, Chhotu."

Sonya said, "I told you he is very good and very efficient."

They got home and opened the door. Sonya said, "Chhotu, don't go anywhere and I will tell the chefs to give you food."

"Thank you, ma'am, but I brought my own."

"Well, you can have that too."

As soon as they got inside, Sonya called the server and said, "Bring a couple of glasses of cold water."

They sat down and waited for Deepak to arrive, and Sonya asked, "Is the food ready?"

"Yes, ma'am. The table is laid, and whenever you say, we will start serving within five minutes."

Deepak arrived and asked, "Is this your friend from England?"

"This is Bharti, and this is my husband, Deepak."

"Hello, Deepak, nice to meet you."

"So nice to meet you, and I have heard so much about you."

"Do you always come home for lunch?"

"Oh no, I have come especially to meet you, and I have to be right back."

"You could have just come in the evening."

"But I wanted to meet you. And where is your fiancé?"

"He's at work."

"Have you made any plans, and have you seen any part of Mumbai?"

"Yes, your driver was very good and he gave us a tour."

"Sonya, is the food ready?"

"Yes."

She told the server to bring the food. "We will wash up and come to the table."

They sat at the dining table, and Bharti remarked, "You have a beautiful house! Did you just buy it, or is the bank providing you with this house?"

"Actually, this house belongs to my grandfather. He built it for my father. My father and I both spent our childhood here."

"Your father is not from Maharashtra?"

"No, my grandfather was a theater artist, and he came to Mumbai because Mumbai was becoming the hub of art and culture. He worked with the famous actor Prithviraj Kapoor."

"You are from the frontiers?"

"Yes, we are. My last name is Khanna."

"You know we are from the frontiers too."

"What a small world!"

"Sir, the lunch is served," informed the server.

They started eating, and Bharti asked, "So do you have any brothers and sisters?"

"No, I am an only son, and my parents are living here with us."

"You went to study in the USA?"

"I did my MBA, was there for about three years, and I got this job with the bank and I wanted to come back to India."

Bharti put some food in a plate and started eating.

Sonya said, "Is that all you want to eat?"

"I'm not pregnant like you. You have to eat for two."

"It's very delicious, but it is a bit spicy."

"In England, you never used to eat any spices."

"I know, but I love the spicy food now," Sonya said.

"So, Deepak, you came back from New York and the bank gave you accommodation?"

"Yes, at first I lived there for six months, but my dad was having a problem with the builders as they wanted to buy the property at any cost and my dad would not sell it. They even threatened him. So I talked to my bank and decided to lease the property to them as long as they renovated it. The understanding was they renovate the property and after that I will live in it."

"So what happened to all the builders?"

"When they found out the property had been leased to the bank, they left us alone."

"This property has a lot of land with it."

"Yes, about two acres."

"Very nice, my father was looking for a property in Mumbai, but he said it is too expensive."

"Okay, Bharti, I must leave. I have a meeting to attend, and I'm keeping the evening free for you. If Vijay phones, please invite him for us so that we can spend some time together." And he left.

Sonya said, "Let us retire into the bedroom as I'm very tired."

"I am too as I got up at four a.m. to catch the flight."

Sonya told the server to bring tea or coffee into the bedroom.

Sonya said, "I like tea, especially the masala chai Mumbai is famous for."

"Okay, no coffee, just masala chai for both of us."

"So tell me, Bharti, how did you meet Vijay?"

"It was about three years ago. I had come from England with the contingent of artists and other people to take part in a youth festival."

"I remember you came to India to attend the youth festival. You used to sing and dance when you were young. Are you still carrying on with that?"

"Not actively anymore, but three years ago I did."

"So were you one of the performers?"

"I wanted to give a Kathak performance but ended up with semiclassical Hindi song performance."

"Is he the same guy that you told me about when you returned after attending the festival in India?"

"Yes, you know the story that I wanted to perform and my name was on the list of performers not chosen."

"I remember now you were infatuated to this guy, and what was his name?"

"His name is Vijay, and it is the same person I am in love with now."

"Did you fall in love right then?"

"No. But I just fell in love with his extra helpful and nice nature."

"What happened then?"

"I was infatuated, and he invited me out for coffee. I agreed right away, and then he told me what he was doing academically."

"What did he do?"

"He was in the new program of law and MBA together."

"Oh really! He is a lawyer!"

"A lawyer and a business executive. He is now working in charge of mergers and acquisitions, and that's the reason we've come here."

"Can I ask you a personal question?"

"Go ahead. You are my old friend."

"Are you going to stay in the same room in the hotel?"

"Yes. I am engaged to him, He's my soul mate and a partner for life."

"That's very nice."

"Now, I can't wait to meet him this evening."

Just at that time, Bharti's cell phone rang.

"Hi, honey, is that you?"

"Yes. I'm sorry for calling so late. We are just going for lunch now, and it seems like it is going to be about six p.m. before I can get away from here. Are you getting bored?"

"No, I'm with my friend Sonya and we have a lot to catch up on. Her husband came home for lunch and was inviting us to be together with him for the evening."

"That's fine, whatever program you make is fine by me. Do you want me to get you picked up?"

"No, in fact, I will go to the hotel about four p.m., sleep for a while, and finalize the program with Sonya for the evening."

"Okay, see you in the evening."

Sonya said, "You don't have to go home. You can change right here and wear my clothes, even get freshened up here."

"I am not going home now. Like I said, I would like to go about four if that's okay with you. You can have your driver drop me off at the hotel."

"That's okay with me, but really you don't have to go."

"No, I would like to go to sleep for a while, take a shower, and change."

Sonya requested, "Tell me more about what happened after that."

"I gave my performance. His sister was there too. She complimented me a lot and invited me to their home."

"And did you go?"

"Yes, I went there for dinner and thought what a beautiful family it was. They were totally unassuming. I felt as if I had known them for years. They treated me like one of their own family."

"Tell me, when did the love start?"

"He invited me to go with him to see the Taj Mahal, and I agreed. He booked a ticket for the Taj Express train. We went in the morning, spent the whole day together, and came back the same night. While we were at the Taj, he told me not to mind him being forward but my eyes were bewitchingly beautiful and so was I and he would like to be friends with me. I started laughing and said, 'Vijay, that's not being forward. I will show you what's being forward!' And I hugged and kissed him and asked him if that is what he wanted to do. Sheepishly he said yes, but he could not gather enough courage to do so. So he came back and gave me a hug and kissed me twice and said he liked me, and that was the start."

"And he only said he likes you?"

"He is the reserved kind."

"What happened then?"

"I was in India for two months, out of which I spent one month doing a rotation at the hospital. We met a few times, and soon it was time for me to go back to England. He came to see me one night before I was leaving. We went to a café, and there he said we can keep in touch with each other chatting online. I said that's fine, and I took down his e-mail address. He said he had a Webcam installed and we could see each other too while chatting if I installed one too. I asked him if that was all he had to say to me. He said he was very sad that I was leaving and that we had a fantastic time for the last two months. He loved me and would always remember me and hoped that I would come back one day."

"Oh, that was nice!" Sonya said.

"Yes, it was. It touched my heart, and I hugged and kissed him on his lips right in the restaurant, and with a sad heart, we parted. I thought about him all the way on the flight back to England."

"So what happened then?"

"I kept in touch with him. The whole year I kept chatting with him and called him a number of times. I grew closer and closer to him, like it is said, absence makes the heart grow fonder, and I desperately wanted to come back to India to meet him."

"And did you?"

"Yes, the next Christmas holidays. When we met each other, we felt like we had known each other for centuries because we had exchanged all our ideas and views while chatting."

"Tell me that juicy stuff. When did you first get intimate with him?"

"We wanted to spend New Year's Eve in Jaipur. I told my cousin Raju to book two rooms for us. When we got there, the hotel management apologized to us and said that they could only give us one super deluxe room with a king-size bed. The other one could not be vacated as the person living in that room was a relative of the minister. The rest of the hotel was full. Vijay and I looked at each other. I quickly said that was fine. We went into the room. Vijay remarked that we were going to stay in one room together, yet we were not married. So I told him that I knew that we were not married but I knew he was a thorough gentleman and I could trust him. I mentioned that we could just sleep arm in arm. He said that he would sleep on the sofa. I told him if that was what he wanted to do, he could do so. So we went to the New Year's Eve party in a different hotel. We danced and had a drink together. I slipped a couple of shots into his drink, and he got a bit tipsy. We got back to our hotel. He kept telling me again and again how much he had missed me. He must have repeated this at least half a dozen times. Then he said that he really loved me. He changed into his pajamas and went to bed with me. I just could not control myself. I kissed him again and again, and he responded by kissing me. He said he would like to make love to me, but he could not because he didn't have any protection. He did not want me to get pregnant. At that, I told him I had the protection. I reminded him that when we checked in to the hotel and before going to the New Year's celebration, I'd told the driver to stop at a drug store. He asked me if I wanted something. I said no. I knew what to get as I was a doctor. I left the car, went and picked up a packet of contraceptives. Vijay kept quiet for a minute and said he wasn't sure if he wanted to make love to me then. I turned my face away, started crying, and asked if he thought that I was a whore? Then he grabbed me from the back, started kissing me on my neck, and said he didn't think that I was a whore, but I was too forward for him. I told him that I had never gone to bed with anybody before. Did he want me to take a virginity test? He apologized for upsetting me. He kept hugging me and kissing me from the back. He said we had known each other for one year and he loved me very much. I responded by saying, for the last one year or so, I had never thought of another man, I had built my dreams around him, and I started crying more. He forcibly turned me around, kissed me repeatedly on my lips, and after a few minutes, he said, 'Give me that contraceptive.' He made love to me, and I was in seventh heaven."

"That is quite a story!"

"It's your turn now. Tell me all about your husband."

"You know I was living in England. My cousin was studying with Deepak. When his bank moved to India from New York, he stayed for two days in England and he called me up. He said he was my cousin's friend from New York and would like to meet me and asked me if my cousin had called me to tell me that he was coming to England. I told him I was expecting his call and asked him where he was staying. He told me the hotel name, and I said I'd be there in about an hour. So I went to see him and took him out for dinner. Next day, I showed him around London, spent the whole day with him, and then we were together for the evening. He asked if we could go together to a nightclub. So we went to a nightclub. There we wined, dined, and danced. I dropped him at his hotel, and next morning he took a flight to Mumbai."

"So did you fall in love with him?"

"No, but I liked him, especially that he was a good spender."

"What happened then?"

"One fine day, his father called my father and they found a connection between the two families. Then his father asked for my hand for his son, whom I have already met. My father said he had to ask me. So my father asked me if I wanted to get married to that boy, my cousin's friend. 'He's nice, but I hadn't really thought about it,' I said to my father. 'Well, think about it,' he said. After a couple of days, I thought he was nice and I said yes. So I came to Mumbai from England, and I got married to him. After the first few days, he showed his real American colors. He would measure everything in money, brag about his position, and generally be bigheaded. When I told him to have some consideration for others, he became wild and started using abusive language. His own mother and father tried to correct him, but he would not listen to anybody. So one fine day, I told him I'm going back to England unless he changed his ways. He improved slightly, tried to be nice to me, and then later on, he became the same."

"So what happened then?"

"My father came to Mumbai, and I went with him to New Delhi to see my relatives. That made a nice change for me, and while I was gone, for about two to three weeks, he had realized that it was no fun living without me. He started calling me every day and asking me as to when was I coming back."

"Did you tell your father that he was being a jerk?"

"I told my father everything, and my father said let's spend a couple more weeks travelling, and by that time, he will come to his senses. When we got back, I observed he was a changed man. Then he became very loving to me, and now I have become pregnant and he has become the most considerate man on this earth."

"It is three thirty, do you want to sleep?" Bharti asked.

"No, I'm lying down and I'm fine. Tell me what happened in the last one and half years?"

"He passed his law and MBA exam in April, two years ago, and started a job with a multinational company. Last year in August, they sent him to London for training and studies in mergers and acquisitions."

"He must have had a good time in London?"

"He had classes and seminars twelve hours a day, six days a week, and had to study for six hours for the next day. I tell you he has a capacity to work hard and he could have taken this course over three months, but his company asked him if he could do it over a month as it was costing them a lot. He decided to do it in a month. For four weeks, I could only see him on Sundays, and we made the best of it. He passed his exam, and it was during the last weekend. We had the time of our life, and luckily, my father was away from London that weekend so he stayed over at my house."

"So you had a mini honeymoon?"

"Not quite, we had a good time."

"Did you visit any of the old places we used to go to?"

"Oh yes, I showed him all our favorite hangouts: my medical school, the university, and the local pubs we used to hang out in and have lunches in. I will never forget those two days."

"So when did you meet him next?"

"I came again at Christmastime, and by this time, his company had given him a very nice flat. At that time, I only came for ten days and went to Khajuraho – you know, the place with all the statues and carvings."

"Yes, I've been there too, and it is fantastic. Centuries ago, they had these nude carvings and poses to make love, on the walls of the temple."

"It was quite enlightening for us, and especially for him."

"Why do you say that?"

"He is not very knowledgeable about sex. He has had a very straight life as compared to me. I know differently, being a doctor and brought up in England. Well, he will learn. I finished my specialization in April, waited for my license, had to do a few things there, and came here in July this year. I got a job with a really good Indian hospital. I have known him for the last three years, and the more I know him, the more I love him, and now I have decided in my heart that he is my partner for life, and I love him from the very core of my heart. And that's my love story."

"That was very touching, and I think you have found the right one. I know you were always very conservative and did not go steady with any boy or, for that matter, never got close to a boy!" Sonya said in a sarcastic tone.

"I was focused on my studies, especially after losing my mother. I wanted to look after my father, and I felt if I had a steady relationship with a boy, my father would not get the attention that he deserves as he gave me all the attention I needed. Especially that he sacrificed and never got married again."

"That is really heartening."

"It is about four now. I should go before I hit rush hour."

"Don't worry too much about rush hour because my driver knows all the ways."

"I want to go my hotel and rest if it's okay with you. Anyway, you need to rest too, and this is my advice as a doctor."

"Okay, thanks for coming and I'll see you again."

Bharti left, and the driver went through the back lanes and dropped her at the hotel.

She handed him a five-hundred-rupee note, but he refused to take it and said, "I get enough from Sonya Maim Sahib, and they look after me really well, and it is my duty to look after their friends."

"You're a very nice man," Bharti said. "If there is anything I can do for you, please let me know."

She went back to her room and went to sleep.

At about 6:00 p.m., Vijay called and said, "I will leave the office in about half an hour and expect to be with you at seven. What is the program for the evening?"

"Sonya's husband was asking to spend the evening with them."

"We can spend this evening with them."

"I will have to ask Sonya what is happening tonight."

"Our division manager, Mr. Mukherjee, has invited us to his home, and he would like us to have dinner there tomorrow."

"Okay, but I don't really have anything formal to wear."

"You can make a plan with Sonya and go shopping tomorrow."

"Okay, will do, and see you soon, honey."

Bharti called up Sonya and asked, "Are you available to go for shopping with me tomorrow?"

"Of course, I have kept these three days free for you."

"Great! We will go shopping tomorrow. Also, Vijay was saying either we can spend tonight or Saturday night with you."

"What is happening tomorrow night?"

"Tomorrow night we are going for dinner to Vijay's division manager's home."

"I will have to ask Deepak and get back to you in a little while."

Bharti took a shower, freshened up, and was ready to go when Vijay arrived and said, "Hi, sweetheart, I am home, and how was your day?"

"As you know, I went to see my friend Sonya. Her driver gave me a mini tour of Mumbai, and I spent the afternoon chatting with her."

"What is the plan for tonight?"

"I don't know yet. I am waiting for Sonya to call. And how was your day?"

"Very busy! I have to learn a lot by tomorrow or by Saturday. If I finish everything tomorrow, then Saturday would be off, but I think I might have to go for a couple of hours on Saturday too. Mr. Mukherjee, the division manager, has been really nice to me. He has given me a driver and a car till Sunday."

"That's really great. We can be independent."

"I'm really tired today. I would like to take a shower and get freshened up. It is a nice evening. Why don't we just go to Chowpatty Beach and have a walk?"

"We have to wait for Sonya to call us because I have given the option of tonight or Saturday night."

"Okay, I'm going to take a shower."

Sonya called and said, "Deepak is not home yet, and when I talked to him on the phone, he was saying he might get home late and Saturday evening is really good for him. He was apologizing because he had told you to keep the evening free."

"No, that's fine."

"Do you want me to send a car with the driver?"

"No, Vijay has his driver today and he will be with us for the evening."

"Are you sure, Bharti? I can easily send Chhotu."

"No, Sonya, we have the driver and we will be fine."

"What time do you want me to pick you up for shopping? Is ten thirty good for you?"

"Yes, that's fine, see you tomorrow."

Vijay came out of the shower wearing a robe.

Bharti hugged him and said, "You smell nice." She kissed him and continued, "The evening is ours to spend alone."

"Yes, my queen. Has Sonya agreed to Saturday evening?"

"Yes, somehow Deepak got delayed at the bank, so it all worked out perfect for us."

"No more conversation, first we are going to make love."

"Yes, my *aaka* [king], your wish is my command."

They grabbed each other and kissed passionately.

Bharti asked, "The driver is not going to come up, is he?"

"No, sweetheart. I told him I will see him in one hour."

"You are brilliant, my sweetheart, and I love you for that." And she kissed him passionately, took his robe off, kissed him on the chest and the neck. And in turn, he took her gown off and said, "You have a beautiful smooth and silky body."

And they made love.

After a little while, Bharti said, "I'm hungry."

"Okay, let us get ready and go to Chowpatty Beach. I'll get you *paani poori* and *pow bhaji* [both traditional Indian snacks]."

They both got ready and went down, and the driver was waiting for them.

Vijay asked the driver, "Do you know how to get to Chowpatty Beach?"

"Yes, of course. That is the most popular place in Mumbai."

Bharti said, "On the way back, can you stop at the bridge so that we can see the view of the beach and the Queen's Necklace?"

"Yes, of course, ma'am. Ever been to Mumbai before?"

"Yes, when I was small. By the way, I went sightseeing with my friend's driver, and he seems to know a lot about Mumbai and the history of Mumbai."

"What was his name, madam?"

"His name is Chhotu."

"Oh, I know him. He's working for Deepak Sir. He is from my colony. He could get a much better job somewhere with a tour company, but he refuses to leave them."

"I guess he likes working for them," Bharti said.

The driver took them to Chowpatty Beach.

Then he said, "Write down my cell phone number. I will leave you at the beach, and then I will have to park the car in the parking lot. When you're ready to go, just call me on my cell phone and I will pick you up."

Vijay took out a five-hundred-rupee bill and gave it to the driver and said, "Go and have dinner."

"The company pays my expense account, sir."

"Keep it anyway, and buy something for your kids."

"Okay, sir, if you insist, and thank you."

Vijay and Bharti got out, and the driver gave them instructions as to where to go and what not to eat.

They followed his advice, and Bharti said, "We should eat only the cooked food."

So they sampled a few things and walked on the beach, holding hands. There was a nice sea breeze blowing, and the sun was setting down. Vijay took a picture of Bharti against the sunset with the orange flame glowing in the background and said, "It is so beautiful and peaceful here."

"Yes, it really is beautiful."

After a couple of hours, Bharti said, "I'm getting tired now. Let's go home."

The driver picked them up. He took them on the bridge from where they could see all the beaches, and with the lights along the beaches, it looked like a necklace. The driver stopped the car right on top of the bridge and said, "You can take a photograph from here."

"It really is a beautiful sight and looks like a giant necklace. No wonder they call it the Queen's Necklace," Bharti said. They looked for a little while, and the driver said, "We have to go as we are not allowed to park for a long time here."

The driver brought them back and asked, "What time do you want me here in the morning, sir?"

"Eight a.m. should be fine."

"Yes, sir." And he left.

"Are you hungry, Bharti?"

"I had so much to eat there. If you're hungry, we can go to the coffee shop."

"No, it is nine thirty p.m. I would rather go to the room and get something from room service." And they ordered a small pizza and two lemon teas.

Vijay said, "As usual, I have to get up in the morning, and I have a very busy day tomorrow. I want to finish my work tomorrow itself, if possible."

"In fact, for some reason, I'm also very tired, and tell me, what should I buy tomorrow?"

"I don't know, whatever you like."

"You're a big help in shopping."

"I was never much of a shopper."

"We are going over for dinner to Mukherjee, and they are Bengalis. I was thinking of buying a *churidar* pajama and a shirt."

"Do you want me to buy something for Pooja, Mom, and Dad?"

"It is up to you, but it is not necessary. Mom and Dad have very simple tastes, but Pooja likes artificial jewelry."

Room service arrived; they had the meal, put the tray outside the door, and got into bed after slipping into pajamas.

Vijay wrapped his arm around Bharti and said, "Did you get bored today, and did I neglect you?"

"No, I had a good time with my friend and loved the Chowpatty Beach."

"One more day tomorrow and I will finish my work by the evening, and you can spend the day shopping with your friend."

"Yes, of course. I'm fine with it. Don't worry about it. I will be fine, and I will see you in the evening, and now you go to bed because you have a busy day tomorrow."

He kissed her good night and went to sleep.

In the morning, he was up at six as usual, did his regular yoga, and got ready. Bharti was still sleeping. He came in the room, and she suddenly woke up and said, "Are you going now?"

"Yes, honey. It is eight o'clock, and I came in here to say bye to you, will call you in a couple of hours."

"Bye, sweetheart, and I will talk to you later."

In about half an hour, Bharti got up and took a shower, got ready and went for breakfast. While having breakfast, one man approached her and asked, "Are you alone, and can I give you company?"

"No, I'm not alone, and I don't need your company because I have my husband with me."

"Where is he?"

"It's none of your business, please leave me alone."

She called the waiter, and the man said, "I was trying to be helpful to show you Mumbai."

In the meantime, the waiter arrived, and Bharti said, "This man is bothering me."

The waiter took him out and handed him over to the management.

Later the manager came to Bharti and apologized and said, "You did the right thing, madam, by handing him over to us."

"How do you get unscrupulous guys like this in the hotel?"

"He was well dressed, and it is hard for us to know as to whether he is a genuine guest or not, but from now on, we will not let him in. Please accept our apologies again."

In a few minutes, she got a call from Sonya.

"Hello, Sonya, how are you?"

"Are you ready, Bharti, to buy the town?"

"Not quite. But I have made a list of what I want to buy."

"Okay. I'll be there in fifteen to twenty minutes."

"That's fine. I'm just finishing off breakfast."

"You're not going to have breakfast with me?"

"Well, you can have breakfast and I'll have a coffee."

"Okay, see you."

Sonya picked her up, and they went shopping.

"How are you, Chhotu?" Bharti asked.

"I am fine, madam."

"And how are your kids?"

"They're fine too, thanks to Sonya Madam."

"Why are you saying thanks to Sonya Madam?"

"Sonya Madam is paying for them to go to school, and she has got them admitted into a good school. I wish there were more people like her to look after us poor people. If it wasn't for her, my children would never get a chance to get ahead in life."

"Yes, I know. There's a real problem in the country."

"Do you have any idea, madam, as to how many children cannot go to school? In this day and age when India is doing so well, there are millions of people living in the *chaals* [slums]. These poor people see that the rich people are getting richer and they have no chance to break the shackles of poverty. Our government is not doing anything for us. The politicians are only there to fill up their pockets. I am scared that one of these days, there is going to be bloodshed or a revolution."

Sonya said, "He should be a leader."

"No, madam, they are all thieves, and I don't want to be one of them. I'm very happy working hard, and I'm so glad that my children will not become criminals and they will have a chance in life to get ahead, and it is all because of you, madam."

"No, Chhotu, we must all do our part. And I'm so glad that you're so hardworking and I feel that God has given me a good opportunity to help somebody."

"Where do you want to go for shopping, madam?"

"First, take us to a good restaurant because I want to have breakfast."

They stopped at a restaurant. Sonya ordered an omelet, and Bharti, a cup of coffee.

"So, Bharti, what do you want to buy?"

"I want to get a sari for Vijay's mother, artificial jewelry for Vijay's sister, possibly a hat for my father and Vijay's father, and for myself maybe a sari or a suit."

"Okay, I will take you to all the shops."

They shopped all afternoon, and at about three thirty, Bharti said, "I think we've done enough shopping. Can you leave me at the hotel?"

"No, Bharti, we will go home, chat for a while, have a little something to eat, and Chhotu will leave you at the hotel."

"Okay, because you know we're going to Mr. Mukherjee's, Vijay's area manager, for dinner."

"So when are you coming to us for dinner, or when do you want to go out for dinner with us?"

"We are free tomorrow evening if you're free."

"Tomorrow is Saturday, and Deepak works half day. I think it should be okay." Sonya called Deepak. "When do you want to see Bharti and Vijay?"

"Tonight or tomorrow night or both nights 'cause I'm free."

"Bharti is saying they're busy tonight as they are going for some official dinner."

"That's fine then, tomorrow night is confirmed from my side for sure."

"Okay, that's fine, see you in the evening."

"There you have it, Bharti. You are coming for sure tomorrow evening. What are you doing during the daytime?"

"I hope I will be spending the day with Vijay."

They got home, and Sonya said to her maid, "First, we will have water then tea. Make it masala chai, and if possible, we would like to have some *pakoras* [cut-up vegetables battered and deep-fried]."

"Yes, madam, and would you like some *paneer pakoras* [ricotta cheese, battered and deep-fried]?"

"Yes, if you have *paneer* at home. Otherwise, vegetable *pakoras* would do."

"Okay, madam."

Sonya said, "So are you excited about the wedding?"

"Yes, in fact, I will send you a card, and both Deepak and you have to come. The engagement is on the fifth of October, and the wedding is on the ninth of November."

"Okay, I will note down the dates and we will see you. You know the baby is due in December."

"You see how you feel, having a baby is the only legitimate excuse, and I'm the only friend you have in India."

"You are right, and you are the only old friend I have. I have made a few friends in Mumbai, but nobody is like you."

"Thank you. Do you know it is almost four thirty?"

Sonya called out for her maid Millie and rang the bell.

Millie came and said, "The tea is almost ready, and I will bring it in five minutes."

"Okay, that's fine."

"Millie's is another story. Her mother and father were killed in a train accident, and she was in the hospital and had nowhere to go. A friend of Deepak's, who is a doctor, asked us if we could do something for her. I felt really sad, and we told him that we would take care of her. Deepak even said if she were educated, he would get her a job at the bank. The doctor said that she was from a very poor family. She used to work cleaning the house and dishes with her mother. We asked the doctor when she could start work at our house and that we would give her a room to stay. So the very next day, I picked up Millie from the hospital, about five years ago, and she's been with us ever since. In fact, she goes to school in the morning and learns various things like stitching, cooking, embroidery, etc."

"You are a very good person, Sonya."

"When I came from England, I felt very bad for the poor people in Mumbai, so I decided whatever little I can do, I will do."

Millie brought the tea and *pakoras.*

They both had it, and Bharti said, "The *pakoras* are delicious. Did you make them yourself?"

"Yes, Bharti Didi, I made them because the cook is off for the afternoon."

"Do you like working for Sonya?"

"Yes, Sonya Didi has replaced my mother and father both and I live like a member of the family and I can speak and write English."

"Oh, that is wonderful! Sonya, I want to go. It is five now, and I will get stuck in the traffic."

"I told you the other day as well. You don't worry about the traffic. Chhotu will take care of that."

Bharti left, and they reached the hotel just before six, and Chhotu brought all her shopping.

Bharti said, "Thank you, Chhotu, you can go home."

Bharti went to her room, and just at that time, her cell phone rang. "Hi, sweetheart, when are you coming?"

"I'm on my way, and you get ready."

"Yes, boss. I bought a nice pantsuit because I could not get a nice *kurta pyjama* suit."

"That's fine." And Vijay opened the door.

"Who is it?"

"Don't worry, it is only me, honey."

"You scared me!"

"I thought it was the guy in the morning who was trying to pick me up."

"Who was it?"

"While I was having breakfast, some guy wanted to sit with me. So I called the waiter and handed him over to the management, that's all."

"Good, I hope the hotel management handed him over to the police."

"What time do we have to reach the Mukherjees' house?"

"We have to reach there by seven thirty p.m. because they have dinner early."

"How far away is it from here?"

"I don't know how far it is, but my driver said it will take about forty-five minutes, so please get ready."

Bharti suggested they get into the shower together to save time. She had been away from him all day and had other naughty plans in her mind. They got into the shower together and soon started making love.

Finally, they come out, got ready quickly, came down, and got into the car as their driver, Kalu, was waiting.

Bharti inquired, "Did you finish your work?"

"I'm all finished, and we have tomorrow to ourselves, and our friend Kalu is going to be with us."

"Yes, sir, I will be at your service, but, sir, I want to warn you of something that I heard through the grapevine. There is trouble brewing in the city!"

"I was in the office all day, and we heard the news at lunchtime. There was nothing like that."

"I know there is some demonstration against a certain builder who tried to clear the newly built *jhuggies* [mud huts] from his plot of land, which had been lying there vacant for a while."

"So what is wrong with that?"

"Well, the government had earmarked that land for a playground for children as it is next to the slum and it is owned by the government. Apparently, some builder in collusion with the corrupt government officials changed the use of the land, and he bought the land to construct a shopping mall and an apartment complex."

"How far away is that?"

"That's on the edge of the city, but you know what happens in Mumbai. Poor people take to the streets as an effect of the frustration. They have nothing to lose and are not scared to die."

"Well, that is very sad. The same thing is happening around Delhi. It is like dynamite, and with the least little provocation, they are ready to explode. The situation is going from bad to worse, and the government is not prepared to do anything. The politicians are busy filling their pockets. I don't know what will happen."

"I will tell you, sir, their patience has run out. You understand very well the economy is growing for the rich, and the poor man is falling behind now. People in the slums are thinking about grabbing and killing and talking about a revolution. Good people like you will suffer, and for that I feel very sad."

"You seem very well-informed. I wish I could find a solution for you."

Bharti butted in, "You know Vijay sir's father has a school, and he's expanding the school to take on more poor children to educate them and to give them a level of education the same as other children have, but this is not going to happen overnight. It is going to take time."

"Madam, you are very nice, but unless the government and the politicians join hands, nothing is going to be achieved."

"You're right. Vijay's father is trying to get the next-door land allotted to him for years even though it was earmarked for a school."

"That's what I mean. Anyway, sir, I will come to know before the news media would as I have some friends in the colony who would call me on my cell phone."

"Okay, I would appreciate it, and are you going to take us back to the hotel?"

"Yes, of course, sir. I like you, sir, and I like your thoughts. Don't worry about the time, but I will let you know if there's a problem."

"Thanks."

They went to Mr. Mukherjee's house and rang the bell. Mr. Mukherjee came out and said, "Welcome, Vijay!"

"This is Bharti, my fiancée."

"I am very pleased to meet you."

"Pleased to meet you too, sir."

"Just call me Romesh."

"No, sir, I cannot do that. My father's teachings were not to call the elders by their first name."

"Okay, I would not argue about that, please come in."

They went in, and he introduced her and Vijay to his wife and his daughter and said, "My son is studying in America to be a doctor."

Vijay said, "Bharti is a doctor too."

"Really! What kind of a doctor?"

"She is a pediatrician."

"So I'd better call you doctor, *sahiba* [madam]."

"No, I'm just Bharti for you."

"Mausami, is the food ready?" asked Mr. Mukherjee to his wife.

"Yes, it is almost ready."

"Vijay and Bharti, would you like to have a drink?"

"No, we are fine, thanks."

"I'm going to have a glass of beer. Do you drink beer?"

"Okay then, we'd have a glass each."

He asked his daughter, Reema, to pour the beer for everybody.

Everybody said, "Cheers!"

Mr. Mukherjee said, "My wife and daughter run a music academy."

Bharti said, "That's interesting because I learned a little bit of music too."

Vijay said, "She is quite good in both singing and dancing."

"Bharti, you have a very English accent. Did you spend most of your life in England?"

"Yes, I did my medicine there. My mother was a good singer and dancer. I learned a bit from her, and later on after her death, I continued my music education."

"Then after dinner, we will have a singsong session."

"Agreed."

They sat down for dinner, and Bharti said, "It is delicious, especially the pan-fried fish and rice."

"My wife is a good cook."

"So is my husband," said Mausami.

After dinner, Mr. Mukherjee said, "Would you like some Bengali sweets?"

"I would not pass it for a million dollars."

"We will move to the sitting room and have it there along with some coffee or tea."

They moved to the sitting room, and Reema, Mr. Mukherjee's daughter, brought in *rashagulla* and *sondesh* (both traditional Bengali desserts).

Bharti said, "These are true Bengali dishes, and I love them!"

Mausami said, "Would you like some tea or coffee?"

They all were having tea, and Bharti said, "I am curious. You don't have a cook or a maid in the house?"

"My wife and I – we both cook, but we do have a maid, but she has gone back to Calcutta for a week."

"Doesn't Reema cook?"

"Oh yes, she does, and she is a very good cook, but she doesn't have time from the music academy."

Bharti got up and said she would help clear the table with Reema.

"No, you are our guest. Please sit down," Mausami said.

"No, Auntie. I'm like a daughter, and please let me help."

Bharti and Reema cleared the table.

Mr. Mukherjee said, "Let's go to our music room."

"You have a room for that?"

"Yes, we have the tabla and harmonium all there."

They all went to the room. Reema played the sitar. Mr. Mukherjee played the tabla and said, "Bharti, you sing a song."

Bharti took the harmonium and sang a semiclassical song. Vijay joined in.

"Oh, you are a dark horse!" Mr. Mukherjee praised her in a backhanded way.

They all had a good time, and just at that time, the bell rang. Reema went out to open the door.

"It is the driver, Papa."

Mr. Mukherjee came over and asked, "What is it, Kalu?"

"Sir, there is a problem growing. There has been some shooting in the slum, and I think Vijay Sir should go back to his hotel."

"Really!"

Vijay and Bharti came over to the door, and Mr. Mukherjee said, "Kalu thinks you should go back to your hotel. Kalu said not only that you should go back to your hotel, but also he thinks it is going to be unsafe for the next two or three days to live in Mumbai as there are going to be some big demonstrations in the city because there was a shooting by the police in the slum." He looked at Kalu and asked, "Is it that serious?"

"Yes, sir."

"We will watch news on the television, and I think Vijay and Bharti should head back to the hotel. Vijay, you've done all your work as far I'm concerned. You should book a flight back to Delhi. You know, Bharti, I must tell you that your fiancé is a brilliant man. Not only did he learn all about the business, but he also gave us some really good suggestions."

"No, sir, I have learned a lot from you," Vijay remarked, appreciating his senior.

Bharti and Vijay said bye to everybody, and they said they had had the most wonderful time of their life. "It was like a family gathering, and you must come to our wedding. We will send you our wedding card," Bharti said.

They got in the car, and Vijay asked Kalu, "What happened?"

"Like I said, the police and the bulldozers went to the colony in the evening and started demolishing the huts. All the colony people got together and sat down in front of the bulldozers. A scuffle started, and the police resorted to a *lathi* [baton] charge. One of the slum dwellers threw a gasoline bomb, which resulted in the police firing. I heard that several people are dead and many more injured due to the stampede that occurred."

"But you said the slum is on the edge of the city?"

"Yes, it is, sir, but a lot of people in that colony work in the city, and they're calling for Mumbai *bandh* [lockdown]."

"You think there's going to be trouble in the city?"

"I'm almost certain, sir, but you can watch the news tonight. My suggestion is tonight you should get a booking done for a tomorrow early-morning flight, and if everything settles down, you can always cancel it early in the morning."

"It's a very good suggestion."

"I will call you tonight. Please give me your cell phone number, sir."

"Thank you very much, Kalu!"

"At this time on Friday night, there is a lot of traffic, but today the roads are empty. What does it tell you, sir?"

"I think people are scared to go out tonight, and they must have heard something on the TV."

They reached the hotel in twenty minutes, and Kalu said, "It is ten p.m. now, and I'll call you at about eleven thirty p.m., or if you get the booking done earlier, you can call me on my cell phone."

Kalu gave his cell number to Vijay, and Vijay entered it into his cell.

"Thank you. I will get back to you for sure." He gave one thousand rupees to Kalu and said, "This is for your kids."

"No, I cannot take it."

"Please, Kalu. I would have liked to meet your kids and would have given this personally to them."

"Okay, sir, if you insist."

Bharti and Vijay went to the room, and Bharti said, "Let me call up Raju."

Vijay said, "We can do it ourselves."

"No, let us not waste time." And Bharti called Raju. He didn't pick up the phone, so Bharti sent him a message. "Where are you, Raju? I need your help. It is an emergency. Please respond immediately."

Bharti and Vijay waited anxiously for fifteen minutes. Vijay decided to call the hotel management, and he said, "I need to get to Delhi tomorrow morning, could you help me book a ticket?"

"Yes, sir. We will put you through to the Indian Airlines office at the airport."

"Thank you very much."

Vijay said, "My flight was booked for Sunday afternoon, but I want to change it to tomorrow morning to two first-class tickets."

The booking agent said, "It's all full except for a twelve noon flight."

"Please book me on that."

The booking agent gave him the confirmation number and said, "You have to be there two hours before the flight."

In the meantime, Raju saw the message and called Bharti.

"What is the matter, Bharti Didi, you scared me."

"Where were you that it took you half an hour to call me?"

"I was at a party, and my cell phone was off."

"There is going to be trouble in Mumbai, and we have to get out from the city in the morning, so Vijay booked a flight for twelve noon with Indian Airlines as that was the earliest flight available."

"Okay, leave it with me, and I will ask my agent to get your flight at seven a.m. with any airline because he deals with all the airlines. Just give me your confirmation number with Indian Airlines, and I will call you back in fifteen minutes."

Raju called back and said, "Your flight is booked for six forty a.m. Can you be at the airport at five a.m.?" He gave her the confirmation number of the Indian Airlines flight.

"You got an Indian Airlines flight, and they told us that there were no seats."

"This happens, maybe they thought you didn't want to fly that early. That is taken care of anyway, my driver, Ranbir, will pick you up from the airport and bring you home, and I haven't told Uncle yet."

"Thank you very much, Raju Bhaiya [brother]."

"You're welcome, and have a good flight."

Kalu called back in an inebriated condition and said, "Hello, sir, did you get your booking done?"

"Actually no, I think we might have to catch the ten thirty a.m. flight. We are on the waiting list."

"Do you want me to call you in the morning, or you can call me whenever you have the confirmation done."

"We will call you in the morning when the confirmation is done."

"Okay, sir, don't forget I will take you."

Bharti said, "Why did you lie to him?"

"He was sounding drunk and somehow I don't trust him, and from his conversation, he sounds like a radical. I even felt uncomfortable about his remark that people would have to grab if they don't get what they want. Now we have two choices: either we take a taxi from here or we call your friend and ask for Chhotu."

"Well, I'll call up Sonya, and if she offers strongly, we will take the offer."

It was about eleven p.m., and Bharti called Sonya.

"Hi, Bharti, I was waiting for your call all evening."

"Are you sleeping?"

"No, it is Friday night. We are watching the television, but did you hear the news that they are calling for Mumbai *bandh*?"

"Yes, we heard it, and I'm sorry to disappoint you, but we're heading back to New Delhi by tomorrow morning's flight. I'm sorry we could not have dinner with you."

"That is all right. Actually, Deepak was suggesting that you go back because you might be stuck in the hotel for two to three days. Do you want Chhotu to pick you up in the morning?"

"No, we will take a cab."

"I think it might be safer. I can call Chhotu on his cell phone and ask him if he can come in the morning. What time do you have to be at the airport?"

"We have to be there by five a.m."

"Okay, I'll call you right back."

Sonya called Chhotu. "Are you sleeping?"

"No, ma'am, but I was just awake, watching the eleven o'clock news."

"It is really bad what happened, and they are calling for a Mumbai *bandh*."

"Yes, ma'am, I was thinking of Vijay and Bharti Maim Saab."

"But they're leaving early now. They will be going by six o'clock flight and have to be at the airport at five a.m."

"I can pick them up at four thirty."

"You would not get enough sleep tonight, but you can take the day off tomorrow as it is going to be a Mumbai *bandh* anyway."

"That is fine, madam. They are very nice people, and it will be my pleasure to be of service to them. I have a sister living in New Delhi, as you know, and her child is quite sick. Do you think it is okay for me to ask Bharti Madam to examine her son?"

"Yes, of course! Ask her yourself and give your sister the cell number of Bharti Madam."

"Do you want me to call Bharti Madam now? I'll call her and then you can call her too."

Sonya called Bharti. "Everything is all set. Chhotu will pick you up at four thirty a.m., and he said it will be his pleasure, but he has a favor to ask you, and he will talk to you about that himself."

"That's fine, and thank you very much for spending two days with me. It is a shame that Deepak and Vijay never got together."

"Deepak is planning to go to Delhi, and I will tag along with him too."

"Okay, thanks a lot and we'll see you soon."

"Bon voyage!"

In a couple of minutes, Chhotu called and said, "Bharti Madam, are you there?"

"Yes, Chhotu, you don't have to come. We can take a taxi in the morning as it is too early for you to come."

"No, madam. I would like to come, and I will be there at four thirty a.m. to pick you up. Thank you very much, madam, and I will see you in the morning."

They rang the reception for a wake-up call at four a.m. and went to bed.

Bharti said, "I'm very tired. I have been shopping all day and have not rested even for a minute."

"Bharti, you go to bed, and I will do the packing."

"Are you sure, honey?"

"Yes, very sure. Good night, sweet dreams, and I love you."

He set an alarm for four and got up before the hotel staff called.

He kissed Bharti and said, "It is time to wake up, sweetheart."

Bharti got up and freshened up. They had tea, and he called up the bell captain. "Please send somebody up to our room to pick up the baggage as we are checking out."

Vijay said, "I'll go down first and pay the bill, and you come after."

"I will pay the bill."

"No, my company will pay the bill."

He went down and cleared the bill, and Bharti came down and saw Chhotu. "Hello, Chhotu, you are right on time."

On the way to the airport, Chhotu said, "I have a favor to ask you."

"What is it?"

"I have a sister living in New Delhi, and her son is always sick. She has shown him to many doctors, but nobody has been able to help her."

"Is that all? Give her my cell number, and I will see her immediately, don't worry."

Chhotu dropped them off at the airport. They caught the flight, and once the plane took off, Bharti said, "I'm very sleepy, and please don't wake me up for breakfast."

They both went off to sleep, and in a little while, the air hostess brought breakfast.

Vijay said, "I will have tea, juice, and a toast with some cheese. And please don't wake up my fiancée."

Bharti was fast asleep. Vijay said, "We are landing now. We are already there, and you were sleeping the whole time."

They picked up the baggage and came out.

"There is Ranbir, Raju's driver."

"Where do you want to go, Bharti Madam?"

"Please take me to Golf Links house, and how is Raju Sir?"

"He's fine and waiting to hear from you."

Bharti called Raju. "Hi, Raju Bhaiya, how are you?"

"I'm fine, and how about you, and how was your journey?"

"Everything is fine, thanks to you. Where is Papa?"

"He must have gone to play golf in the morning. I told him about the whole situation, and he wants you to call him."

"Okay bye, Raju, and thanks again."

Bharti called her father. "Hi, Papa, I am back."

"Good to hear your voice again, and do you want to join me for lunch at the golf club?"

"No, Papa. I'm tired, and I want to rest for a while."

"Okay, I am having lunch with some friends here. Do you want me to bring something home?"

"No, Papa, I am fine and Vijay is with me."

"Did you have a good time in Mumbai?"

"Yes, Papa, most of the time I spent with my old friend Sonya. However, we went together on Chowpatty Beach and had a fantastic time walking on the beach and eating *pow bhaji*, *bhel poori*, and other snacks."

"I'm glad you had a good time and you were able to meet your old friend Sonya."

"Yes, we had a lot to catch up on."

"Okay, I will talk to you later."

"I will call you later and tell you my program. Bye for now, Papa."

Vijay said, "Why don't you come with me and we will go out in the evening and have a date."

"Okay, that sounds like a good idea. Why don't we go home together? I will pick up my car, and we go together to your house, and then we'll make a program there."

On the way, Vijay remarked, "When you were in England, you told me that you wanted to help the poor."

"Yes, I still want to but I don't know how to?"

"Well, there is a slum in the close proximity of my father's school and the area where we used to live. You can open a clinic to help the children of the slum."

"That sounds exciting, but do you know anybody there?"

"Yes, I have some friends living close to the slum who are involved in social work at the colony, and you will have a good opportunity to meet them at the Independence Day celebration."

"When is that taking place?"

"On the fourteenth of August, a day before India's Independence Day."

"Let's go there tomorrow, and I'll meet all your friends as well."

At night, Vijay took Bharti to a nightclub where they danced the night away and came back late after drinking one too many, still made love, and got up with a hangover in the morning.

In the evening, Bharti and Vijay went to Vijay's friend, Ajay's house where they met his friend Joy who was also very involved in social work and taught music to the children of the slum. He was the main organizer of the Independence Day celebration, and Vijay and Bharti became excited to help him organize the show. After spending a few hours with Ajay and Joy, Vijay dropped Bharti home and came back to his flat.

Bharti got busy in the sick kid's hospital, where she had started a clinic, and Vijay got busy in his office after the training in Mumbai. They met a couple of times during the week and talked about various issues including one about living together and left it to be settled at a later time.

CHAPTER 4

Friday, August 14, 2013

BHARTI DROVE TO Vijay's house early in the morning, left her car there, and went with Vijay to the slum to organize the function of the Independence Day celebrations.

On the way, Bharti said, "I have a surprise for you. My father is going to see your parents tomorrow. He phoned your father and asked if he could see him, and your father said that he was most welcome to come."

"Really, I did not know that. I guess he had a busy day at school today. I know there was a missed call from my sister. So what is your father going to talk about with my parents?"

"He's going to propose to them that we get officially engaged and married by Diwali this year. He asked me to ask you, if it was possible and acceptable to you. He's going away for a foreign trip after Diwali," Bharti whispered in a very sweet and loving voice.

Vijay was taken aback and said, "So soon! My parents will never agree to that as they want to prepare so much for my wedding and call all our relatives."

"Let's see what happens, but you are agreeable, aren't you?"

"Yes, honey, if you ask me to marry you tomorrow, I will."

"Then it is all settled. We will leave it to our parents to decide."

"That's the best thing to do, and my parents will be very happy that they're making the decision."

Joy, a music teacher who lived next to the slum, Vijay, and Bharti, along with residents of the slum, worked very hard to organize the show for India's Independence Day celebrations taking place in the middle of the slum.

The road leading to the slum was through a beautifully developed colony called Anand Enclave, which had large individually designed houses landscaped with trees on both sides. One could hear parrots whistling, birds singing, and see the lovebirds kissing while sitting on the trees. Straight ahead on this road was the slum where the houses became smaller and the road became narrower, lined up with small shops on both sides. Moving farther along was the open ground surrounded by over ten thousand mud huts and tin shacks.

Flowers and colorful decorations decorated the stage. *Rangoli* made from flower petals of marigold, white roses, and green leaves covered the front of the stage, which represented the colors of the Indian flag. On the stage were the children all dressed like flowers on this gorgeous cloudy day with a mild cool damp breeze blowing. Men, women, and children were all happy to see the children singing and performing on the stage, which was erected and decorated by the people of the slum with their ingenuity and effort. Normally, this was the playground for children, but now they were sitting on burlap mats in front of the stage, and behind them were some folding *chai*rs for women. Menfolk were all standing behind the *chai*rs enjoying, clapping, and cheering while watching the show.

It looked like the stage of a birthday party, and why not? It was the sixty-sixth birthday of India's independence.

Joy, Vijay, and Bharti were the main organizers of the show. The show was already more than half-finished. "Where is the minister?" the visibly upset Bharti asked.

Vijay remarked with a quick reply, "These people are always late, and I don't know how they can run the country!"

In the next few minutes, a large motorcade arrived on the scene, leaving a cloud of dust behind it. Personal bodyguards and the police came out of the cars followed by the minister. People shouted slogans, "Long live the minister." The minister came to the microphone and said to continue the program after his speech was over. He started by saying, "I have given you toilets, water, roads, and electricity even though your colony was unauthorized, and all I asked for in return was simply your vote. Is that too much to ask for?"

The minister had a feeling that people were unhappy with him and that they were not ready to listen to his speech. Just at that time, somebody shouted, "The toilets never functioned as they were substandard, and the water was sold to us for money!"

Hearing that, the hoodlums working for the minister started going through the public to see who shouted and started beating up the man who was complaining.

The public became furious and started beating up the minister's hoods. This started a brawl; and in the melee, one of the men walked up to the stage and threw a knife at the minister, missing him narrowly. The celebration went into a chaos. The police tried to calm the public, and then there was a brawl between the minister's men and the public. To control the public, the police fired tear gas. The public started rushing to the stage; the police started a baton charge, ordered the public to be calm and to sit down, but to no avail.

There were some militants also present in the public who did not like the corrupt minister and believed in violence to deal with the matter. One of those men fired at the minister and shot him.

The police started firing in the air and announcing on the speaker for the public to lie down so that they could catch the culprits; however, the minister's bodyguards fired at the people, killing several men, women, and children.

Many reporters were covering the event, but the most prominent was the champion of the poor, Nandita Basu of the National TV Network.

"The minister has been shot; thousands of panic-stricken men, women, and children are running to take cover from the bullets. The police have started firing in the air and are announcing on the speaker for the public to lie down to avoid a stampede so that they can apprehend the culprits. However, the minister's bodyguards fired at the people, killing several people. A couple of ambulances have arrived. The minister has been rushed to the hospital. The shot and injured are lying around in pain, and there are no ambulances for them. Women and children are crying for help. Dodging the bullets, this is Nandita Basu, taking cover and reporting live from the site of the bloodshed of the innocent poor people."

Bharti, being a doctor, went with the minister. The ground was cleared. In about an hour, the ambulances arrived to take the injured and the dead to the hospital. After a couple of hours, calm returned and most of the police personnel left, but a few stayed back. Ajay came home and turned on the TV.

"Now we bring to you a report of Nandita Basu from the slum where the Independence Day celebrations were going on, and during the celebrations, a minister was shot," broadcasted the anchorman.

"This is Nandita Basu live from the scene of killings and bloodshed, and now it is all but calm in the slum. Vijay has taken the microphone in his hands and is requesting the people to calm down and go home. The police have the situation under control and are telling everybody to go home so that they can take care of the injured."

Vijay went with his friends to Ajay's house. "This should not have happened. I was going to give a petition to the minister," Vijay said, disappointed and shaking his head.

"What would have the petition achieved?" shot back Ajay.

"I went to invite the minister. I told him that some of his people were charging money for the water. The minister looked surprised. He said that he was not aware of that and suggested me to submit a petition to him, pointing out all the problems, and he will see what can be done?"

At that, Ajay emphatically said, "You don't believe that liar. Do you know that knife attack was a stage show and it was done by one of his own men!"

"How do you know that?" Vijay asked in an unbelieving tone.

"I recognized the man. He's one of the minister's hoods," Ajay replied in an asserting way.

"And the firing?" inquired Vijay.

"I don't know!"

(Vijay and Ajay were good friends, and they grew up together in Anand Enclave. Vijay wanted to study as his father was a schoolteacher and encouraged Vijay to study. Ajay was the son of a shopkeeper, who did not encourage his son to study as he wanted him to give a hand in the business. Vijay moved out of the colony when he went to college. Ajay stayed in the colony with his father, mother, and one sister and helped his father with the family business. Ajay knew the politics of the colony. Vijay kept visiting the colony to visit his friends and to carry out social work in the adjoining slum. He was considered a member of Ajay's family. Ajay's father used to treat Vijay as his older son and took his advice on all matters. Ajay's father had expanded his business to a milk-vending booth called the Mother Dairy milk booth, and he had to bribe the local politicians to get that booth.)

Just at that time, Joy and Ali walked in and broke the news, "I know who shot the minister. I think it was Mohan or one of his friends."

"Why would he want to shoot the minister?" Vijay asked.

Ali said, "Four years ago, Mohan lost his father in a train accident, and he was still waiting for the compensation that the minister had announced. He has had tragedies one after the other. Three years ago, he had a dairy farm, and in 2009, the government acquired the farm to build roads for the 2010 Commonwealth Games. At that time, the minister, who got shot today, had promised to give him compensation as well as an alternate piece of land to start the farm again. His land was taken away, but to date, he hasn't got another site for the farm. He goes repeatedly to the minister's office, and the minister's staff does not even let him in. The crux of the matter is that they are demanding a bribe – and a very large sum at that. The poor guy doesn't have any money to pay them. He is totally frustrated and is now living in our slum whereas earlier, he had a big house and a farm in a village close by."

"I feel very bad for this guy," Vijay said sadly. "There is a very serious problem with this country. The politicians are filling up their pockets, and the poor people are totally ignored. The country is going through an economic boom for the last ten years. The middle class is growing, the rich are becoming richer, and the poor people are trying to survive and managing with just enough to feed the family. *Slum's* population is increasing. Due to shortage of work, people are leaving their villages and moving to cities in the search of jobs and they end up in slums like this to live in deplorable conditions," he continued.

"Here, at least, they're able to make a living to feed the family," remarked Ajay.

"There's unrest in the whole country, people are getting frustrated. A couple of months ago, I went to a communist's meeting. It was a very large meeting, and there were representatives from all the states of India. Naxalites from Bengal and Andhra Pradesh were present. They were all talking about a revolution. They were saying that a Russian type of revolution is needed to fix this country's problems," Joy said in a very sad tone.

"Can you tell me about the episode of toilets and the hand pumps?" Vijay asked.

"Joy knows everything about it because the communist party protested when the toilets were not working," Ajay said.

"It is a shame that millions of rupees were spent to build the complex in the middle of the slum to provide one hundred toilets and fifty showers for the poor. They could use the facility by paying the usage fee of just one rupee. At first, it was very popular, everybody was very happy, and in fact, they had a function to celebrate the opening of the toilets. But the inside story is that the contractor had to pay a large sum of money to the minister's fund and said he was not making any money. So he decided to leave the work 90 percent finished. The local municipality had to finish the work, but they did not know that the contractor had not connected this system to the main sewer system, resulting in the system being clogged up in a month or so," explained Joy.

"I understand now," Vijay said. "And what about the hand pumps?"

"That's another long story. You know how corrupt the whole system is! A contract was given to one of the minister's known men. The fair system of tenders was bypassed in the name of urgency of the matter," Joy informed.

"So what went wrong?" Vijay asked.

"Well, they did a geological survey to find out as to where the hand pumps and tube wells should be placed," Joy said in a cynical tone.

"So what was wrong with that?" inquired Vijay.

"The geological survey was rigged. They placed all the hand pumps outside or in the vicinity of the party workers' houses so that they could charge money for the water from the poor people of the colony," explained Joy.

"I heard in the evening news that the media is now demanding a CBI [Central Bureau of Investigations] inquiry into the whole affair of the toilets and hand pumps," said Ajay's sister, Geeta, who just entered the room.

Joy was one of the friends of Vijay and Ajay. He belonged to the communist party, but he was not the militant type. He was steering the communist party away from violence.

"We cannot let this happen, and we must do something about it. I mean about the poverty, and there must not be a revolution. You realize that millions will be homeless. In the end, poor people will suffer," Vijay emphasized to Joy. "You must not let this happen, and I suggest you keep a tab on your party," Vijay said very firmly.

"I wonder what happened to Bharti?" inquired Ajay.

Vijay was just thinking the same thing, so he called Bharti on her cell phone and asked, "Where are you, we're getting worried about you, I hope the minister lives!"

"I'm just leaving the hospital in the hospital van for doctors, and the minister is fine. The bullet just grazed him. You know bad people don't die that easily."

Bharti arrived at about 8:00 p.m. She had been away for four hours. "Let's go home," Vijay said.

"No, you cannot go without eating," Ajay said.

Ajay called his sister and asked her to serve dinner for everybody. Ali got up and said, "My father will be waiting for me, and he won't eat without me."

"My mother is waiting for me too," Joy said.

Bharti emphasized, "I'm not going without eating as I'm starving. I'll go and help in the kitchen."

"I met Ali just a few years ago, but I have not had the chance to introduce Ali to you. His father is a hakim who makes herbal medicines, and Ali and his mother give him a hand," Ajay said. "Do you know," he continued, "his father has a cure for cancer, diabetes, and many other diseases, but he does not want fame. He does not even talk to reporters as he thinks that fame would distract him from his work and he won't be able to do the work that needs to done, which Allah has sent him to do."

"I know Joy seems like a very educated person. How come he's a communist?" Vijay inquired.

"He has his story. When he was in Calcutta, studying in school, he was influenced by the Karl Marx idea of communism and was very impressed by it. He read the book and started going to the communist party meetings. He feels that everybody should be equal and thinks that if everything was state controlled, there will be no poverty. However, after seeing that the Russian system failed, he has turned socialist now," Ajay explained.

"I understand that Joy and his mother live alone. Where is his father?" Vijay inquired.

"His father was in foreign services, went to America alone, and left his wife in India, and at that time, he didn't know that she was pregnant. He fell in love with an American girl, married her in America, and never came back. Joy's mother was a singer and used to teach and still teaches music to make a living. At first, she was in Calcutta, staying with her brother. Three years ago, she moved to New Delhi, where she was given a flat in the foreign services colony. She did not like being in a flat, so she sold the flat, which fetched good money, and decided to move to this colony where she could be of service to poor people. She started teaching music to children of the colony. The show you saw today was a result of all her hard work."

Bharti took a small amount of food.

"Take some more, Bharti, you eat very little, you must eat more to get stronger," insisted Ajay's mother.

"I'm strong enough, Mommy. Look at my muscles," Bharti said jokingly. She continued, "Why don't you have more, Mom."

In India, mothers are always telling everybody to eat more, and everybody gets a little annoyed. But it is a part of the Indian culture and the hospitality.

Ajay's mom turned around, pointing at herself. "Look at me, I'm so fat and I don't need any more, but you do, Bharti, as you are very skinny and you need to get healthy!"

"Mommy, don't forget I am a doctor," Bharti said politely. And she continued, "I may not be fat but I am healthy!"

After finishing her food, Bharti got up and said, "It is very late, and we must leave."

"No, you cannot go without eating dessert," Ajay's mom lovingly but emphatically said.

"It's your favorite dessert," Geeta said.

"I see the dessert is *kheer* [rice pudding]," Bharti said, smiling.

"In that case, I must have it and forget about dieting for one day," Bharti remarked.

After having dessert, Bharti and Vijay hugged everybody and left in the small car provided by the company where Vijay was working as a legal advisor.

CHAPTER 5

THEY REACHED HOME, and Vijay switched on the TV.

"Earlier in the breaking news, it was reported that the minister was hurt and possibly dead. What we know now is that the minister is alive and he is still in a critical stage, but nobody is commenting on that in the hospital. We believe at least half a dozen people are dead and several dozens injured as there were six ambulances which took the people from the colony to various hospitals. The police are saying that there were two dead and about ten people injured. The final count will come out in the next few hours. We are still outside the hospital and waiting for doctors to comment. This is Nandita Basu reporting with cameraman Tony Fernandez."

"Poverty must be removed, and if the government is not willing to do anything about it, there will be violence in this country, and to stop that, we must do our part in helping the government to remove poverty," Vijay said in a speechlike manner.

"I don't know about you, but I'm very tired and am going to bed."

"Actually, I'm tired too and will be right over to cuddle up with you."

"I thought you're going to all solve the problems of the country as you are all wired up about it," sang Bharti jokingly.

"These problems will not be solved overnight. I'm not going to let you sleep unless you make love to me."

"I'm always ready for that, sweetie, so I'm waiting."

After a few minutes, Vijay got into the bed. They made love and then went to sleep.

The next morning, Vijay got up bright and early at six, brought the newspaper, and the headlines read that the minister survived. On the inside page, it was written that his bodyguards, the Black Cat Commandos, did a fantastic job of shooting the culprits; however, a few innocent people were shot in the process. After the normal morning chores, Vijay started practicing his usual morning yoga in the other bedroom.

Bharti, without making a noise, slipped into the kitchen and made some tea and got breakfast going. Vijay finished his yoga and was surprised to find Bharti in the kitchen. He grabbed and hugged her from behind and whispered, "I love you, honey. I did know you were up and, look at you, making tea and breakfast."

"Yes, I'm trying to be a good partner." And she turned around, kissed and hugged him, and asked, "Do you want to have tea first, or do you want have it with breakfast."

"Anyway, you like it, honey, but I want to make love to you first."

"Breakfast is almost ready, let's finish breakfast and then make love in peace."

Vijay kept grabbing and kissing her; Bharti was showing anger on the surface, but really was happy in her mind. She switched off the cooking range, turned around while showing anger, and said, "Let me see your stuff." She grabbed and kissed him passionately.

Vijay picked her up and took her to the bedroom and made love with her passionately.

"Vijay, I'm starving now, make breakfast for me."

"Yes, my queen."

He kissed her and went to make breakfast. After breakfast, Bharti asked, "What's the plan today?"

"Well, we are going for lunch to my parents, and is your father coming there?"

"I'm not sure of the plan my father made with them," Bharti remarked.

Vijay called his parents.

His father answered the phone and said, "What took you so long to call?"

"I was caught in the mess at the slum function. I'm sure you must have heard about it. I came home very late, and I am going to pick up Bharti, and we're coming for lunch. What time is Bharti's father coming over?" Vijay asked.

"We have invited him for lunch as well as we knew you were coming," Vijay's father said. He inquired, "Isn't Bharti coming with her father?"

"No, Papa, she stayed over at her friend's in the next building, where they had a little get-together."

"Come soon as you have a lot of work to do at home. Your mom is not very well, and your sisters, Pooja and Chemeli, are looking after the cooking."

They quickly got ready, and as they were leaving, Vijay asked, "What are you wearing, my dear? Wear a nice flashy red suit."

"But I didn't bring one."

"You knew we were going to my parents' house. Anyway, no big deal, show me what you have."

"So you're going to choose my clothes even before getting married?"

"No, of course not! Wear any suit. I know my mother. It is going to be a very special day for you."

"All right, I will show you the clothes I brought. You can help me choose the one you like."

Vijay picked out a flame-colored suit. Bharti wore it, and they were out of the flat within minutes.

Vijay's parents lived about fifteen minutes away.

Bharti asked Vijay, "Do you think your father is going to agree to an early wedding?"

"I don't know. It depends on what your father is proposing. I know my sister is not getting married till March because her fiancé has gone to the United States for some training, and he's coming back in March next year, so that can't be a problem," Vijay said.

"You know my father is leaving just after Diwali to open up an office in Canada, and he's planning to buy some hotels there through his London office. He told me he'll be away at least until Christmas. That's why he wants me to be married before he leaves," explained Bharti.

Vijay's father opened the door. Vijay and Bharti both greeted him in the old-fashioned way of touching his feet, but he didn't let them and said, "You are all grown-up now." He hugged and kissed them on the cheek, placed his hand on her shoulder, and said, "Come on in, my *beti* [daughter]."

Vijay and Bharti asked, "Where is Bejee [Mom]?"

"In the kitchen, of course, despite my telling her so many times not to exert," father remarked, sounding very frustrated.

Both of them went into the kitchen, hugged mom, and Bharti said, "I don't know much about cooking, but I'm going to give you a hand."

"No, no, you go out, and please sit with Papaji," Vijay's mom said.

Vijay's father handed a grocery list to Vijay and said, "I know it is Independence Day, but a few stores are open. I phoned one store. He said he could not deliver today as he doesn't have very much help, but he'd have everything ready. You can go and pick them up. Here's the list for you to double-check."

Vijay went to pick up the groceries and came back in time for Bharti's father to arrive. Bharti went to the kitchen and insisted on helping. At that, Vijay's mother said, "Okay, if you want to help, lay the table and Pooja will help you find the dishes and cutlery."

Vijay's father had a very nice house in a group housing complex outside the city of Gurgaon. They were provided with water and an electricity supply 24-7 by the housing society management, and Vijay's father was the president of the society. They had security at the gate to screen all the visitors. In a few minutes, Bharti's father, Mr. Kapoor, arrived at the gate, and the security guard phoned and asked, "Mr. Kapoor is here to see you, Mr. Shastri. Should I let him in?"

Mr. Shastri replied, "Please let him in and send somebody with him to show him my house."

Vijay's father kept the front door open for Bharti's father. "Welcome, Mr. Kapoor." He hugged him and asked him to come inside.

They sat down, and Vijay's father called Vijay's mother, Shanti. "Come over and meet Mr. Kapoor."

She greeted him in the traditional Indian way, "Namaste."

Bharti and Pooja came and met Bharti's father.

"So you're getting married in March next year," Bharti's father asked Pooja. "Do you ever talk to your fiancé?"

"I talk to him when he calls me. Otherwise, I'm in touch with him on the computer every day. Before going, he set up a Webcam for me, and we see each other every time we chat online."

"Things have really changed in India in the last ten years. I remember calling my sister long-distance ten years ago and she would be shouting on the phone and I would say, 'Why are you shouting?' And now we have Webcams and cell phones even for international callers. Do you know, the other day, a street vendor was talking to his wife on a cell phone and he had a Bluetooth on his ear? I guess everybody has cell phones now," remarked Bharti's father.

"I'm also here, Dad," Bharti said.

"Oh, my dear, did I ignore you? You know when I start talking, I get carried away." He got up and hugged her and made her sit down next to him.

"Mr. Shastri, I have come here to propose a marriage between my daughter and your son. I request that we should get these two lovebirds married off as soon as possible. You see, I am opening up an office in Canada and the meetings are set from the middle of November to the end of December. I will probably be back by the end of December 2013," Mr. Kapoor said.

Vijay's father said, "You have put me on the spot. When do you propose the wedding should be?"

"Sometime in October, if possible before Diwali, or just after Diwali in November."

"It gives us very little time to prepare. We have to consult all the relatives, and Vijay is very busy these days. Pooja is the only one who can help. Also Pooja's mom is not feeling too well these days."

Just at that time, Chemeli, the maid, walked in from the kitchen and said, "Mommyji will be fine, and all she needs is a little excitement as well as something to do. You see, she's bored at home. Pooja goes away to her college to teach, Papaji goes to his school, and I'm the only one left home with Mommyji. Bharti Didi came the other day and checked Mommy out and said except for a little high blood pressure, there is nothing wrong with her, and told me to make sure she takes her medicines regularly."

'Who is this girl?" Mr. Kapoor inquired.

"She is our maid, but we consider her a part of our family as she has been with us for more than ten years. She has her own bedroom and is treated just like a family member."

Mr. Kapoor was very impressed and said, "I know of many families who treat their maids and house help very badly. These people spend thousands of rupees to have one meal and yet would not give their maids and house help more than a few hundred a month."

Vijay said, "This is the biggest problem in this country that we do not have any dignity of labor. One day, it is going to lead us to disaster if we don't change our ways."

Vijay's father said, "We have an immediate problem that Mr. Kapoor wants us to address, so let us find a solution to that problem."

Bharti's father remarked, "I can help you if you'd let me. I have the whole thing planned for you, Mr. Shastri. If it helps, I can ask Raj to help you with all the running around for the wedding. He is like a family member, and I have raised him like my own son. You have not met him yet. He should be arriving here any minute. Lovingly we call him Raju, and the best thing about him is that he's very resourceful."

"I've never heard about him before, even from Vijay!" Vijay's father said.

"Like I said, he's just like my own son, and he lives with his mother where my office is in South Delhi. Vijay has seen my office. It is in that house on the ground floor, and the whole of the first- and second-floor duplex is where Raju and his mother live. When I'm away from India, he is in charge of everything," asserted Mr. Kapoor.

"But he seems like too important a person for you to give up."

"No, not really, because I'm going to be in the office and I have a lot of other boys to do the work. Besides, he will be upset if I don't use his help for his sister's wedding," assured Bharti's father.

"Please give us a little bit of time to think and consult our relatives," Vijay's father requested Mr. Kapoor.

"That's fine! But I also want to request you that I would like to have two functions: one for their engagement and the other for the wedding. I can host both of them in the Marriott Hotel because the manager of Marriott is a very good friend of mine, but you have to decide quickly as I want to make reservations as soon as possible."

"Oh yes, I will not take very long. Give us three days to decide, and Vijay will get back to you after that."

The telephone rang, and the security guard said, "There are three cars and one Mr. Raju to see you."

Mr. Shastri was surprised. "Three cars and one person did you say?"

"No, sir, three cars with three drivers and Mr. Raju."

"Please send a man with them and bring them to our house," Mr. Shastri said.

"What is all this, Mr. Kapoor?" Vijay's father asked.

"I believe it is called *thaka* [initial confirmation of union between bride and groom], isn't it?" replied Bharti's father.

Raju walked in and genuflected to touch Mr. Shastri's feet, but before he could do so, Mr. Shastri hugged him.

Raju asked Mr. Kapoor, "Shall I tell the drivers to bring in the goods."

"Yes, of course," Mr. Kapoor said.

Raju went out and told the drivers, "Bring in the baskets and trays one by one so that we have a chance to place them inside." And then he came back, and Mr. Shastri asked to give them some room for the baskets, trays, and boxes.

Mr. Shastri asked Pooja to help them.

Pooja showed him Vijay's room and cleared the tables and said, "You can stack them here."

"Well, I'll try," Raju answered with a smile.

Raju went out and instructed the drivers to start bringing in the fruit baskets, followed by trays of dried fruit and thereafter the sweet packets in the most orderly fashion. Everybody watched with stunned faces as they brought the goods. It seemed like they were given training by Raju to meticulously perform this task.

A stunned Mrs. Shastri questioned, "Mr. Kapoor, what will we do with all that? We are only four people here!"

"Oh no! You have the whole colony here, and besides, you are not going to share the news with your relatives empty-handed. I wanted to do more, but Bharti stopped me and said to me that this might be considered a show of our wealth."

"We cannot accept all this," Vijay's mother said.

"No, Bhehnji, we will not take this back, but if you don't want it, please distribute it to the poor in the name of Vijay and Bharti's happiness," Mr. Kapoor requested.

Chemeli came in and announced, "The food is ready. Just tell me when to serve it."

"I must be leaving now," Mr. Kapoor said.

"No, you cannot go without eating as we had invited you for lunch," said Mr. and Mrs. Shastri together.

"I cannot eat food in my daughter's house," Mr. Kapoor exclaimed.

Mr. Shastri retorted, "We thought you're a modern man, but you're sounding more orthodox than my father. Come on, Mr. Kapoor, and please join us so that we don't feel that this is a small house and you do not want to eat with us, or we might feel that it is below your dignity to share a meal with us poor people."

Mr. Kapoor was so humbled that he got up from the *chair*, stood with his hands folded, and pleaded to Mr. Shastri, "Please don't say that! I'm like a younger brother to you." He then announced, "Let's all have lunch, and I will lead the way."

Everybody came along, including Raju, to eat lunch.

"What about the drivers?" Mr. Shastri asked.

"They don't usually have lunch as they have a heavy breakfast in the morning."

"Well, I'll send them something anyway," Mr. Shastri said and instructed Pooja and Chemeli to prepare three plates with food and sweets for the drivers.

"It is our tradition to feed our guests first, especially the drivers," informed Mrs. Shastri.

"We are vegetarians, and the food is totally vegetarian. I hope you'll like it, Mr. Kapoor."

"Oh yes, most of the time, I am vegetarian as I have a heart problem and my dear Bharti is a doctor who preaches that nonvegetarian food is not good for you."

They all ate together, and Mr. Kapoor could not stop praising, "I have never had such good food in my life before!"

After a little while, Mr. Kapoor and Raju got up. They hugged everybody, and while going, Mr. Kapoor said, "Now I look forward to hearing from you," and hugged Mr. Shastri. "We are now brothers for life."

After they left, everybody sat down and praised Mr. Kapoor. Mrs. Shastri said to Bharti, "Your father is a very nice man. However, he should not have brought so much."

Bharti changed the topic very cleverly and inquired, "Where is the kite-flying competition?"

"It is where the shooting took place yesterday, but I'm not sure if they are still going to have one."

Vijay called Ajay. "Why didn't you come for lunch. I asked you to come for lunch for a reason, and I was missing you."

"Well, today's the fifteenth of August and we still had to keep the Mother Dairy open for milk. We did not have any help today. So the whole family is working today. We haven't even had the time for lunch today."

"Oh my god! I'm going to bring some food for you. Just tell me if the kite-flying competition is on, or is it cancelled because of the shooting yesterday?"

"Yes, it is still on. However, it will be fairly low-key, and as I understand, only two people died in yesterday's shooting. In this colony of over fifty-thousand, people forget very quickly. It seems that life is cheap here."

"Bharti and I are coming over right now with some food, and I am not taking no for an answer!"

Vijay asked Pooja and Chemeli to pack some food, sweets, and fruits.

"Mr. Kapoor brought so much. Let us start the distribution with Ajay as he's Vijay's best friend," said Mrs Shastri, who then instructed Pooja and Chemeli to pack the food, two boxes of sweets, and some dried fruits.

Bharti said, "I'll give you a hand. Let Chemeli have her food."

"Oh no, Bharti Didi, I had some when I was cooking," replied Chemeli.

"No, you must have a proper meal," insisted Bharti.

"How come we're not giving any fruit to them?" inquired Pooja.

"Well, they have so much fruit in the shop. It'll be like giving water to the ocean," replied her mom.

CHAPTER 6

A JAY'S HOUSE WAS twenty minutes away by car. While travelling, Bharti inquired, "What did you think of my father's behavior?"

"I think it was fine. He was very polite and handled the situation really well. Tell me more about your brother, Raju. You don't ever talk about him."

"When my father opened an office in Greater Kailash in 1992, he bought a house on a three-hundred-yard lot and converted the ground floor and the basement into his office. We moved from London to live on the first- and second-floor duplex after renovating it. He said India will be one of the economic powers of the world, so he expanded his business into the software market and serviced the London market from India."

"So when did Raju and his mother move into the duplex?"

"In 1995, my father's business was so successful that he bought a house in Golf Links and we moved back to England. I started studying in England and lived with my mother and father. At that time, Raju was still in school and was having a problem in his neighborhood, so he decided to give the first- and second-floor duplex to Raju and his mother."

"Oh, I see! Does he have any higher education?"

"Oh yes, he went to university in India, graduated at the top of his class, and then my father called him to England for a one-year program in software programming. In the GK office, we have approximately twenty-five programmers working in the basement with two shifts on hand, and Raju single-handedly oversees everybody because he himself knows programming."

"How is your relationship with him?"

"I don't have a real brother. I tie *rakhi* [a protection thread] on him, and he treats me like a real sister and calls me Didi."

"It seems like he is a very busy man and your father wants him to organize our wedding?"

"Raju will not have it any other way. In fact, he's the one who was suggesting all that to my father, and you know he will argue with my father until he has his way, especially on the point when he's right. So respecting his sentiments, I took his side."

"Okay, I understand now, you're right, and I'm sorry if I hurt your feelings."

"Are we going to tell Ajay about the *thaka*?"

"Of course, I'm going to tell him. Ajay is my best friend, and I asked him to come for lunch, but he could not as he had to give a hand to his father. They didn't have any help because of the fifteenth of August being a national holiday."

They arrived at Ajay's house. All the shops were closed now, but were open for half day. They went into the house, hugged everybody, and asked Ajay to give a hand.

"What do you have there, my friend?" inquired Ajay.

"We did not know that Bharti's father was going to bring in the *thaka*. He was merely invited for lunch. He told my father he wanted to come and talk to them about Bharti and me getting married," Vijay explained.

"Congratulations!" spoke out Ajay's father and mother, Ajay, and Geeta.

"So when is the wedding taking place?" Ajay's father asked.

"We don't know yet. They haven't decided anything yet," Vijay and Bharti spoke together.

Vijay and Ajay went out to get the food and the sweets from Vijay's car.

"What is all this?" inquired Ajay's father and mother.

"Well, it's part of the *thaka*, and you are the first people to get it," Vijay said.

"Congratulate your father and mother for us," Ajay's parents said.

"The food is here. My mom and dad have sent the food with love."

"Your auntie cooked and we all ate, except Ajay who has been too busy to eat."

Ajay's mom and dad went to have a rest while Geeta, Ajay, Vijay, and Bharti all sat down to eat.

"The food is delicious," Ajay said.

Vijay started off by asking, "So what happened there yesterday? You must have known about it."

Ajay said, "The police arrested Mohan. Apparently, it was Mohan's ex-employee who shot the minister. He was an employee at the dairy farm, and he was very upset when the dairy farm closed. Mohan didn't know anything about this man's involvement in the shooting. They took Mohan into custody and kept him there overnight. We didn't know about it. Mohan called and said that he is at the police station. My father has a lot of influence there. They call him Pehalwanji [Mr. Wrestler] as he was a wrestler in his young days and he won lots of medals. His real name is Mr. Anand. He even went to the Olympics. Besides, he also supplies fruits and vegetables to the officer in charge. Once you please the senior officers, you do not have to worry about the junior officers. My father went in the morning and released him on bail."

"Do they know who shot the minister?" Bharti asked.

"Yes, the police know, but just to tell the newspapers and to please the chief honcho, they arrested Mohan. The police knew even then the shooter was one of the two men shot dead as they found the gun on him. There were ten others injured, and almost all of the injured were innocent," Ajay replied.

"How is your father so well-known to the police and the politicians?" Bharti asked.

"Well, it's a long story, but I'll try to be brief. My father bought this land about twenty years ago from some politicians who were dividing up farmland into plots and selling them. They were saying that this will be an authorized colony and they were selling these plots really cheap. So my father went ahead and bought a plot. It was about five to six hundred yards, and it was at the same time that Mr. Shastri had bought land for his house and school. He sold his old house, and other people also sold their old properties to build houses on their newly acquired plots of land. My father and Mr. Shastri were the first people to build houses. The politicians kept promising that the colony would be regularized and the sewers would be put in as they were still trying to sell all the land. They were selling the land for a hundred times more than the price of farmland. Anyway, there were hundreds of people who built their houses, and my father built this house with his life savings. We put in septic tanks and a tube well for our house. A temporary connection was given to us for electricity. Three years later, we got a demolition notice. My father was very upset. He went to the courts and said that he was told by the politicians that this was going to be an authorized developed colony. The politicians were supposed to file papers in the court to obtain approval for this to be converted to a residential colony. The judge told him that no papers were filed and that this was still considered farmland. The courts asked him to show proof of promises made by the politician who sold him the land. He could not show any proof and was told that the demolition will be carried out. And sure enough, one fine morning, the demolition machines arrived. By this time, about five hundred people had built their houses and they all supported my father," Ajay said.

"So what happened then?"

"He lay down on the floor in front of the demolition machine and told them that they will have to go over him before demolishing his house. At that time, I was about twelve years old. I supported my father, and I also lay down on the ground with my father. It was so heartening that even my little sister lay down with us. There was a big noise in the colony, and everybody joined in. In fact, the police had to be called. They couldn't control the house owners, and the demolition machines had to go back. It was at that time all the home owners got together and filed petitions to the lieutenant governor and the chief minister to get everything authorized."

"So how did your colony get regularized. Now, you have sewers, electricity, and water, how did that come about?" Bharti asked.

"Well, there was a big scene after that. A week later, the demolition machines arrived again. This time, my father was prepared. He went and got a stay order – an injunction to stay from the court. He handed the court order to them. But that did not deter them. A week later, they returned again, overruling the injunction, and they started breaking up houses of the colony."

"Vijay, what happened to your house?"

"They did not have an order to break my house because we had a school and the judge did not give an order against that. You see, when my father bought our land, it was not farmland but it was part of the village. So we were exempted for a while."

"Ajay, what happened then?" Bharti asked.

"Well, my father went and appealed to the court again. He fought the case, and the judge ordered a stay until the judgment was given. So for six to seven months, we had some respite. Behind this drama, there were some big builders who were buying the land to build multistory buildings. The judge was totally corrupt. The judge again issued demolition orders to demolish the colony, and the demolition machines came in once again! By this time, there were over five hundred houses built in the colony by the owners who had initially bought the plots. When the machines arrived to demolish the houses in the colony, all the home owners got together and there was a big demonstration. At that time, my father went on a hunger strike. The machines had to go back. He was on a hunger strike for twenty-one days. He nearly died," Ajay replied with tears in his eyes. He paused and went on, "I nearly lost my father."

"So what happened then?" Bharti asked, feeling very sad.

"It caught the media's attention. Major newspapers in the world said that Mr. Anand (a.k.a. Pehalwanji) was on a fast for twenty-one days and he would be dead soon. The court issued an order to give him juice and glucose through intravenous injections. I did not even oppose that because I felt that it would save my father's life. We were crying and praying to God every day. My mother and sister lost half their weight. Even I became skinny. I requested my father to stop the fast, and I told him to eat, drink, and live for us and continue to fight after he was better. My father is a big man. He is over six feet tall and was a wrestler. It was heart wrenching to watch him turn into a skeleton of bones!" Ajay replied with tears in his eyes as he recalled the sad memories.

"So obviously, he lived. What happened with the case?"

"After that, the courts ordered a CBI inquiry. By then, politicians had changed. New politicians had come into power. There was a new air in politics. The CBI inquiry report came out in three months, and they agreed that the residents were promised a regularized colony, and the politicians were corrupt at that time. Therefore, the judge ordered a commission to regularize the colony, provide drinking water, electric connections, and sewers with immediate effect.

"I understand, so did it happen right away?"

"It is not so simple. It took a few years for the wheels of justice to turn. Something good came out of that in that they provided electricity and water within months, if not weeks. Drinking water was brought in from the city's filtration plant. In the years to come, they put in the sewers. The colony people had to bribe the local municipal authorities. Finally, this colony was regularized and we had water, sewers, and electricity and the residents named the colony Anand Enclave after my father's name."

"What is the story about the slum at the back side of this colony," Bharti inquired.

"That is the slum also known as the Jhuggi-Jhopri Colony. There are over fifty thousand people living in this colony, and you can get anything you want from booze to drugs and women," answered Vijay.

"Don't the police do anything about it?"

"It happens under the watchful eye of the police as they are a part of all these operations and work under the umbrella of the politicians," Vijay informed.

"So how did this come about?"

"At that time, there was a provincial election. A new set of hungry politicians came into power. At first, they seemed all nice, but soon they showed their teeth. They bought the farmland with the blessing of the minister who was shot yesterday. They started dividing the 'unserviced' farmland into tiny plots, some as small as twenty square yards but no bigger than one hundred. There were no sewers, no water, and no electricity. They promised the buyers that one day this would be regularized as was the adjoining colony. Poor people came from villages, where they had no jobs, and used all their life savings to build houses on these small plots. The politicians provided some hand pumps, one for every ten to twenty jhuggies. People had to line up for hours to get a couple of buckets of water. Electricity was stolen from the nearby light poles by the hoods of politicians. It turned into a slum. There are ten thousand or more of these jhuggies, and now they have television sets and cell phones," Ajay explained.

"Oh my god, this is disgusting. So what happened about the toilets, and where do people go to relieve themselves?" Bharti asked.

"There is a greenbelt preservation area adjoining that slum where people go every morning with a bottle of water to relieve themselves," Vijay explained.

"With that many people living in that slum, can you imagine the stench it will have, let alone the danger of a major epidemic in this area?" Bharti said.

"Yes, absolutely, there is a danger of an epidemic. In fact, it was only a year ago in the summer, there was an epidemic of food poisoning and diarrhea. Many children, the old and the weak, died. It is at that time that this minister came in and told the health department to do something about the sanitary conditions. Emergency action was taken, and it was at that time they constructed the complex of toilets, which you have heard about before," Vijay said.

"How can people live like this?" Bharti asked.

"I have a very simple answer to this, and that is that poverty has turned people into this condition. They were not like this in the villages, but they left their villages because of drought, shortage of food and work. They have come in search of employment from poor states like Bihar, Uttar Pradesh, and even from neighboring countries like Bangladesh and Nepal, and they end up in this slum as there is work close by. They can at least feed their families here. The problem is our politicians and the government. They are so corrupt that they cannot see beyond their own pockets."

"Tell me why the minister was so upset when he was giving the speech and why did he think that people were not going to vote for him?"

"People were not listening to him. They are fed up of his lies, and his hoods are informing him about people being upset with him as he has not fulfilled any of the promises he made five years ago. Now everybody is asking Mr. Shastri to stand in the elections, and the minister is afraid of Mr. Shastri as he commands a lot of respect in this colony. He has been teaching the children for the last forty years, and even Vijay looks after the legal problems of the jhuggie dwellers. Although Mr. Shastri is not agreeing, every now and then, there is a delegation sent to him from the colony, requesting him to stand in the election," Ajay explained.

"I think it's a great idea."

"I think it is a great idea too, but somebody needs to convince Mr. Shastri, and the only person who can do that is you, Bharti."

"I know Vijay is doing a lot of social work in the slum. I was thinking of spending a couple of days giving medical attention to the children of the slum," Bharti said.

"It is a fantastic idea. I was going to ask you because you are a pediatrician. You would be a big help to the children of the slum," Ajay said.

"I'm sure we can find a place clean enough for you to run a clinic for a few hours a week," Vijay said.

"No, Bharti, you cannot sit in the slum. I have a room by the side of my house, which was used by my mother for sewing classes for the destitute women. Now that my mother is not too well, we have stopped the sewing classes."

"I will let you know the days I am free to hold a clinic for children in the slum."

In turn, Ajay said, "I'll get the room all cleaned up and ready for you in a couple days."

CHAPTER 7

"IT IS ALMOST a quarter to four. We should go as the kite completion is about to start," Vijay said.

Bharti said, "I'm just itching to see the sky full of kites."

Then while walking, Bharti asked, "How many competitors are there, and how does it work?"

"Okay, there are a set of ground rules, and first of all, you can only take part in the competition if you make the kites and the *manja* [string] yourself. You're allowed two helpers, fifty kites, and unlimited *manja*. You fly your kite and try to tangle with other kites with a point of view of cutting the *dore* [string] of the opponent's kite. Once the string is cut off, the flyer loses control of the kite. The kite falls free, and the kite runners run after the cut kite to catch it. The principle is, whosoever catches the kite and/or the dore attached to it, the kite is his or her property," Ajay explained.

"It is not unusual for kite catchers to fall and break their arms or legs. Sometimes, two or three catchers catch the same kite, and since there are no rules, they fight with each other and sometimes the kite gets torn into bits. I remember once I was flying a kite on my roof and one cut kite came wavering above my head. I tried to catch the dore, and running after it, I fell off the roof, but luckily I got away with just a bruised arm and shoulder," Vijay said.

"But a real expert in kite flying is one who can cut the opponent's kite and, after cutting it, can loop it with his own kite and bring both the kites home," Ajay said.

"When we were young, we were quite the kite fliers. Ajay and I used to fly kites at the same time. Ajay used to be on top of his roof, and I used to be on top of my roof. We used to cut off all other kites in the sky till only our two kites remained," Vijay said very proudly.

"At the end of the day, Vijay and I used to end up with more kites as we would not only cut the opponents' kites but also loop them and bring them home."

"Oh really! One day, I want to see you both in action," Bharti remarked.

"It is a done deal!" both of them said together.

"So what makes the string so sharp that it actually cuts the other string?" Bharti asked.

"That's what I mean by making the dore or *manja*. A strong special sewing thread is tied over poles, and a paste made of ground glass, glue, and a few other ingredients are applied over this thread. After it is dry, it is wound on a *cherkhee*, which is typically like a wheel with one stick coming out of each end so that you can hold it in both hands."

Vijay inquired from Ajay, "Who is taking part this year besides Ali? I know he was the champion the year before last."

"I don't know, there are some new players in the game."

"Can we go close to Ali's booth?" Bharti inquired.

"Very much so, and he would be delighted to see us supporting him. We can actually go and stand behind his booth and get a grandstand view of what is happening," Ajay said.

They started walking toward the center of the slum where the shooting took place a day before. "People are going about their way as if nothing happened yesterday," Bharti remarked sadly.

After about a ten-minute walk into the slum, they arrived at the scene and Bharti looked at the sky. The wind direction was from the south, which meant to look at the kites, one would have to at the north side with the sun behind them on the south side. That gave them a very clear picture of the sky.

"Wow! Look at the kites. They are flying in the sky as if they own the sky and rule it. There is every color imaginable, but mostly, they are green, white, and saffron – the tricolor on the flag of India. Look at that! I see one cut off, and it's falling freely from the sky to the earth, but, Vijay, it seems to be going slowly and wavering."

"Yes, it is because it has a long string attached to it and that is not letting it fall freely," replied Vijay.

They reached Ali's booth and greeted him with hugs.

"I am glad that all you guys have come," a jubilant Ali said.

He told his helpers to bring some *chairs* and place them about twenty feet behind his booth.

"So how does the competition end, and how do they declare the winner?" Bharti inquired.

"All the competitors keep flying their kites, and as they tangle with each other and the kites get cut off, one person, who is the referee, keeps track of the number of kites lost by each competitor in the competition. Any competitor who has lost all his fifty kites is out of the competition. The competition ends about half an hour before sunset. They count up all the kites left with each competitor, and the competitor with the maximum number of kites is declared the winner," Vijay explained.

"This is the basic rule of the competition in this slum and agreed by all the competitors. Competition rules may vary from one place to another," Ajay interjected.

"So what if one of the competitors gets his kite cut off by a noncompetitor?" Bharti asked.

"Oh no, that doesn't happen because these competitors really know what they're doing and noncompetitors don't even fly their kites close to the competitors' kites as most of them are keen and want to learn the competitors' techniques," Ajay said.

"You said techniques, are there any techniques?" Bharti inquired.

"Yes, of course, there are two basic techniques. One is *dheel dena* [to give slack] that means that any two engaging competitors will try to put his kite above the other and they both give slack of the string. The kite will carry the string, and it will rub against the competitor's string, causing the competitor's string to be cut off. The other technique is called *khecha marna* [pulling the string]. This is a bit harder, and Ali uses that technique. He would fly his kite underneath the other competitor's kite. At first, the other competitor feels very happy and he turns the nose of the kite downward and lets off the slack, hoping he would cut off Ali's kite, but that doesn't happen as Ali goes into action and pulls on the dore, shortening the slack, and starts bringing the kite home while his helper is busy winding up the dore. He turns the nose of the kite from vertical to forty-five degrees toward the other kite, resulting in the kite being pulled up and travelling up with his dore rubbing against the opponent's dore, thereby cutting it," Ajay informed.

"There goes the *bigul* [sounding of the conch] that means the kite competition has officially started," Vijay said.

Excited, Bharti looked at the sky and said, "Look in the distance, there are hundreds of multicolored kites in the backdrop of the blue sky. It looks like somebody has painted the sky in a design of a huge tapestry. It looks so beautiful."

Bharti pulled out the binoculars from her handbag and looked at the sky, excited like a child, pointing. "Look, look in the distance. There is that kite with a long tail, and if you look on the right, there are six kites attached vertically. If you see farther right, there are two heart-shaped kites and there is something written on them. I'm trying to read it. I cannot say for sure, but there are two names written on it. I get it. It says Raju loves Rita."

"Can I have your binoculars?" Vijay asked.

"Yes, of course." And she handed over the binoculars to Vijay.

"Yes, I see that kite, and the writing is 'Raju loves Rita.' You spent most of your time in England. I guess they don't have the weather for kite flying."

"Did you know that they have been flying kites for four thousand years in India? In fact, they have been flying kites in China too, but not the way we cut each other's kites and not the way we fly them in India," Ajay said.

"Oh really, how many kites do you think fly on the fifteenth of August in the evening?"

"It is hard to guess, but I would say more than half a million kites will be flying in the evening, but the major kite festivals in the country are on the Hindu festival of Basant Panchami, which is also called the Festival of Colors. I remember getting up at six a.m. to start flying kites."

"Are there competitions on that day as well?"

"Yes, of course, most of the competitions are on that day."

Vijay went on, "Once my father told me that when he used to live in Sargodha, kite flying was a big thing and my father and his brothers, together with my grandfather, all used to fly kites. They had two teams. One team comprised of my grandfather and one son, and the other team had my father and his brother. My maternal grandfather was in the dried fruit business, and he used to have dried fruit traders coming in from Afghanistan and Iran to trade, among other things, kites and dore with dried fruit."

"When was that?" Bharti asked.

"It was in the 1920s. My maternal grandfather, who had a side business of kites and dore, used to buy in bulk and trade them with nuts and dried fruit from Afghani traders. The Afghani traders told him that they could not get as good dore and kites in Afghanistan."

Bharti focused on the competition, looking at the sky and admiring all the different kites that were flying. "I have never seen anything like this! In fact, I would really like to hold a kite."

"Once the competition is over, you can hold Ali's kite."

Ajay was very keenly watching the competition from the point of view that nobody was cheating, and said, "Ali is going to win for sure as he has not even lost a single kite yet whereas some of his opponents have lost thirty out of fifty. I think he should change his dore and rest for a little while. I will go and suggest that to him."

Ajay went and told him, "You have been at it for the last one and a half hours. You need to rest and change the dore."

"I was thinking of doing that. Okay, I will bring in my kite." As he started reeling in the kite, one of his competitors saw this opportunity and tangled his kite with Ali's kite. Ali gave slack but was too late, and Ali's kite got cut off.

"It is all my fault," Ajay said.

"No, you may have saved me from a bigger disaster. My dore was getting worn-out, and I might have lost a few more kites."

"Our friend has lost one," Bharti said.

"No big deal! He's got one more to go, and this is his first break, and he is allowed two fifteen-minute breaks," Vijay said.

"Why's that?"

"You could have a situation where one of the competitors keeps taking a break and he spends most of his time on breaks and ends up winning the competition.

Therefore, they made the rule that nobody takes more than two breaks in the competition."

"What happens if one of the competitors loses kites and takes too long to start flying the next kite?"

"Well, if the referee feels that somebody is taking too long, he gets a warning, and three warnings mean he's out."

At the end of the competition, as expected, Ali won. He got the trophy, and Bharti wanted to hold his kite.

Vijay then put a kite in the air and let Bharti hold it and said, "Be careful, you might cut your hand as this is a very sharp dore. This is Ali's dore."

The competition finished, they all got together, and Ajay said, "Let's go to my house and celebrate there." They all went to Ajay's house to have tea and sweets.

Bharti said, "I had a lot of fun, but I must go. I have a long day tomorrow."

Bharti and Vijay left.

CHAPTER 8

O N THE WAY to Vijay's condo, he asked, "You have not eaten yet, Bharti. Should we go to my parents' house to have food?"

"No, after the tea and sweets at Ajay's house, I am quite full," Bharti said.

"Okay, we can go to my house, and if you feel like a pizza, we will order one."

"That's a great idea, and if you have any beer in the fridge, maybe we can have beer and pizza. I'm thirsty as I didn't drink any water over there."

"You are right, it's not a good idea to drink water in Anand Enclave, especially these days, after the rainy season, it could be contaminated. And yes, I have half a dozen beer bottles in the fridge. Remember, I told you the other day that I brought beer and wine."

"That's great, let us hope the pizza place is open today, being the fifteenth of August?"

"Oh yes, they never close."

Bharti called and ordered a pizza.

"It is about eight p.m. now. What time do you want to go home, or do you want to stay at my place?"

"No, I really cannot stay as I have to go to the hospital at eight in the morning."

"My cell phone is ringing." Bharti answered the phone.

"Is that you, Bharti?"

"Yes, Papa."

"Where is your phone? I was trying to call your number for a long time!"

"My battery was dead, so I switched it off for a while."

"Where are you?"

"I am with Vijay, we're going to his flat to have a quick bite, and then I will come home."

"Do you want me to send a driver to pick you up?"

"No, Papa, I have my car."

"You know it is the fifteenth of August, there are a lot of parties, and there are a lot of drunks on the road, and I'm a little concerned about you and it being nighttime."

Vijay interjected and said, "Bharti, you could stay the night with me and can go early in the morning. I get up at the crack of dawn anyway."

Bharti, in her heart, really wanted to stay with Vijay, so she asked, "So, Papa, do you want me to stay at Vijay's one more night?"

"You always know what you want to do, Bharti. I'm only looking at the security angle."

"Okay, Papa, I think that's the best thing to do, and I'm very tired anyway to travel thirty kilometers."

"Say hello to Vijay for me, and I love you."

"I love you too, Papa, and will see you tomorrow."

"I'm so glad that you made a decision to stay. We can be together for at least one more night."

"I really wanted to stay, but I wanted an excuse, and when Papa told me to stay, my heart was jumping with joy."

She moved closer to Vijay and kissed him.

They arrived at the flat and were about to take the elevator when a security guard approached them and said, "There is a pizza delivery guy waiting for you, sir."

"Great! Send him in, and would you please tell the control room that madam's car will be here tonight."

"Yes, sir."

They went to the flat. "Could you please take care of the pizza guy, and I'm going in for a shower because I'm very tired and a shower always relaxes me," Bharti said.

"Of course, my dear, and do you want me to open a beer for you?"

"They have big bottles here. I will only have one glass."

Bharti went in for a shower, and Vijay followed her and asked, "Do you want me to scrub your back?"

"Oh my god, you are here. Do you want to have a shower with me?"

"If you want, I would love that!"

They got to the shower in each other's arms, and Bharti said, "I will never forget these moments because these are the best moments of my life!"

"I just can't wait to get married to you."

"Neither can I!"

"But we have to do it right and with the blessings of our parents."

They made love passionately in the shower, came out, and put on their nightwear. Bharti remarked, "I am starving, open that beer and let's have the pizza."

Next morning, Vijay got up, first made a couple of cups of tea, and then woke Bharti up.

"Tea for you, madam."

"You are so sweet, will you be like this forever?"

She kissed and hugged him.

"Forever and ever."

They both got ready, and a sad Bharti whispered, "Every moment from now on will seem like a year."

"I will go to my parents to help them decide on an earlier date."

"That will be fantastic! I just can't keep away from you anymore."

Late in the evening, Bharti called Vijay on his cell phone. "I was trying to call you earlier, but your phone was switched off."

"Yes, I was working late in the office, attending this high-profile meeting, and I just got home."

"I miss you and love you."

"I miss you and love you too, honey."

"I was talking to Papa, and he remarked he hardly knows anything about you and if you are free on Sunday, he would like to spend some time with you."

"What time does your father want me to come on Sunday?"

"Well, he was saying Sunday evening."

"That's fine with me."

"So you are not going to meet me on Saturday?" Vijay asked.

"I am working half day on Saturday."

"We're going to a party, and Papa was saying to invite you on Saturday night to go with us."

"I'm going to talk about our wedding with my parents on Saturday, and if I come to you, I would not be able to finalize that matter. How about you go to the party with your dad and let's have dinner together on Friday night somewhere nice and cozy?"

"Only on one condition – that you will go where I ask you to go and I will pay for dinner," Bharti said.

"That doesn't work too well with me."

"I know because you'd never let me pay for anything. I want to spend out of my own hard-earned money and not my papa's money."

"I know you want to go to a five-star hotel, and you know my point of view on spending so much money for one dinner, which could feed a hundred poor people."

Bharti got upset. "If I buy anything, let us say I buy some jewelry, are you going to say the same thing every time?"

"I am sorry, I didn't mean it that way. Please don't be upset. I will go wherever you want me to go."

"I feel for the poor people too, and I want to help them, and that's the reason I was talking to Ajay about opening a clinic in the slum. If I start thinking of how much money I can make in the hospital as against spending time in the slum, I will never be able to work there. I genuinely feel from my heart that I want to help poor people, and the best way I know is to use my profession because these poor people never have access to specialists like me."

"Yes, I understand, we have to have our life too."

"I was brought up as an independent person. I have always made my own decisions, with the help of my father, of course. I love you very much, Vijay, but at the same time, I should have independence as to what to wear and where to spend. You will see that I'm a careful spender, and we have gone through some hard times too. There was a time when my father was working for somebody in India and he used to work eighty hours a week. We were living in a small flat in West Delhi. I know the value of money, which is why I want to help the poor."

"I fully understand your sentiments. I apologize for my mistake. I promise you that this will never happen again. You are the best thing that's ever happened to me," Vijay said emotionally.

Bharti responded, "I love you, honey, and I don't want these little things to come in between us."

"So do we have a date tomorrow?"

"Yes, absolutely, and would you be kind enough to pick me up from my house?"

"Yes, of course, sweetheart, you don't even need to ask," Vijay said.

"Okay, then good night. I love you, and remember I cannot live without you, and I believe in falling in love only once in life."

"I believe that relationships are made in heaven and we don't have any control over them."

"I agree, love you, and see you tomorrow."

CHAPTER 9

V IJAY WENT TO work in the morning and was busy attending meetings all day. He called Bharti at 7:00 p.m. from home; Ajay, Joy, and Ali were sitting with him.

Vijay said, "Hi, sweetheart, how are you?"

"Hi, sweetheart, I'm fine. How was your day?" Bharti asked.

"It started with a surprise. I'll tell you all about it when I meet you."

"You are coming to pick me up, aren't you?"

"Yes, of course, I have a date with you!"

"Ajay, Joy, and Ali are here, and they've brought a petition regarding the toilets and need for water in the slum for me to read over and for you to sign. I'll read the part they want you to sign."

"Why don't you bring the whole petition with you, I'll read it and sign it, and say hello to our friends for me."

"I might be a little late and will probably get there between eight and eight thirty depending upon traffic. Love you and see you soon."

Vijay told his friends, "Leave the petition with me, and I'll show it to Bharti tonight and will bring it back for you tomorrow as I'm coming here anyway."

"It's great that you're coming to see us tomorrow. We will finalize the petition tomorrow and hand it in first thing Monday morning. We are also approaching the media as we want them to follow it up. Nandita is a well-known reporter, and she has promised me that she will not leave any stone unturned and is thankful to us for giving the story exclusively to her," Joy informed.

"Oh, that is really good news. Now we can get some things going for the slum, especially that now the whole affair of toilets, the minister's, and what is going on in the slum is out in the open," mentioned Vijay.

"Well, we'll be on our way and let you go. Give a hug to Bharti for us."

"Thanks, I will."

He arrived at Bharti's place and rang the bell. A doorman opened the door and said, "Bharti Ma'am and Mr. Kapoor are waiting for you in the drawing room."

Bharti and her father got up and hugged Vijay.

Mr. Kapoor said, "Come and sit down here and have a drink with me."

"No, Mr. Kapoor, I won't drink as I don't drink very much."

"All right then, have some juice."

"That I will, thank you."

"Bharti, I have good news to tell you, and I might as well tell you in front of your father."

She said, 'Well, go on, Vijay, and tell me the good news as I'm itching to hear it."

"This morning, when I went into the office, the president's personal assistant came to me and told me that the president of my company wanted to see me, so I got really scared. The personal assistant told me not to worry about anything as there was good news for me, but he couldn't tell me as the president wanted to give me the good news personally. The president told me that he was giving me a promotion and was making me in charge of all the mergers and acquisitions. That means I would report directly to him. He was doing this because of my background of having two degrees, MBA and law, an unusual combination. He further told me, not only that I am a brilliant man, but that he was also very impressed by the manner in which I have applied myself to come up with some innovative ideas to do the work in a very efficient way. He was very pleased with my work. The details of my own entitlements, salary increases, etc., will be worked out as per the company policy, and his personal assistant, Diane, will inform me of that later."

"That's wonderful, and congratulations!" Bharti and her father said together.

In the meantime, the server brought the juice and offered it to Bharti and Vijay.

Bharti's father said, "Cheers! Here's to you, my son."

"Cheers," Vijay and Bharti said.

"We must leave now, and, Papa, you have to go to see your friend too."

"Take one of the drivers as it will be easier for parking, and you won't have to walk from the car to the restaurant," suggested Bharti's father.

"Okay, Papa, that is a great idea and thanks."

"You're most welcome!"

They went outside, and the driver was waiting. Bharti said, "I have made reservations for our special night tonight in the Indian restaurant in a five-star hotel."

She instructed the driver to take them to the Taj Hotel.

The car arrived at the hotel entrance. The bell captain's staff in the porch, a tall Sikh in red uniform looking very majestic like an old king of a bygone era, opened the door of the car and said, "Welcome, sir and madam!" Walking through the granite-and-marble halls and maneuvering through the hustle and bustle of the hotel guests, finally they arrived at the door of the Indian restaurant, where an usher seated them.

"Would you like to start off with the drinks?" asked the waiter.

Bharti asked Vijay, "Would you like to drink something?"

"I'll take a glass of juice."

"Why don't we have one glass of wine each because it is a celebration for you?"

"Okay, if you insist, but only one glass because I have to work tomorrow morning."

"Do you have any red Italian wine?"

"Yes, ma'am. We have several choices."

"We would like a glass each of Chianti. How long will it take to get the food?"

"It depends on what you order, say between fifteen to twenty minutes."

"Okay, in that case, we'll have a glass of beer each and have the wine after dinner."

"Would you like a draft beer? We have Kingfisher on tap."

"That will do, and we'll order the food when you bring the beer."

"Yes, ma'am."

"What would you like to have some snacks with beer?"

"Anything vegetarian or maybe I would like to have some chicken tikka."

"Chicken tikka is our speciality," the waiter informed.

"What was the petition about?" Bharti asked.

"It is the same old problem of water, roads, and toilets, and there is a note from you being a doctor, confirming that the conditions in the slum are unhygienic and not fit for living for human beings. There is a danger of a major epidemic in the slum. If that happens, fifty thousand men, women, and children could become sick and some may even die."

"You are right, but it has a lot to do with personal hygiene of the people, and it seems to me that these people don't even keep themselves clean."

"No, they just look dirty because their clothes are old, tattered, and torn. They don't have the resources. It is the scourge of poverty that is forcing them to live like this, and if they had a chance, they would live just like you and me. I'll tell you an interesting story."

"Go on."

"There was a man living in the slum complex, and he won the lottery last year of one crore [ten million] rupees. The very next day, he moved out of the slum, rented a big house, bought a plot, and six months later, he had the most beautiful and modern house. I've been to his house, and you could not believe it was the same man."

"Oh really, that's great! Did he not help the other slum people?"

"Oh yes, he helped his neighbors and he keeps helping the needy. He has also opened up a business, a fabric-dyeing unit for the exporters, and has employed about ten people from the slum."

"I think we need to do some work in the slum to make them aware of the need for cleanliness and personal hygiene," Bharti said.

"Actually, we do work in the slum from time to time and teach them about cleanliness and personal hygiene through the student volunteers. The people who attend these hygiene camps are provided with soaps, towels, and contraceptives."

"What about the children? How are they looked after?"

"Most of the children are going to schools and have access to showers, toilets, and a washing facility in the school. My father has been a big help in that. Although he has retired as a teacher, he is still very active in social work. He manages the whole affair of the school, and for the children, he has built toilets and showers so that if they can come early to school, they can take a shower right in school."

"That really is wonderful!"

"What do you want to do with that petition?"

"Why don't you leave it with me? It has to be typed on my letterhead. I may want to change this to make it better. That way we don't have to discuss it tonight, and in the morning, I will send this document to Ajay by courier."

"I think that is a great idea, and call me if you want Ajay's address."

"You can give me that now."

Vijay gave Ajay's address to Bharti so that she could courier the petition to him.

The waiter brought the beer and the chicken tikka.

Bharti held Vijay's hand and said, "Let us talk about the wedding plans."

"What do you want to talk about?"

"For example, where are we going to stay after we get married?"

"Well, for the time being, we can stay in my two-bedroom flat, and from what I understand from the company policy, with my promotion, I will be entitled to a four-bedroom super deluxe suite with a chauffeur-driven car and a cook."

"That's awesome!"

"All this is happening because of you. My luck changed three years ago when I met you. I got this job last year, and when you came back from England, I got one promotion, and now we talked about getting married, and I got this promotion. You are very lucky for me, and all this is happening because Almighty God wants you to live well."

"Stop, this is your hard work paying off."

"I never dreamt that my life would change so much. I still say that it is all because of you, and I love you very much."

"When we move into the super deluxe suite, we will have to buy more furniture to furnish it properly."

"Oh no, this furniture belongs to the company, and for the new suite, the company will give us a separate budget to furnish and decorate it properly."

"They spend that much money for their executives?"

"Yes, because sometimes they expect you to entertain the senior officials of the company, especially when the officials come from abroad."

"Oh, I see!"

"Doesn't your father entertain people from abroad?"

"All the time."

The waiter placed the prewarmed plates on the table and served the food from the serving bowls one by one.

After they finished eating, the waiter brought the wine they ordered and asked, "Any dessert for you?"

Both of them spontaneously said, "No, thanks!"

Vijay took a sip of the wine and said, "I cannot finish this."

"I can't either."

"Let's pay the bill and go."

"The music is going to start now. Why don't you have some coffee, cheese, and biscuits? It's on the house, and I will bring the bill soon."

In the restaurant, the lights were dimmed and the musicians started playing a tune of old-time waltz.

"I love that tune," Bharti said.

"It is nice."

"Do you want to dance with me?"

"Well, I'm not much of a dancer, but I can try."

"Let's go."

They went to the small dance floor in front of the stage with a nice ambiance and romantic atmosphere where a four-man band played on the stage with a background of blue sky with stars and hills; Bharti and Vijay started dancing cheek to cheek, holding each other close.

"In England, it is quite a fashion to dance on the floor. Most of the time, we did *bhangra*, but I like ballroom dancing too. When I was a teenager, I took some dancing lessons at school."

"I thought you were a Kathak dancer?"

"That too."

"I just love music and dancing. I hope you like it too."

"Oh, I love *bhangra* music and dance. Every time there was a wedding in the colony, Ajay and I used to get invited. We would have a great time doing the *bhangra*."

"You dance quite well. Where did you learn that?"

"In my college days when we used to take part in plays and variety programs, just for fun, we used to pretend to dance like English people."

"Did you officially learn dancing?"

"No, I guess I'm a fast learner."

The music stopped, and the DJ announced, "This tune is for Madam Dr. Kapoor and her fiancé."

Vijay was surprised. "How did he know that?"

"This is my father's doing. I asked him to make a reservation for us, and he knows that I like the old-time tunes, so he told them to play the old-time tunes for us and announce it."

"That's nice of him, but I feel like he is watching us."

"No, he's not. He has gone to meet his friends."

Anyway, it was very nice. They walked back arm in arm. The waiter already had the bill on the table.

They told the bell captain to call the driver. In a short while, the car arrived, and they went home.

Bharti said, "It was a wonderful evening. I'm so glad you came, and see, I learned more about you. I was kind of scared that you might not like this kind of English atmosphere, but I learned you are a man for all seasons."

"I am more of an Indian man, but I believe there is no harm in trying out new things."

"Are you happy tonight because when you're happy, I feel happy too?"

"What a shame the evening has to end like this."

They arrived at the house.

"Are you not coming in?"

"No, it is very late already. You know, Bharti, I get up early and have to reach the office tomorrow at eight a.m. because we have a meeting."

She opened the door with her key, pulled him in the door, shut the door, hugged and kissed him, and said, "I didn't want to do this in front of the driver."

"You did the right thing." He hugged and kissed her and said, "I love you, but I must go, and I will call you tomorrow."

CHAPTER 10

NEXT DAY, VIJAY first went to Ajay's house in the afternoon, rang the bell, and Geeta opened the door and said, "Hi, Vijay Bhaiya, I didn't know you were coming."

"I told Ajay I will come on Saturday afternoon, where is he?"

"He's away with Joy and Ali. They must be in the back part of the colony. I heard somebody committed suicide."

"Oh really!"

"I'll call him in his cell phone."

She called Ajay and said, "Vijay Bhaiya is here."

"We are coming. Please make some tea for all of us."

"How is Bharti Didi?"

"She is fine. You know you'll be seeing more of Bharti here as she is planning to open a clinic in the room where you used to teach sewing classes."

Ajay, Ali, and Joy arrived, shook hands, greeted each other, and sat down.

"Did Bharti sign the petition and give it to you?"

"No, she sent it by courier. Didn't you get it?"

Geeta said from the kitchen, "Yes, the courier came, and I have placed the envelope on the side table."

Ajay opened the petition, read it, and gave it to Vijay. Vijay then read the petition, and Ajay asked, "What do you think of it?" He then gave the petition to Joy and Ali to read it.

After about five minutes, they all agreed and remarked, "Bharti did a great job with it. After all, she's a professional, and don't forget she studied in England."

Geeta brought the tea and said, "Guys, come and get it, here is your masala tea."

Everybody appreciated Geeta for making such good tea.

Vijay asked, "What is the plan with the petition?"

"On Monday morning, we will present this petition to the minister of rehabilitation, in front of Nandita Basu," Ajay said.

"Is she interested in what we're doing?"

"Yes, very much so, and she has promised to help us in every way."

"I heard somebody committed suicide?" Vijay asked.

"Yes, that's right."

"Who was it?"

"One of the guys went to a party in the colony and drank some illicit booze. That spurious booze was supplied by the bootlegger who works for the minister's head honcho, Shakti. He was sick for a while, and yesterday, they declared him blind. He was very upset, so today, he committed suicide. He leaves behind a wife and two children."

"So what is going to happen to his children, and how old are they?"

"They are going to school. I believe they go to your father's school, and for the time being, we have asked their neighbors to look after them. We then went to the police to see if they had taken any action against the bootlegger," Ajay said.

"As usual, they say they have no proof," Joy said.

"We have to stop this activity in the slum," said Ali.

"Okay, we will think about it, but I must leave now to go to my parents to work out the wedding plans."

"What are your wedding plans? You did not tell us about that."

"I'm going to tell you when they are finalized."

Geeta said, "I noticed the ring on Bharti Didi's finger, but I didn't say anything."

"Yes, I gave her that ring a fortnight ago and proposed to her to be my 50 percent partner, friend, soul mate, and wife, and she replied that the pleasure was all hers. On the fifteenth of August, her father came to our house and proposed the marriage of Bharti to me."

"So what happened?"

"My father needed time to consult with our relatives and to think."

"What is there to think about?"

"Well, Bharti's father wanted the wedding very quickly as he's going away after Diwali for a long foreign trip, and my father called me to discuss certain things with him and to work out the details. Can I please leave now, and I promise you will be the first ones to know, after Bharti of course."

"Of course."

He shook hands and left.

A short time later, he arrived at his parents' house; Chemeli opened the door and announced, "Vijay Bhaiya is here."

Vijay went inside, hugged his parents and his sister, Pooja.

His mother asked, "Would you like something to eat?"

"No, Mom, I ate at the office, but I will have a cup of tea."

Chemeli went to make tea.

"So, Papa, what have you decided?"

"When we discussed the matter with your uncles and aunts, they all agreed that they'll be able to attend the wedding just after Diwali. I then phoned Mr. Kapoor to ask Bharti's date, place, and time of birth. I got her *kundli* [horoscope] made to compare with your horoscope."

"Did they match?"

"Yes, very well. The only thing I found out was that you both are *manglik* and you both are born under the same stars. I also asked Punditji to give us an auspicious day for you to get married."

"So did he?"

"Yes, he said a week after Diwali, and that is on the ninth or tenth of November 2013 or the next auspicious day is in January 2014."

"That's wonderful!"

"But to get you married off that quickly, you'd have to do a lot of work."

"Yes, Papa, I will do what I can, but Ajay will be a big help in this. We should make a list of things to be done and call him tomorrow and ask him how he can help us."

"What about the engagement? When does Mr. Kapoor want to have the engagement ceremony?"

"I'm going there tomorrow night to tell him about the possible wedding dates and to finalize plans for the engagement and wedding."

"I have already made a list of things, and here it is. I would rather you deal with Ajay yourself. I don't need to be there. Between the two of you, you can decide who wants to do what."

"Yes, that makes it easy. In that case, I will go to see Ajay tomorrow afternoon."

"As far as the shopping is concerned, I will leave that to your sister, Pooja, and your mother. It'll be nice if Mr. Kapoor sends his chauffeur-driven car to take Pooja, Bharti, and your mother for shopping since most of the shopping is for Bharti. She might as well choose the clothes and the jewelry herself."

"No, I don't have to talk to Mr. Kapoor. Bharti will arrange all that, or even I might be able to arrange it."

"You don't have a driver, do you?"

"I may have one soon. Papa and Mama, I want to give you some good news. I have been given a promotion at work, and this promotion will mean I will be entitled to a larger flat, a cook, and a chauffeur-driven car."

"What is this promotion?"

"Vice president, in charge of all acquisitions and mergers."

"Bhaiya, that is fantastic! Bharti Didi is lucky for you," Pooja remarked.

"Yes, I agree with Pooja," said their mother.

Their father joined in and said, "That really is very good news."

"We hope you don't have to move out of the city!" inquired his mother.

"No, the head office is here, and I will be reporting to the president directly. But I may have to travel more because they are thinking of expanding to Canada. Even Mr. Kapoor is thinking of expanding to Canada. Canada has been ranked as one of the best countries to do business with," Vijay remarked.

"Vijay, do you want to look at the list now?" Vijay's father asked.

"Yes, I might as well see it now."

"The first item on the list is invitation cards. Papa, do you know Krishna Grover?"

"Is he related to Mr. Grover who died last year and was fasting with Ajay's father?"

"Yes, he is his son and he runs a printing press from the basement of his house and is a good friend of Ajay."

"You write up the matter for the card and give it to Ajay, and he will get it done in a week's time. You know Ajay is very responsible."

"Oh yes, I know he is a responsible chap."

"Next on the list is the tent. How long do you need it for?"

"I think we need a small tent for one week for the caterers and a large tent to be set up for two days. The small one will go at the back of the kitchen in the open space and the large one will go on the grounds around the corner from our house. I think the best person for the tent is Madan Tent House in Lajpat Nagar as he knows me very well. At one time, he was our next-door neighbor."

"Do you want to handle that yourself, Papa?"

"Okay, I'll look after that. I will call him up and tell him to come here."

"The next item on the list is the caterers."

"I will look after that too because he's a friend of Madan's. I know him quite well too, and I know he has a good chef."

"Next is the arrangement of the buses. I know Pappu. He supplies minibuses to our school, and he has expanded his business to tour buses and cars. How many buses do we need?"

"I think we need two buses."

"Are there going to be that many people without cars?"

"Yes, some people in the colony and my school staff do not have cars."

"How many people are we inviting for the wedding?"

"I estimate the total to be about three hundred to four hundred people."

"Oh really, that many!"

"Well, we have to invite people from our family. There are going to be people from our colony where we live now and people from the other colony where the school is, friends, and relatives. In fact, I'm making a complete list."

"When you're making the list, Papa, make sure you put down beside it as to whether they have a car or not."

"Okay, noted."

"We need one chef for the house to look after day to day, cooking for the close relatives who would come and stay with us for about a week."

"For one whole week!"

"Yes, son, your aunts are coming from out of town, and this is the first wedding in the family! We have to make arrangements for accommodation for some of the other relatives too."

"Yes, but that is not a problem because all our neighbors are offering accommodation for our relatives to stay with them."

"What about the bangle vendor, the *mehandi* [henna] artist, and the makeup artist?" asked Pooja.

"You can look after that. When you go to the market for shopping, inquire there and fix it up with somebody," replied Vijay.

"Don't worry about it. I will talk to my friends, and they will suggest somebody."

"One thing is left and that is to get sweets, which are to be distributed with the cards," said his father.

"Yes, of course, I think we should get some good quality sweets. One place I can think of is in GK 2. So once you decide how many cards are to be distributed and how many boxes of sweets we need, I will arrange to get that."

"Pooja and you should make a list of the friends that you both want to invite, and I will combine it with my list."

"I will do that and will give you the list tomorrow morning," Vijay said.

Pooja said, "I will give you the list tomorrow morning as well."

Vijay called Ajay. "Hi, Ajay, we're making arrangements for my wedding. There are certain tasks assigned to you, and it will be your responsibility to get them done."

"The pleasure will be all mine. Tell me what I have to do," Ajay said.

"I think the best idea is that you come here in the morning."

"I can come after ten a.m. because in the morning, I have to go to the *mundi* [fruit-and-vegetable wholesale market] like I do on most mornings."

"That's fine. Ten a.m. suits me as well. And how is everything in the colony?"

"It is quiet for a change."

"See you tomorrow then."

Their mother called Chemeli. "When are you going to serve the dinner, Chemeli?"

"In about ten minutes."

Pooja and her mother went to help Chemeli.

"I'm going to my room to change into my pajamas."

Vijay went to his room and called Bharti. "Hi, sweetheart, how is the party?"

"It is very nice, but I wish you were here."

"But you know I came here to finalize our wedding plans."

"Yes, I'm itching to find out the details."

"There are two dates suggested by the pundit, and they are either the ninth or tenth of November, a week after Diwali. Your father can decide which day suits him."

"Oh, that's fantastic. I will tell him in the car on our way home."

"If he wants to have an official engagement party, he can do it two weeks before that, that is a week before Diwali."

"Your father asked my father for my time and date of birth."

"Yes, he wanted to match the horoscopes. They match perfectly, and the pundit said it is not very often that he sees such a perfect match and said that we are both born under the same set of stars. He further said that either we get married a week after Diwali or the next auspicious day is in January 2014."

"It will be a week after Diwali for sure as it suits my father too."

"Enjoy the party, my dear, and I will meet you tomorrow evening."

"Why not in the afternoon?"

"Okay, I will see you tomorrow afternoon, and then your father can talk to me in the evening."

"It's a date."

Ajay came to see them in the morning, and Vijay and his father briefed him about the work that needed to be done.

"When you have finalized the matter, call me and I will get the cards printed. I will get them distributed afterward in the colony as well. Have you made any arrangements for the horse or mare? As you know, it is a tradition for a groom to go to the bride's house on a horse or mare even if it is for a short distance."

"We totally forgot about that!" Vijay and his father said.

"There's a guy in the slum, his name is Badal, who has three horses. He rents them out for weddings. One time, he used to operate a tonga [a horse-driven buggy], and when they abolished the animal-driven carts, he did not want to let go of his horses as he loved them so much. So he came to me for some ideas. I told him that he could start a horse rental business for wedding purposes, and now his business is booming."

"So I'll let you know the date, and you can fix it up with him."

"He knows you very well, Vijay, and he'll only be too glad to provide a horse or a mare for your wedding."

"How does he know me?"

"You seem to have forgotten, but he's the same man who was thrown in jail for an accident with a car three years ago, and your father and you bailed him out. Afterward, the charges were dropped because you talked to the owner of the car in front of me."

"Yes, I remember that clearly, but at that time, he was operating a tonga."

"Well, that is all fixed now. Come and have lunch with us."

"No, I have got to go home and must have lunch at home. My mother and Geeta are waiting for me, and I have to take care of a few things for them."

"Ajay, you can't go without having some sweets. This is the wedding house now," Vijay's mother said.

Pooja brought a box of sweets and offered it to Ajay.

He took one *gulab jamun* (an Indian dessert), put it in his mouth, and said, "This is my most favorite sweet." And then he left after hugging everybody.

Vijay had lunch with his family; and a short time after, he hugged Pooja, his mother, and his father and said, "You have a nap and I have to go and see Bharti."

They all said, "Give our love to Bharti."

CHAPTER 11

V IJAY ARRIVED AT Bharti's house at about 3:00 p.m., and the Gurkha gate man at the door said, "I know who you are. Bharti Madam told me about you this morning."

Gurkha phoned Bharti and said, "Vijay Saab is coming in."

Vijay drove the car to the porch, parked the car on the side, and walked to the front door.

Bharti was waiting for him. She hugged and kissed him and asked him to come in.

The housemaid, Tara, brought water and offered it to Vijay and Bharti.

Bharti said, "Tara, you can go home now, and we'll see you back at five."

"Thank you, Bharti Didi, and shall I bring tea at five?"

"Yes, that's fine."

Bharti took Vijay's hand and walked him to show her clinic. Her clinic was in one corner of the ground floor of the house, which was accessible from outside the house. "I see very few patients here, see them one day a week on Tuesdays for about two hours, from six to eight p.m. Otherwise, they come to the front gate, and if I am available, I see them. Mostly, they are children of the chefs and drivers of the colony."

"It is very nice. You have a nice desk in the middle and examination table on the side with all the gadgets necessary for examination. It is all very high-tech."

"My father set it up for me. Now let's go to my bedroom."

They climbed up the stairs, and her bedroom was in the corner directly above her clinic.

They entered the bedroom, and Vijay said, "Wow, it is massive! It is three times the size of my bedrooms. My whole flat could fit in your one bedroom."

Bharti had other designs and was itching to grab him and to make love to him.

"I didn't bring you here for the appreciation. I brought you here to make love to you. At this time, nobody's home. All the house help has gone, and my father is away to the golf club. The house help will start returning at five, and my father would come back after tea at about six thirty."

"That's why you were saying to come in the afternoon."

"Yes, of course, honey."

She hugged and kissed him and locked the bedroom door from inside.

"I feel so good to know that your father has agreed to an early wedding, don't you?"

"Absolutely! I'm delighted too, but let me tell you something about my parents. Actually, I talked to my mother and she convinced my father for such an early wedding. He was insistent that my wedding should be after Pooja's."

"Is it all settled now?"

"Yes, it is final, but I'm not sure now after looking at your bedroom and the decor in it whether I'll be able to provide all the amenities that you are used to!"

"You are being silly now. Your bedroom was fine. I slept there with you, didn't I?" She became emotional and continued, "Sometimes, I think you don't know me at all. It is not the bedroom which makes me happy. It is you who makes me happy. I don't care where I live with you." And she started crying.

"Oh, I'm sorry, honey, I did not mean it that way. You see, I want to provide the best for you."

He kissed and hugged her and promised her he would never bring that topic up again. She kissed and hugged him, and she took her clothes off in a frenzy. He did the same, and they made love passionately.

For a little while, they lay in the bed arm in arm, and Vijay remarked, "Your room is really beautiful, and it is decorated with taste." He paused for a while and then asked, "Who decorated it?"

"I did it all by myself, a lot of these little paintings and handicrafts are made by me."

"You're very talented, aren't you, Bharti?"

"It is because my father encouraged me when I lost my mother fifteen years ago."

"How did she die?"

"She died of ovarian cancer and was diagnosed only a few months before she died."

"It is very sad. You were just a teenager, how did you cope with that?"

"I was very depressed for a while and spent all my time in music, and thanks to my papa. He did not want me to miss my mother, so he spent a lot of time with me. He took interest in my hobbies and in the things I did."

"He's such a big businessman. How could he do that?"

"He was a small businessman at that time. All his spare time, he spent with me, and if I phoned him in his office and said that I was lonely, he would leave everything and come home. Ever since my mother died, I wanted to be a doctor to help others and went to medical school for about nine years. I got really busy in medical school, and then he was the one always complaining about my not sparing time for him, so he had no choice but to concentrate on his business."

"It is almost five p.m. Let us get ready as your maid will be coming soon."

Bharti kissed Vijay and whispered, "I wish we didn't have to get up."

They both got dressed and came down, and a few minutes later, Tara rang the bell and asked, "Should I bring the tea?"

"Yes, of course, Tara."

A few minutes later, Bharti's father arrived and said, "Hi, Vijay, and how are you both?"

"I am fine, Papa."

Vijay got up and hugged him and said, "I'm fine, Uncle."

"Would you like some tea, Papa?"

"No, beta, I had some at the club."

Bharti's father sat down and asked, "Vijay, so what is your father's decision?"

"He talked to some pundits, my aunts, and my uncles. He said that the wedding can be a week after Diwali."

"That's wonderful! That suits me down to the ground."

"And you wanted to have the engagement two to four weeks before the wedding?"

"That's fine with me too."

"Then I'll go ahead and make the hotel bookings. I prefer the wedding on Saturday night, so the final dates are Saturday, fifth of October, for the engagement and Saturday, ninth of November, for the wedding."

"So what about Raju? Does your father want his help?"

"No, Uncle, not for now. However, they have to do a lot of shopping with Bharti, and if she could go with the chauffeur-driven car, it will be a lot easier."

"Of course, no problem, and do you need two chauffeur-driven cars?"

"Well, we were thinking of renting one."

"Oh no, I won't let you do that. I have so many cars and chauffeurs in my staff. I can always spare one. So it is final. I will send a chauffeur-driven car from tomorrow, and he will be reporting to your father every day. As far as Bharti is concerned, she can make her own program with your mother. So are you both happy now?"

Together they said, "Yes, we are very happy."

"Let us talk about you, Vijay."

"What do you want to know, Uncle?"

"I have met your father twice, once here, for Bharti's birthday, and the second time in your house. I don't really know very much about your family and yourself, so in brief, if you could give background of yourself and your family."

"I don't know where to start."

"Okay, start with yourself."

"I grew up in the old colony that was sold to us as serviced land, but the politicians and the land developers did not develop the land and sold us the plots, promising that the land would be developed after. They had left the provisions for sewers, electricity and water, etc."

"You went ahead and built the house without all the facilities?"

"Yes, we did because my father had already bought the plot after selling our house in Lajpat Nagar. At the same time, he bought a very large plot for the school, which was given to us at a very cheap price due to the fact that there was no school for the two adjoining villages."

"So what did you do for sewers, water, and electricity?"

"We put in septic tanks and put in a tube well for water. By the time, the house was half-built. We got a temporary connection for electricity after bribing the local authorities, of course."

"Was the colony ever regularized?"

"Oh yes, but not without a struggle. Finally, we got the sewers, water, and regular connection of electricity."

"So how many residents were in that colony?"

"There were about five hundred or so, and all of them became very close to each other because of the problems and lawsuits we had with the authorities."

"What happened? How did your colony get so many jhuggies next to it?"

"Just imagine, on one side, there were these two villages, then the school, and after that was our colony. Farther down from our colony, the corrupt politicians, hand in hand with the local authorities, started selling small pieces of land to poor people coming from the villages from all over India in search of employment, as there was a big boom in the construction industry close by, in Gurgaon."

"I see, so did you go to your father's school?"

"No, my father's school was a primary school. There were a bunch of children from our colony who were going to schools close to Gurgaon, so all the residents of the colony got together and hired a couple of buses to take us to school and bring us back."

"What about your father's school?"

"At first, it was till grade 5, but now it is up to grade 10 and he wants to make it into a high school."

"When did you move in to this new house in the cooperative housing society?"

"Ten years ago when I started going to the university."

"So what did you do at the university?"

"I finished my bachelor of business administration first, then I found out that Delhi University was offering a new program in which you could do law and an MBA together."

All this time, Bharti was sitting quietly and listening to the conversation between her father and Vijay. She interjected, "Vijay stood first in that program."

"Oh really, you are a brilliant man!"

"No, I just studied and left everything to Lord Krishna."

"That is very nice. So you believe in what Krishna preached, 'Do your work without thinking about the reward.'"

"Yes, Uncle."

"Now you are being rewarded in your job for your hard work," remarked Mr. Kapoor.

"That's all God's will."

"Now it's your turn, Vijay."

"I'd like to know a bit of your family background."

"Yes sure. I can tell you in short. We are from the northwest frontiers of India, that area is in Pakistan now, and it is very close to the borders of Afghanistan. My great-grandfather was in the wholesale business of clothing and dried fruit. They had very large properties in that area and had been well settled for generations. Then six months before the partition when Pakistan was carved out of India, my great-grandfather, with his family, moved to Delhi because he had a vision that there will be bloodshed in that area."

"So were you refugees like my father, who left everything in Pakistan?" Vijay asked.

"No, we were not. My great-grandfather had a vision that India will be divided into Pakistan and India. He also knew that northwest frontiers being the Pakhtoon Territory would definitely be a part of Pakistan. So he sold his business for whatever he could get and moved to Delhi. My grandfather had to reestablish himself. At that time, my father was very young. He finished school and went to work with my grandfather. Later on, my father got married, and I was born in 1955."

"Which school did you go to?"

"I went to Modern School because my father was a friend of the principal of the school, who later on opened Gyan Bharti School. I finished my schooling and then went to Shri Ram College of Commerce, finished my B.Com (Honors), and joined father in his business. After a few years, my father sent me to England to get my MBA. There I met Bharti's mother."

"So when did you get married, Uncle?"

"I got married in 1984 in India because all my family was in India and my father insisted that I get married here."

"The parents of Bharti's mother were in England at that time?"

"Yes, they were, but they readily agreed to a wedding in India."

"Did you go back to England right away?"

"Yes, I had started a job with an advertising company and had to go back."

"When did you start your business?"

"In 1990, software business was the upcoming business and everybody was sourcing out to India. I was in between jobs. This being the opportune time, I decided to open my business with a small office in England. I got enough orders, so I moved back to India with Bharti and her mother in 1992, bought that house in GK 2, and started living in it. We were living on the first and second floor with an office on the ground floor. I employed ten software engineers and provided offices for them in the basement. Within three years, my business was booming and I bought this house in Golf Links and moved back to England in 1995."

"So did Bharti go to school in India?"

"Yes, she went to Gyan Bharti School. As you know, it is difficult to get admission in good private schools in India. Bharti was admitted because the principal was known to me."

"Bharti, you didn't tell me before that you went to school in India?"

"Well, it never came up. I started in grade 2 and I loved the school."

"So what was so special about the school?"

"Well, they emphasized music, drama, and sports with a good standard of education."

"Were you interested in music even when you were a little girl?"

"Yes, I was, and so was my mother. She was a good semiclassical singer, and she taught me from the time I was in her womb. She taught me Hindi language too because she believed that music and culture comes through the language."

"Tell me, is your father music minded too?"

Mr. Kapoor was smiling, and he interjected, "I can sing some Punjabi songs and do the *bhangra* dance. Actually, I learned how to play the tabla when Bharti's mother used to sing."

"I used to play the harmonium, and he used to play the tabla, and those were the best years of my life."

Tears started rolling down Mr. Kapoor's cheeks, and he went into a song, "Those were the days my friend, I thought they would never end."

Bharti was already feeling emotional, and she started crying too.

Vijay said, "I'm sorry I touched your soft spot."

"I'm okay. You know sometimes Bharti used to join us too, with her baby voice. Bharti is a very good singer."

"Tell me why you liked that school so much, Bharti?"

"I didn't want to leave the school to go back to England. I remember I was in school the first year and I was selected to perform on the stage. I was very nervous. There was this head girl of the school. She encouraged me a lot. She herself was in a play. I still remember it. It was called *paisa bolta hai* [money talks]. While watching it, I started crying."

"Do you remember her name?"

"Yes, I do. Her name was Meera Didi, and she lived in our colony. I remember we used to go to the market and sometimes I would bump into her. She was always very pleasant to me and to all the children of the school. I still remember her father used to drive an imported yellow car with Le Car written on it, and that was the only yellow car in our colony."

"Do you know where she went?"

"After she finished high school in 1993, we heard she went to Canada."

"Oh well, one day we will trace her."

"I wonder if she would remember me."

"Vijay, I want to talk to you about your father's school as I'm very interested in donating some money. So who runs your father's school?"

"He manages it. He has a principal and several teachers who run the school."

"So is he the owner of the school?"

"He was at first, but a few years ago, he converted it into a trust and took on some trustees who also contributed some money. Then he was able to renovate the school, build some more toilets, and add the shower facilities as he was getting some children from the slum."

"The reason I ask is that I want to help the poor by donating one hundred million rupees to the school and your father could make Bharti and you trustees of the school. What do you think, Vijay?"

"Awesome, I think it is a fantastic idea! Isn't it a rather large sum?"

"Not really, I would like to see the children getting the most up-to-date education."

"My father is like that too. Do you know he has provided computers to grade 2 and above?"

"So he's very modern in his outlook."

Bharti said, "I didn't know that little kids in your father's school have access to computers!"

"Yes, Bharti, we didn't talk about this before."

Tara came in and said the food was ready to be served.

"Yes, serve it in the dining room."

"Would you like to have a glass of beer, Vijay? And what would you like to drink, Bharti?"

"Nothing," both said together, "we have work to do tomorrow, let's go to the dining room."

The dining room was beautifully decorated with paintings of Indian kings of a bygone era and valuables of art with special effects lighting all around. A large crystal chandelier hung from the ceiling in the middle that accentuated the decorations of the dining room, which had a large rectangular table and twelve *chairs*, upholstered with maroon velvet. They sat on same side of the table. The server and the chef brought the dishes in several courses, starting with the salad and yogurt, next came the main dish, the fish, and chicken tikka, then came the vegetables, roti, and rice pilaf.

"Wow, so many dishes! Do you always eat food like this? If so, how do you remain so skinny, Bharti?"

"Not always like this. I admit there is a little extra today, but then you don't come for dinner every day, do you? Just take what you want and eat."

After dinner, Bharti told Tara to serve dessert in the family room.

They retired to the family room; and a few minutes later, Tara brought fruit and ice cream, cheese and biscuits, and coffee on a trolley.

"That's a healthy dessert," Vijay remarked.

"Papa will just have the fruit, and both of us can have ice cream with fruit."

"Why are you so strict on your papa?"

"No, I don't want to eat ice cream. I don't like sweet things very much. However, I do like a *rasmalai* [an Indian dessert] every now and then," Mr. Kapoor informed.

"Do you have diabetes?" Vijay asked.

"No. But he has a family history of diabetes, and his sugar level is close to the top limit. If he keeps watching himself, he will be okay. He has other problems, like blood pressure and high cholesterol," replied Bharti.

"But she has it totally under control," Mr. Kapoor asserted.

They finished dessert. Vijay and Bharti had a cup of tea whereas their father had a cup of coffee.

Bharti's father asked, "Would you like some wine?"

Vijay said, "I'm not a wine drinker, but I'll have a glass with you, Uncle. I will have one glass today because I ate a lot."

"In that case, I'll have a glass of white wine. Do you want the same, Vijay?"

"Yes, I would like that."

Bharti commented, "That goes nice with the fish."

Tara brought in a nice vintage chardonnay, and they all enjoyed a glass of wine.

To be hospitable, Mr. Kapoor asked, "Vijay, would you like another glass?"

"No. Thank you very much for the wine and the dinner. I really must be going now because I have to get up very early."

He got up and hugged Mr. Kapoor. Bharti walked him to the door, and while kissing him, she whispered, "When will I see you again?"

"I will call you tomorrow."

CHAPTER 12

HE REACHED HOME and received a call from Ajay.

"Hi, Vijay, turn on the news. The minister who was shot is having a news conference."

Vijay turned on the TV and watched the news conference.

The minister said, "It was a very unfortunate incident, and despite the fact that I was shot, I'm not holding a grudge against the slum dwellers. It was an isolated event."

One reporter inquired, "How are you feeling now, sir?"

"I feel okay, and I will recover."

"Who did you think shot you?"

"The police think that they know, but I think it was politically motivated. It is either the opposition party or a new player in politics who wants to show his muscle."

"Do you know the new player?"

"I'm not sure. What my party workers tell me is that there is one schoolteacher, but time will tell. The chief minister is about to announce the elections, and then we'll find out who files the nominations."

"Are the police still looking for the man behind the shooting?"

"Oh yes, they will keep looking, and when they do have the proof, I will be the first one to know."

"What are you doing for the colony?" Nandita asked.

"As soon as I resume my office, the first thing I'll do is to take action against the contractor who constructed the toilets."

"That's fine, you can take action against the contractor if he's available, but what will you do to fix the toilets, showers, and the water situation?" Nandita asked.

"I'll have to look into it."

"There has already been an inquiry into the matter, and it was concluded that the contractor did not connect the toilets' sewers into the main sewers. Why waste time looking into it and taking action against the contractor who has disappeared?" Nandita said.

"I've had enough questions from you for one day, and I'm getting tired. Don't forget I was the one who was shot."

"The conference ends here," the TV newscaster said.

The minister went to his farm for a few days to think, form a strategy for the upcoming election, and rest.

He called his hoods to the farmhouse and said, "We have to do something about this slum. This is a major vote bank in my constituency. Throw a couple of gasoline bombs or burn down a few jhuggies, and then I will come in and announce compensation for the burnt-down jhuggies, and in the meantime, I will talk to the municipality concerned to see what they can do about the toilets in the slum complex."

"What about Mr. Shastri? We understand that he is the most popular man in the colony, and if he stands in the election, he is sure to win," his main honcho said.

"It will be dangerous to touch him at this time. Leave him alone for now. We will deal with him later if he stands up against me."

"When do you want us to bomb the slum?"

"At a time when there are firecrackers. I would say on Dushehra because on that day, there are firecrackers, and for all intents and purposes, jhuggies could catch fire from one of those crackers."

"In fact, sir, I have news that they are staging the *Ram Leela* and they intend to burn the effigies of Ravan, Megnath, and Kumbhakarna [the three evil brothers in the epic of Ramayana]."

"That'll be the perfect timing, and on that day, call the police guys from the local police station, give them a party somewhere on a farmhouse, and show them the dancing girls so they get drunk and cannot come after you," the minister said.

"So shall be done," said the main honcho.

"Go on, boys, have a drink and enjoy."

The next day, Vijay's father called on his cell phone. "Vijay, this is your father."

"Yes, Papa. I recognize your voice, and how is everybody?"

"Everybody's fine. Did you talk to Mr. Kapoor?"

"Yes, he has tentatively fixed the dates. He was supposed to check with the hotel manager and get back to me, but you know, Father, the hotel manager is his friend and he will oblige Mr. Kapoor to have the dates he wants."

"So what are the dates?"

"He wants to have the engagement on the fifth of October and wedding on the ninth of November. He said that we don't have to prepare anything for the engagement. He wants to do that early as I have already given an engagement ring to Bharti, and if his friends see the ring, they are going to ask him questions as to when the engagement was and how come they were not invited."

"That's okay with us. Just reconfirm the dates so that we can get the invitation cards printed."

"As soon as he calls me, I'll call you back."

"Vijay, you know something good happened today while I was in school."

"What happened that was so good, Papa?"

"One of my old students called me and said that he has become a district magistrate of our area and he wants to visit the school along with the deputy commissioner of police and the collector regarding our application for allotment of land next to the school so that we can build an extension of the school on it."

"Oh really, who was that student? Do I know him?"

"I think so. He was a very brilliant student and was senior to you by about five years. He was my student at DAV School in Lajpat Nagar, and his name is Amit Malik."

"Yes, I remember him. He was quite an all-rounder, and he was the captain of our cricket team."

"Yes, he was in grade 10 and you were grade 5."

"I loved playing cricket, and he used to teach me."

"You know he told me that whatever he is, it's because of me. I told him it is not true. You are the diamonds, and we are the polishers. You can polish a piece of glass all you want, but it will never glitter as the diamond. He is going to call me next week to set up a time to visit the school."

"Did you tell him of all the problems and all the illegal activity going on in the slum?"

"Yes, I did, and that's why he wants to bring the deputy commissioner of police."

"That's excellent, Papa. I will call you back."

A few minutes later, Bharti's father called him and said, "It's all fixed. The engagement is on Saturday, the fifth of October, and the wedding on Saturday, the ninth of November, and tell your father the dates."

"Yes, I did, and he is waiting for a confirmation so that he can get the invitation cards printed."

"Excellent! It's all settled now, and I look forward to you both being engaged officially."

"Yes, Uncle, I do too. Is Bharti there?"

"No, I'm not speaking from home. I don't know where she is."

"Okay, Uncle, I will try on her cell phone. Thanks and good night."

Vijay called his father and said, "It is all finalized. The engagement is fixed for the fifth of October and the wedding for the ninth of November. You can go ahead and get the invitation cards printed. Please call up Ajay when you're ready with the matter to be printed on the invitations cards. Please let me know the date and time of the district magistrate coming to see you, and it will be a good idea to get Mr. Kapoor there as well because he wants to get involved in the school as he wants to donate one hundred million rupees [ten crore] right away to expand and upgrade the school."

"A hundred million rupees?"

"Yes, Papa, he really means it, and it is a fantastic opportunity for our school, especially now that you're very close to getting the plot next door and you were thinking of various schemes to raise money for it. Now you don't have to think about fund-raising and can just spend your time making the budget of what you want."

"Oh, that is wonderful!"

"I'll gladly get him in on that day, except that I don't want to talk about this donation in front of the district magistrate and especially the DCP."

"Okay, I will tell him that you'll let me know the date and the time they're coming. And when do you need the chauffeur-driven car?"

"We could start shopping this Saturday."

"That's fine. Just tell Pooja and Mommy to make their lists, and priority for shopping should be the things for the engagement only."

"Why do you say that?"

"I know Pooja. She would buy anything and everything."

"Yes, she is a bit spoilt, and I will give her your message."

"Okay, Papa. I will talk to you again."

CHAPTER 13

NEXT MORNING, VIJAY went to Bharti's house. Bharti opened the door, kissed him, and rang the bell to tell her maid, Tara, to make some of tea.

"So what is your plan for the day?" inquired Vijay.

"Either we hang around here till evening, get ready here, and go for dinner somewhere in Delhi, or we can go to your condo in Gurgaon."

"Since there is a lot of time for dinner, I think it would be better if we go to my condo, relax for a while, and then go out in the evening."

"Okay, that makes sense. In that case, I'll get changed and come back with a small night bag. I will stay the night with you and will come back tomorrow afternoon to spend some time with my papa."

"That sounds like a plan."

Bharti went over to the kitchen and told Tara not to make tea as they were leaving, and they left in Bharti's car.

Vijay asked Bharti, "Do you want to go to my parents' house for lunch?"

"I don't mind if they don't mind."

"Why should they mind? It is my house too, and I can go there whenever I want. Besides, they wanted to discuss the shopping with you."

"What do they want to discuss?"

"They want to buy some clothes and jewelry for you for our engagement and wedding, and that is a tradition."

"Okay, this would be a good opportunity."

Vijay called Pooja, "Hi, Pooja, how is everybody?"

"Everybody's fine. Papa has gone to school apparently for a meeting with the deputy commissioner of police and the district magistrate as they were coming to visit the school."

"Bharti and I are coming home for lunch."

"Great, Bharti Didi likes South Indian food, so I will make a *dosa* for her. Otherwise, I'm making *channa bhatura* [chickpea curry and flatbread]."

"That's lovely, see you later."

Bharti and Vijay reached the condo. Bharti said, "I will make coffee, you take a shower and get ready."

Vijay went to take a shower. Bharti made the coffee. He put on a bathrobe and came out.

"Do you always put on a bath gown?"

"Yes, pretty well. It is because I am only wearing my undergarments. I didn't like to walk around half-nude in the house as we always had Pooja and Chemeli in the house."

They started drinking coffee. "Honey, that's excellent coffee! I don't drink coffee that often, but I do relish it sometimes."

"I am glad you like it."

"I want to ask you something."

"What is it?"

"You know your maid, Tara, has an English accent? Did you bring her from England?"

"Yes, it's a real sad story of a woman's abuse. Her mother was cheated on, beaten, and abused, and so was Tara. Her father moved from India, and later on, Tara and her mother joined him. Tara was very young when she started going to school in England. Later on, her mother found out that he was having an affair with an Englishwoman as he would stay out many nights. When she confronted him, she was almost beaten to death. The mother was totally uneducated from Punjab, and to make ends meet, she was working in a factory. When Tara turned sixteen, she quit school and started working with her mother at the same factory. Out of the blue, a real tragedy happened. The mother developed breast cancer and died because she was diagnosed very late. Tara was all alone then. She started going out with different boys. Finally, she met a truck driver and got married to him. For a year or so, he was fine, and then he started beating her up after drinking. I was doing my specialization at that time when she was admitted to the hospital. It took her almost six months to recover."

"So how did she end up with you?"

"She told me the whole story, became very affectionate and attached to me. When she was released from the hospital, she had nowhere to go and she wanted to be with me. So I asked her what all she could do, and she said that she knew all kinds of cooking, including Indian cooking, as she used to cook for her mother. She was not very bright in studies, but she could manage the house very well. So I decided to take her in to look after our house as my father was often away."

"Now she has come to India with you?"

"She's like my little sister. She stays in the room right beside my clinic, and she's a member of the family."

"What does she do all day?"

"We have a lot of staff. She manages the staff, and now she has started going to a part-time school of nursing."

"Whose idea was that?"

"It was her own idea. She helps me out with the patients. One day, she decided that she wanted to be a nurse, so I found out if there was a part-time course she could do and she started."

"That's nice of you, Bharti. You have not eaten anything today. Is there anything in the fridge?"

"Only a little bit of milk that I made coffee from."

"Okay, let me order some groceries, and they will deliver in about half an hour."

"You have that facility here?"

"There is a convenience store in our complex, and if you phone in the order, they will deliver."

"The prices must be exorbitant!"

"No more than the normal stores."

Vijay picked up the phone and ordered milk, bread, eggs, and cheese.

"Is there anything else you need, Bharti?"

"No, that's fine. We are going for lunch to your parents."

"I will get ready."

"If you get ready, you will have to take your clothes off again."

"Is that so?"

He came over to Bharti, picked her up, gave her a kiss, and said, "You're naughty!"

They finished making love, and the bell rang.

"Your delivery, sir."

Vijay went inside; Bharti quickly got dressed and opened the door. "How much is it?"

"No, madam. It is on Vijay Sir's account."

She pulled out a fifty-rupee note and gave it to the boy.

"Thanks, madam!" And he went away.

"You know, Bharti, you are spoiling the boy. They're not supposed to get any tips."

"Anyway, that's an issue we will discuss another day."

Bharti got ready while Vijay put the groceries away.

While he was getting ready, she went to the kitchen and made a cheese sandwich and a cup of tea.

Vijay got ready, came out, and said, "Boy, you are quick!"

"I'm not a boy, I am a girl, and did you not know that?"

"Do I ever know that, and I think you are a sexy lady!"

They had their cheese sandwich with tea and went to Vijay's parents.

On the way, Vijay called Pooja. "Has Papa come back yet?"

"No, but he called and said they are on their way into Ajay's colony and then they will go to the slum."

Vijay shut the phone quickly and called Ajay on his cell phone.

"Did you know that my father, the district magistrate, and the deputy commissioner of police are coming to your area?"

"Now I know why there's a big commotion in the slum. Ali phoned and said that all the hoods in the colony were trying to shut off the illegal operations."

"So they have been tipped off."

"Yes, it seems so."

"It cannot be the deputy commissioner of police who tipped them off, so it must the station house officer or the assistant commissioner of police. Okay, you pretend as if you know nothing."

"Just see who is with the deputy commissioner of police, is it the ACP or SHO?"

"Will do and where are you?"

"I'm going to my parent's house, and Bharti is driving."

"That's how you're talking on the cell phone as I know you will not break the law of not talking on the cell phone while driving."

"Where are you?"

"I am at home but will go to our shop and wait for your father to arrive."

"I hope my father will stop at your shop and introduce you to the district magistrate," Vijay said.

"Bye for now, and would you keep me posted, my friend?"

Ajay came out of his house, and he saw the whole entourage of police going through the colony toward the slum. He picked up his scooter and went behind the entourage. They stopped in the middle of the slum. The police officers made a circle around Mr. Shastri, the district magistrate, and the DCP. Assistant commissioner of police Rathore came out of his jeep in front and asked, "Where is Ali's house?"

By that time, the public had gathered around them, and somebody said, "Ali's house is right in front of you."

Ali's father came out of the house and said, "I'm the local hakim, and I am Ali's father. How can I help you?"

ACP Rathore said, "I have a number of complaints against Ali and his friends for intimidation."

"My boy is not a hood. He is a social worker, and who are the friends you have a complaint against?"

"Their names are Mohan, Ajay, Joy, and many more."

"These are all good boys," remarked Ali's father.

In the meantime, the people started greeting Mr. Shastri and started asking what was happening. Some people actually came and touched his feet to show respect and said, "Guruji Ki Jai Ho [long live the teacher]."

Ali's father asked the crowd to be quiet and requested, "Listen to me. Tell the ACP and the DCP in one voice, I repeat, in one voice how are the boys Ali, Ajay, and Joy? Are they hoods, or are they good boys?"

In one voice, they all spoke, "They are our friends. They help us a lot, and they are always on our side."

Ali's father remarked sarcastically to ACP Rathore, "Did you get your answer?"

At that time, people shouted that somebody had made a false complaint against Hakim Saab and Ali. They insisted that Ali was always busy making the medicines all day to cure the sick. These boys were not hoods.

The deputy commissioner of police said, "I'm satisfied that somebody made a false complaint against these people, like Mr. Shastri was saying."

The DCP took the handheld loudspeaker and said, "I'm here to help you, and next to me is the district magistrate of your area, and he is here to help you too. If you have any complaints, I will address them now."

Some people remarked that they still didn't have water and they were being harassed by the hoods of the minister who were carrying on in illegal activities like illicit liquor, prostitution, and operating the illegal bars and gambling joints.

The DCP advised, "The best way to approach this is to write down your complaints and I will take action."

A couple of people shouted, "You will not take action against the hoods. But action will be taken against complainants."

"No, I promise you in front of the district magistrate and in front of Mr. Shastri that your complaint will be handled by me personally and that I will make sure that none of the complainants are harassed."

"In that case, we only trust Vijay Bhaiya and he will bring the complaints to you."

"Where is this Vijay Bhaiya?"

"He is Mr. Shastri's son, and he is not here but will be coming here in a day or two," remarked one of them.

"Very well then, I will wait for your complaints."

They all got in the jeeps and left the slum, and on the way, Mr. Shastri said, "Can we stop a little farther at the Mother Dairy? I want to introduce you to Pehalwanji who owns the Mother Dairy and the vegetable-and-fruit market next to it. He is one of the main pillars of the colony, and we have been asking him to stand in the election for a member of local legislature."

The DCP asked his driver to stop. He, along with the district magistrate and Mr. Shastri, got out. Mr. Shastri went to the vegetable store and asked, "Where is Pehalwanji."

The store manager phoned and informed Pehalwanji, "Some people are here to see you."

"I'm coming right over."

In the meantime, Ajay arrived on his scooter, and Mr. Shastri introduced him, "This is Ajay, Pehalwanji's son."

The DCP said, "Oh! Your name is on one of the complaints."

"What complaint, sir?"

"The complaint about intimidation, that you are intimidating people."

"Somebody has made a false complaint, sir. Every day, I go to the wholesale food market at four a.m. and come back with fresh vegetables and fruits while my father looks after the Mother Dairy. Then we both sleep in the afternoon, and our store stays open till nine p.m."

"I understand now," said the DCP.

In the meantime, Pehalwanji arrived at the scene, and Mr. Shastri said, "He is Pehalwanji."

Pehalwanji asked, "What seems to be the problem?"

The DCP said, "Somebody made a complaint against Ajay and other boys for intimidation. But we found no evidence of that."

"These boys go into the slum to help people and to do social work. I know ACP Rathore and the station in charge, SHO Rawat, quite well, and Ajay is my son."

"There is no problem. You carry on with your work," the DCP said.

"Okay, sir, would you like some water or cold drink?"

"No, it is not necessary, and we must get going."

They left and went back to the school, and after they reached the school, the DCP instructed the ACP to go back and told him that he would be back at his office after lunch.

They sat in Mr. Shastri's office, and the district magistrate asked the DCP, "Are you satisfied with Mr. Shastri's application for the school extension? I am as he is doing a great job, what do you think?"

The DCP said, "I'm quite satisfied too, sir, and we should allow the application to go through. Mr. Shastri, what does your son Vijay do?"

Mr. Shastri replied, "He is a lawyer and has his license to practice, but these days, he's working for a multinational company as a legal advisor."

"So what is his role in the slum?"

"He grew up with those boys you had a complaint against, and he does some social work in the colony. He teaches them about law and arranges the immunization programs. He also helps to organize game competitions, charity programs, music competitions, and many other activities."

"With his job, when does he get the time?"

"In the evenings, but mostly on the weekends. However, his friends are there all the time, and whenever anybody has a problem, they try to help."

"That is very nice."

"But there are some other problems like there are some hoods in the colony who run illegal activities and they must be stopped," Mr. Shastri said.

"I have heard about this before, and every time we catch somebody, nobody comes to give evidence against that person."

"Because they intimidate people, and the people are scared to speak against them, and the only time they speak is in a group, like you heard yourself, so that they cannot be identified."

"I see! We will have to raid them in the dark," the DCP said.

"But they have informants in the police department. Many times, the police has gone in on a complaint. They put up a stage show of a raid."

"I see! Just leave it with me, Mr. Shastri."

"Very well, sir."

"Please don't call me sir. You are my senior, and now I will take your leave, sir."

The DCP left, and Mr. Shastri said to the district magistrate, "It is time for lunch, let's go home."

"Another day, today I'm on an official visit and I will take your leave. Sir, you will get the official sanction of extension of your school in about a week's time, and I will see to it that you get it, but if you haven't received in a week, please call me."

"Thank you, son, and don't forget your promise that you will come home for dinner one day with your wife and the kids."

The district magistrate left, and soon after that, Mr. Shastri picked up his car and went home.

CHAPTER 14

VIJAY AND BHARTI reached home, and after the usual greeting with his mother and Pooja, Vijay turned on the TV.

The news anchor reported, "It was quiet yesterday in Mumbai after one week of disturbances and *bandhs*. However, some people started rioting in the evening and it could be the slum dwellers whose jhuggies were demolished. The news is coming in now that there is widespread looting in some areas and that police had to resort to shooting. The exact number of casualties is unknown at present. The Mumbai mayor told us that he had asked for armed police to control the situation."

Vijay's father arrived, and he hugged Vijay. Just at that time, Bharti came out of his mother's room.

Mr. Shastri said, "What a beautiful surprise!" Bharti tried to touch his feet, but he didn't let her and hugged her instead, then remarked, "Daughters don't touch feet."

"How was your meeting with the DCP and the district magistrate?"

"Amit Malik, the district magistrate, arrived early to explain to me that he has to submit a report on the school extension and whether it is a genuine proposal or not. He wants to ensure that we don't use his land for something else as we're going to get this land way below the market price because it is being used for a school. He was calling the DCP to verify if there was any illegal activity carried out in the school. Soon after that, the DCP arrived. He went for an inspection of the school and asked me to accompany him to my old colony and the slum because he wanted to investigate a complaint of intimidation against certain boys. I asked him to name the boys. He said it was Ali, Ajay, and a few other names. The reason the DCP wanted me to go with him was that he had heard that the slum dwellers have a lot of respect for me."

"Did you tell him that you knew Ali and Ajay?"

"No, I didn't want to bias his opinion as I wanted him to perform an independent investigation."

"So did he find out for himself?"

"Yes, he did. In fact, he also found out that somebody from the police department informed the hoods that we were going there."

"Very good, do you think he's honest? I know for sure that the ACP is dishonest."

"I think I am reasonably sure that the DCP is honest, but let us wait and see."

"So what is the procedure now?"

"The DCP has to give a report to the district magistrate, and the district magistrate will recommend our case to the collector. The district magistrate said it'll be all done in a week."

Pooja and Bharti came in and announced that the food was ready. When they finished eating, Vijay's father said, "There are two people coming to see us today. First, Krishna is bringing in the invitation cards for proofreading and selection of the final card to be printed, and secondly, Madan from the tent house is coming to finalize the kind of tent we want and where we want to place it."

Pooja butted in and said, "Raju is sending a chauffeur-driven car so that we can go shopping later in the afternoon. The car will be here at three p.m."

Bharti said, "That's very good! So you have made arrangements with Raju?"

"Yes, he called. It was nice of him," Pooja said.

"So who's going and where are you going?"

"All the ladies are going, including Chemeli. We are planning to go to our jeweler. He is in Lajpat Nagar. We've been dealing with him for the last thirty years, and if we have time left, we will look at some clothes. Vijay and Papa can look after the cards and the tent."

"When will we be done?" Bharti asked.

"The market closes at seven, so we should head home by that time, why?"

Vijay said, "We will be done here long before that, and I want to see Ajay too. So I will take Bharti's car, visit Ajay, and then come to Lajpat Nagar. I can easily be there by six thirty."

"Great! Then you can take me home, and I can change," Bharti said.

"What about the sweets?" the father asked.

"On the way, I can phone the sweetshop in GK 2, and we can send the driver to pick them up. The only thing I have to know is how many boxes we need and when?"

"Okay, we can talk about that a little later. I'm going to rest now, and so should your mother."

They all went to Vijay's room and started chatting. Vijay asked Pooja, "Have you fixed up with the *mehandi* artist and the beautician?"

"Yes, bhaiya, it is all done."

In a few minutes, they got a call from the gate man, "Sir, there is a Mr. Krishna here."

Vijay said, "Send him in with the car and tell him where our house is."

Krishna arrived and said, "I'm seeing you after a long time."

Vijay hugged him and said, "It is so nice to see you."

He took him into his bedroom and introduced him to Bharti, "She is my fiancée, and he is Krishna, my childhood friend."

"I'm pleased to meet you, Bharti, and here are the sample wedding cards. What I suggest is you choose the card you like and I can put the insert with the details printed separately."

They all looked at the cards. Vijay said, "I don't particularly like that idea. I think the program and invitee's name should be printed right inside the card and there should be another little card for the people we want to invite for *mehandi* and for *sangeet* [an evening of music and dance]. Not everybody invited for the wedding will be invited for *mehandi* and *sangeet*."

Krishna showed another set of cards, and they picked out two, and everybody liked those two cards.

"That's fine. I will show them to Papaji when he gets up, and I had the other matter printed for his proofreading."

They chatted for a while. Vijay's parents came back after resting. Krishna showed the cards to them and said, "These are the cards liked by Pooja, Bharti, and Vijay."

Vijay's father proofread the cards and nodded. "It is fine." Out of the two cards, he picked the card that had the dancing lady with her folded hands, and underneath it said *swagatam* [welcome] in Hindi. On the left inside page of the card with the backdrop of the golden OM, the program was printed in red, and on the right inside page with the backdrop of the golden OM were the names of the bride and groom and of the family.

Vijay's father showed the card to Bharti. "What do you think, Bharti?"

"It is beautiful, and I love the material. Is it some sort of silk and paper mixed?"

Krishna explained, "This is a new kind of card material we have just received, and it comes in all colors, light and dark."

Bharti mentioned, "It will be very nice to see a kind of yellow-brown material, and if you have a gold backdrop of OM, then the red printing will really stand out."

Krishna said, "It will be done."

The gate man informed them, "There is a driver with a car for you, sir."

Pooja, her mother, and Bharti were ready to go. Bharti inquired, "Where is Chemeli?"

Chemeli showed up and said, "What will I do there with you people choosing the jewelry? I'm really not interested in that. I will go when you're buying the clothes, anyway. I'm very tired, and I want to stay and look after Papaji."

The three of them went shopping, and while leaving, Krishna said, "I will show you the final card before printing it."

In a few minutes, the gate man called again and informed them, "Mr. Arun Madan is here."

"Sir, I am Arun Madan, son of Mr. Madan of Madan Tent House."

"I was hoping to meet your father," Mr. Shastri said.

"Sir, I will look after you as I have been involved in the business for the last ten years. Did Vijay not tell you that?"

Vijay and his father went with him to show him the location where the tents were supposed to be put up. Mr. Shastri said, "For the large tent, we need carpeting and about seventy-five *chairs* for people to sit while the *sehra bandi* [covering the face with strings of flowers] ceremony is taking place."

He looked, measured the area, and said, "We can go now, and I'll do the rest in the house."

They sat at the dining table; he wrote everything down and said, "My father will work out the expenses with you. The only thing you have to tell me is whether you want a cloth tent or the waterproof-and-fireproof tent?"

"What is the difference in cost?"

"It's about 10 percent more, but it is a lot better and safer. It does not catch fire very easily, and its structure is made up of aluminum posts rather than wood posts."

Vijay and his father both agreed that it would be better and safer to have the fireproof tent.

"Arun, are you going to be home this evening?"

"Yes, in fact, we are having a little get-together with our old friends from Lajpat Nagar. You know we moved to the big new house."

"Yes, I know you're a big shot now!"

"I'm sorry! I didn't mean it that way."

"So how about Bharti and I join your party?"

"You took the words out of my mouth. I was actually going to invite you, and yes, the pleasure will be all mine."

Mr. Shastri said, "Please don't delay to quote the cost and ask your father to call me as soon as possible."

While leaving, Arun said, "Uncle, it is my old friend's wedding and I will look after you. As you are my father's old friend, we will just charge you our cost, but I will tell him to call you."

Vijay said, "I'm going too, Papa, as I have to go to see Ajay and the boys."

In the meantime, Bharti, Pooja, and her mother were in the car and were about to reach Lajpat Nagar.

Mother asked, "What kind of jewelry do you like to wear, Bharti?"

"Mommy, I don't wear any jewelry, and if I wear some, it is usually very light."

"We have to buy you a heavy jewelry set, it is the tradition."

"In that case, you can buy me a set which is not too heavy and I will give it to Pooja after the wedding because I will never wear it again. Do you know I have so many heavy jewelry sets that my mother left for me and I have never worn them?"

"Oh, dear! This is a very difficult situation."

"There's a way out, and that is you are going to buy some jewelry for Pooja. You buy it for her, and I will borrow the set from her and wear it for my wedding."

"I'm sorry! It does not work like that," Pooja said. And she continued, "You cannot wear borrowed things on your wedding. I'll tell you what we will do. We will tell the jeweler to give us two sets, one with the diamonds for the engagement and the other of gold for the wedding, and because he's known to us, he'll take the gold set back at cost and exchange it for whatever you want from the store later."

Mother said, "I'm glad you girls settled it."

"He will do that?" Bharti asked.

"Yes. We've known him for years, and my father helped him a lot when he had a small unauthorized shop. My father was living in Lajpat Nagar, and he knew all the politicians at that time when the government was allotting shops to the Hindu refugees from Pakistan."

"Was the jeweler not a refugee?" Bharti asked.

"His father was a refugee when he was very small."

"Now his two sons are running the business, and they have a lot of regard for my father."

They got out of the car, and Bharti said to the driver, "We will walk to the jeweler from here. We will call you when we are ready, Satbir."

Vijay reached Ajay's house and asked, "Where is Ajay?"

Geeta called Ajay and said, "Hi, Ajay, Vijay is here to see you."

"Give him a masala chai and make one for me too, and I'll be there shortly."

A couple of minutes later, Ajay arrived, "How are the wedding plans going, Vijay?"

"Everything is going very smoothly. Krishna came today, and we have finalized the invitation cards. Bharti has gone shopping with Mommy and Pooja. What's happening with the petition the DCP asked for?"

"I had gone to the slum only for that reason, and the people are scared. The minister's hoods are already telling them not to sign any evidence against them or there will be dire circumstances. Ali and Deepak are trying to persuade them too, but they are very reluctant."

"How many people are agreeing?"

"Not many, most of them have families and they're scared."

"Yes, we know, but it will take some time to convince the people that the DCP is an honest person. Maybe I'll get my father to call the DCP one evening. I will talk to him too when I give him the invitation card, but tell our friends to be quiet for the time being."

"I think that's a good idea. In the meantime, I'll try to be friendly with the RSS leader here who is starting a *shakha* [martial arts training camp] in our colony and maybe he can extend it to the boys of the slum. These RSS people were very active during the freedom movement, and now they have become active for poor people's rights."

"Is everything else okay in the colony?"

"Yes, everything is fine."

"Bye, Ajay, I will talk to you on the phone in the next couple of days."

CHAPTER 15

VIJAY MET BHARTI at Lajpat Nagar as planned, and Bharti said, "I want to go home to change."

"Okay, dear, your house is not very far from here."

They went to Bharti's house, and while Bharti was trying to open the door, her father opened the door.

"Hello, stranger!" he exclaimed.

"Hi, Papa, what a pleasant surprise?" She hugged him and so did Vijay.

"Papa, were you on your way out?"

"Actually yes, but I can stay for a while and talk with you."

"I'm going for a shower and change as we are going to Vijay's friends for a get-together, but you can talk with Vijay for a while."

"Yes, princess, you go and get ready."

"Vijay, what is happening on the school front? Did your father get the extension permit?"

"No, my father is still waiting for it. The district magistrate and the DCP visited the school and did their investigation. They said that everything seems to be in order, and the district magistrate promised my father that he will hear from him in about a week."

"Tell your father to contact his lawyers as soon as he gets the permission to build the extension. We will do our paperwork, and I will be ready to put in the money. I'm making arrangements now, and the money should be transferred by Tuesday or Wednesday."

"Very good, sir, I will tell my father."

"How was your trip to Mumbai?"

"It was very good. But when it came to spending time with Bharti, we had to cut our trip short and come back."

"That was a good decision. Never stay where you find danger and don't ever try to be a hero because if you are alive, you can always fix things afterward."

"It is a very good advice, I will keep it in mind."

"How are the preparations for the engagement going on, Vijay?"

"Very well at our end. Bharti went shopping with Mommy and Pooja. When my mother is determined, she will get the job done. And how is it going at your end?"

"Very well, we have invited some people from abroad, which include my friends, some of my business associates, and some relatives who live in England, America, and Australia."

"So you are going to have quite an international gathering."

"Yes, after a long time, I'm having a cause for celebration in the house, and I want to make the best of it. A lot of my business associates and my staff in London are all anxious to come to Bharti's wedding, but obviously, I cannot invite them all. Some of my English and Indian friends will come, and these English friends of mine have never seen an Indian wedding, and they are so anxious that they would never miss it for their life. On Bharti's mother's side, they are all over the place in England, America, and Australia, and we are having a hard time making the list and to decide who to invite and who not to invite. Raju knows them all, and I have given this hard task to him. Tomorrow Raju and I are meeting here after my golf game. I must say that Raju is a big help and is making sure that his sister's [godsister] wedding is going to be the best in this continent, and Raju's mother is going to look after all the shopping for Bharti."

Bharti came down and informed, "I am ready to go."

Bharti's father informed her, "I hope you don't have any plans tomorrow because we have to plan the wedding and Raju and his mother are meeting us here after my golf game. We will have lunch together, and then we can plan the engagement and the wedding."

"No, I don't have anything planned for tomorrow and Sunday, Papa. I want to relax and am back to work on Monday unless Vijay has something special planned." She looked at Vijay with an inquisitive look.

Vijay said, "I have nothing planned except for work because I have to prepare a report tomorrow to be submitted to my president by Monday morning."

They both said bye and left to go to Vijay's friend's house.

Bharti asked, "Are these your childhood friends?"

"Yes. They are very basic people, and they are all businessmen. They own the tent and catering business, one is in home electronics, one of them has a retail clothing business, and the fourth one is in the car servicing and repair business. We have another friend who was in the real estate business, but I don't know where he is now and whether he's coming or not."

"So all of these are business people, and you're the only one who went to law school and did MBA?"

"All of those guys went to the university, finished their basic degree, and joined the family business."

Vijay got a call from Arun Madan.

"Where are you, Vijay? We're all waiting for you."

"I'm coming, but give me directions to your new house."

Bharti and Vijay looked at the house. "Wow! That's a huge house."

Arun was standing with the front door open and said, "Welcome, Bharti and Vijay!" And they went in the living room, which was like a big hall. He put an arm around his wife and said, "This is Anu."

They went inside, and there were about six couples sitting with some children running around.

"This is a big party. What is the occasion?" Bharti asked.

Arun replied, "This is in your honor, Bharti, and to welcome you and to introduce you to all the old childhood buddies of Vijay."

They all gathered around, gave a welcome applause, and introduced themselves to Bharti.

Feeling very emotional, humbly she whispered, "I'm honored."

Vijay noticed an old friend at the back of the room, went over to him, and asked, "Are you Chander?"

He turned around and said yes.

"I haven't seen you for years! Where have you been? I remember you used to sing very well, and we thought you would be a big star one day."

"No, nothing like that happened. I tried to go to Mumbai, and it was about who you know rather than what you know, so I came back to my family who had moved to the Dhobi Colony [Washermen's Colony] near the Yamuna River."

"What are you doing now?"

"I'm fighting for the poor, and for that, I became a politician. I'm a member of the State Legislature Assembly."

Just at that time, Arun came over and remarked, "He's a big shot now. Did you notice in front of the house, there is a car with a blue light on top and a black commando standing by the side for his security?"

"No, I'm not a big shot. I'm still that poor *dhobi* boy you used to know, and Vijay gave me all his books to encourage me. Vijay's father helped me a lot by encouraging me to stay in school and telling my parents not to pull me out of the school."

Bharti was standing there listening, and when Vijay noticed Bharti, he turned around and introduced Bharti, "This is my fiancée, Bharti, and this is my old friend from school and his name is Chander."

Chander said, "I could not bring my wife with me as she is pregnant and very close to the delivery time."

"Pleased to meet you, Chander, and it is totally understandable."

Vijay and Chander exchanged their phone numbers with a promise that they would meet again very soon.

Vijay said, "You have to come to my engagement and wedding. I'll have the card sent to you. You must bring your wife and children."

"I will see, but I will come for sure as my wife is due any day."

Arun said, "You must have dinner and then go."

"No, Arun, thank you very much, but I must go."

The party went on. Bharti was the main attraction. They had dinner and left.

Vijay said, "Do you think you can get me a ride home from your chauffeur?"

"No, my dear, I would drop you home personally and be your chauffeur."

Bharti had plans in her mind, but she let Vijay go on.

"It is almost ten p.m. It would take too long to go and come back. You can send the driver, or I can take a cab."

"Did you notice I have a big bag with me today?"

"No, I didn't."

"I slipped in a nightgown and a change of clothes, in case I have to stay the night. Tomorrow is Sunday. I can come back in the morning, and you can do the report all day. Well, are you going to invite me or not?"

Vijay's face lit up, and with a smile, he remarked, "Your wish is my command, my *aaka*."

Bharti said, "Come close to me and give me a hug and a kiss."

He said, "You are driving, it is against the law."

"Oh, you lawyers!"

Quickly he got closer to her, grabbed her by the waist, kissed her on the cheek, and said, "Let's keep the rest for the bedroom."

They reached his condo, and Bharti asked, "Do you have any wine?"

"Yes, I have a bottle from last time as I had bought two bottles."

"Great! Let's open it and celebrate," she said. "Cheers, and here's to our married life."

"We're not married yet."

"But in my mind, I'm married to you, and today I want to talk to you which will give you a better understanding of what, I feel, the married life should be."

"Go ahead. I'm listening."

"Let's talk about your work for a second. You said you are going to be busy tomorrow, writing a report."

"Yes, and when I'm doing intensive work like project analysis reports, I like to be alone."

"So how are you going to be fed? Are you going to get food from outside?"

"I will see, but food is not important for me."

"Being a doctor, what I have learned is that eating food in regular intervals is very important for one's health. For example, if one skips the breakfast and makes a habit of it, it can cause long-term problems of producing too much acid and gas."

"I am young yet, I can take it."

"You have a bad attitude, and you're going to have to fix it. I want to tell you how we used to work it out between my father and me. When I was small, my mother died and my father was busy trying to establish his business. On the other hand, I was very lonely and he wanted to be with me. He used to bring his work home and would ask me nicely if I was going to feed him. So I had no choice but to say yes. That way, he'd get me busy and get his work done too. And then later on when I went to med school, I had too much work. My father was already established, he had more time on his hands, so he used to come home to cook and prepare the food for both of us."

"Didn't you have any maids or chefs?"

"It is not easy to afford them in England. Besides, you have to pay them as much as you earn. Besides, it was very nice to work together and we became great pals. You understand now that's the kind of relationship I want to have with you. I want to be your pal."

"I understand now I will have to change my ways. I have always worked alone. It will be a fantastic experience to have you around. You know, Bharti, I was going to tell you that I will be very busy in the next two to three weeks. My president already told me that I will have to evaluate some companies that we're thinking of taking over. I didn't know how to put it across that I will not be able to meet you for the next couple of weeks, but now I think your system will work and it'll be a great experience."

"You know I could bring my laptop here and I could do my work here as well. I always have to prepare the reports, to give talks to my juniors. I want to share my life with you, and I want you to share your life with me. I want to be your buddy, and I can tell you that life can be very pleasant that way. There will be some adjustments, but you would need to have the right attitude."

"You are so right. What is your plan for tomorrow?"

"I would make lunch for you tomorrow and then leave."

"Why would you go before lunch?"

"Do you remember what my father said? Raju and his mother are coming for lunch, and I have to be there. Besides, we're going to finalize the wedding and engagement plans."

"We'll have brunch together tomorrow. I will get up early in the morning as usual, and after my regular chores, I'll have something for breakfast, and then later on, we can have brunch together."

"That sounds good!"

"Done, and do you want me to pour some more wine for you?"

"Yes, thank you."

"You know, Bharti, I have been looking at you all evening, and when you were telling me about your father, you were looking so beautiful. I was admiring your light green eyes."

"Don't flatter me now. Just come close to me."

Vijay came close to her, put his hand on her hair, and said, "Your hair is so soft and silky." He moved his hand down and continued, "So is your body. God made you a very special person, all for me, and thank you very much for giving me a lesson on how to share life with another unknown person."

"I told you before too that I want to be your lover, your friend, your caregiver, your partner, and your soul mate who can share the joys and the sorrows of life."

"Thank you, Bharti. I am so thankful to God that I'm going to have you as my partner for life."

They lay down with their arms round each other, made love, and went to sleep.

CHAPTER 16

V IJAY WAS UP at the crack of dawn as usual and got down to work. While Bharti was still asleep, Vijay made a couple of cups of masala chai and said, "Chai is ready, my princess."

"Thank you, sweetheart."

She hugged and kissed him and asked, "Did you get any work done?"

"Yes, quite a bit actually."

"Okay, I want to take a shower, get ready, and make brunch for you. Do you have any groceries, or can you order some from the convenience store?"

"Tell me what you need, and what are you going to make for brunch?"

"I can make you a nice cheese-and-mushroom omelet with toast, and you can have it with milk or coffee, or do you want more choices?"

"No, it'll hit the spot like the Americans say."

Vijay looked in the fridge and phoned the convenience store and asked for bread, eggs, mushrooms, cheese, milk, and marmalade and also asked, "Do you have any bananas, mangoes, or apples?"

The store man said, "We have all three, and we have imported English marmalade, but it is a bit expensive."

Vijay said, "Send me the marmalade and five hundred grams of bananas, oranges, and apples, but they have to be good. If they're rotten, I will send them back."

Vijay went back to work on his project. By the time Bharti got ready, the groceries were delivered.

Vijay came to the kitchen, "Is everything okay?"

"Yes, but I am surprised at the marmalade."

"Well, once you told me that you used to take marmalade sandwiches for lunch when you were in school, so I got English marmalade for you."

"Thank you, you are a real darling."

Bharti made the brunch, laid it out on the table, and said, "The brunch is ready, my master."

Vijay looked at the table and said, "On his own, he has never had a brunch that good – a fruit platter, toast, marmalade, butter, coffee, and mushroom-and-cheese omelet with sautéed potatoes."

"Where did you find the potatoes?"

"In the fridge."

"But I never keep them there."

"Last time when I was here, I put the onions and potatoes in the fridge so that they don't rot in the cupboard and smell."

"Now I know I'm getting married to the right person."

"Is that what you think, that I'm only good for cooking and household stuff, and that is why you're marrying me?"

"No, honey, I am marrying you because you're the most unique person in this whole universe. I was surprised that you can cook and do household work considering you are a doctor, musician, and singer. Frankly, I'm feeling intimidated by all the things you can do, and do you know that most of the Indian girls from the rich families here don't know how to cook as they are spoilt with having chefs and servants in the house."

"Okay, I forgive you, I was just joking with you."

They finished their brunch, and while leaving, Bharti kissed him and whispered, "I love you."

"Give me a couple of kisses and hugs to last me the rest of the week as I don't know when I will be able to meet you again," Vijay whispered.

"Why? Are you going away?"

"No, it's just that I will be busy working on my project reports and you will be busy shopping."

"You are right." She hugged and kissed him, and before you knew it, they got into bed and started making love.

"You know how to get your way, and I cannot resist you."

After making love, Bharti went to fix her hair and Vijay started washing the dishes.

"What is the dishwasher for? Just put the dishes in the dishwasher."

She helped him load the dishwasher, and while leaving, she said, "I will call you later."

"Thank you for everything, and if I have more work to do, I will call you," Vijay said jokingly.

"Find another slave as I'm not coming back for that," Bharti whispered with a grin.

Bharti went home and straight into bed. After a little nap just before lunch, she asked, "Tara, is Papa back yet from the golf course?"

"Yes. He is in his study."

Bharti went to the study, hugged him from the back, and said, "Hi, Papa. I love you."

"I love you too. Have a seat as I want to have a chat with you."

Bharti sat down, and he said, "I will come to the point as always. Bharti, you have been staying with Vijay at his condo. I hope you're not doing anything wrong."

"Do you mean am I sleeping with him? And the answer is yes, but I also want to say this. I'm madly in love with him, and he is not the type to take advantage of me. He is always resisting me. In my mind, I'm married to him now and forever. I have taken vows of marriage in my mind, heart, and soul. Whatever is left, you are doing for me, Papa, and I thank you for that."

"I'm satisfied, Bharti, and I will never ask you that again. Sorry for provoking you." He got up and gave her a big hug and a kiss on the cheek, and he whispered with tears in his eyes, "Unfortunately, I have to do the job of your mother too, and this is the time I miss her the most."

Bharti started crying too and whispered, "I miss her too, and you have been such a wonderful father that you've taken good care of me like a mother and a father too."

Just at that time, the bell rang.

"I think it is Auntie and Raju."

They wiped their tears and went to the living room to exchange the customary greetings with Raju and his mother, Mrs. Arora.

Tara said, "Would you like something to drink?"

Mr. Kapoor said, "A glass of cold water for everybody, apple juice for Auntie, two chilled beers for Raju and me, and an extra glass for Bharti as she will share it with me."

"Very well, sir, and would you want me to serve lunch too as it'll take about fifteen minutes?"

"Go ahead."

They went and sat down in the family room, and a few minutes later, Tara brought their drinks.

Mr. Kapoor started off by saying, "Mrs. Arora has agreed to help with all of Bharti's shopping, except for the jewelry. Leave that to me as I will get that. I have made arrangements for the hotel, and Raju is going to decide the menu, etc., with me. We're getting professionals to decorate the halls. Raju is getting the invitation cards printed, and they will be here tomorrow for final proofreading. I have made a list of most of the invitees, and, Bharti, you have to give me your list of people you want to invite. Raju, my son [godson], is going to take care of everything else."

"Just leave it to me, Papa. I will take care of it," assured Raju.

"I'm relying on you, beta. I have nobody else, and you're the only brother Bharti has ever known."

Bharti said, "Raju is one person I can always rely on. He's more than my real younger brother. In fact, he is my friend as well. Isn't that true, Raju Bhaiya?"

"Yes, Bharti Didi."

Mrs. Arora said, "What a wonderful family we have here with a mutual admiration society."

"Yes, thank God for that. Well, the whole thing has been planned, so let's have lunch now," Mr. Kapoor said.

Mrs. Arora said, "Bharti, you have to tell me your schedule, and we will go shopping at your convenience. I'm not doing anything except for some volunteer work at the widows and destitute women's hostel."

"Auntie, I will find out tomorrow as to when I'm scheduled to work, and then we can plan the whole week."

"That's fine, call me tomorrow."

"Papa, don't buy too much jewelry as I never wear it anyway, and I have all of Mommy's jewelry as well."

"All right, beta, but I have to buy you a couple of nice sets for your wedding and reception. I'm also planning to do a reception in England for my friends and staff who cannot come here, but that will be later, after the wedding."

After they finished lunch, Raju and his mother left.

On Wednesday evening, Vijay called Bharti and said, "Have you been very busy?"

"Yes, at work, and today is the first day I have come out for shopping."

"Sorry to disturb you, I wanted to talk to your father. However, I cannot get him on his cell phone."

"Is there anything special?" Bharti asked in a worried tone.

"No, nothing special, I just want to discuss the school extension and his investment, etc."

"He must be busy in a meeting. I'll call him and get him to call you a little later on in the evening. And how is your work going?"

"I am very busy. I have been working till eight in the evening. Today they gave me a new personal secretary, and she has taken a lot of load of office work from me so that I can spend my time completing the analysis of the businesses we are planning to take over."

"New personal secretary, huh! How is everybody at home, and what is happening in the slum?"

Vijay jokingly remarked, "She is good-looking too! Everybody at home is fine. As far as the slum is concerned, I understand the hoods are having a field day, but not for too long as I'm going to the DCP and the district magistrate to invite them for our engagement and wedding."

"Did your father talk to them?"

"Yes, he set up a time for Friday evening for me to see them in their homes."

"Have you thought of what you are going to tell them?"

"Yes, I have a plan, will tell you about it tomorrow. If I can see you and your father both, I will get your father's opinion on it, and this plan was suggested by the district magistrate."

"I'll call my father and try to set up a time for tomorrow evening."

"I will probably get off tomorrow at six p.m. so I can be there for seven."

"Will call you back, and love you."

"I love you too."

A little while later, Bharti called him back and said, "It is totally okay for you to come to see my father tomorrow, and he's inviting you for dinner with us."

"All right, I will, but don't make it too elaborate, please."

"Fine, we will have a quick bite."

"Oh yes."

"See you and love you."

CHAPTER 17

THE NEXT DAY, Vijay arrived at 7:00 p.m. Bharti and her father were waiting for him. Bharti's father said, "I'm sorry, there's been a change in the plan for dinner. We can talk here, but we have to go out for dinner to my golf club as all my friends are anxious to meet you."

"Oh no, I'm not even dressed properly and didn't even wash my face."

Bharti said, "You don't need to wash your face. You are looking great. With a tie and a jacket, you are looking gorgeous."

She turned her face toward her father and asked, "Isn't he looking good, Papa?"

"He certainly is!"

Vijay was embarrassed. "Okay, I will go wherever you want."

Bharti's father said, "Let's get down to business."

Vijay started off and said, "The school extension permit is on hold because of the minister."

"How do you know that?" Mr. Kapoor asked.

"The district magistrate called my father and said he had forwarded the application to HUDA (Haryana Urban Housing Authority), which is the final authority that sanctions the allotment of plots and gives permits to build on it. Finally, my father phoned the HUDA office to inquire, and they told him the application was still pending and it was under scrutiny."

"My father has drafted the entire infrastructure, and his lawyers shall be giving the documents to you for review on Monday," Vijay informed.

"That's very efficient of your father."

"My father wanted me to convey the message to you that he is very happy to have you on board for this noble cause."

Bharti asked, "What is the plan to deal with the hoods of the slum, and what are you going to tell the DCP when you go to him to deliver the invitation cards for our engagement and the wedding?"

Mr. Kapoor interjected, "So your father is inviting the DCP?"

"Yes, the DCP is totally honest and a good friend of the district magistrate who was a student of my father, but nobody knows that." Vijay paused for a minute and then continued, "I will see what the DCP suggests, but I will tell him about all the illegal activities in the slum and give him the list of names of the hoods which Ali and Ajay compiled."

"That sounds like a plan," agreed Mr. Kapoor. He paused for a while and then continued, "That means I should get my funds ready for next week."

"If you like," Vijay said.

"Let us go to the club as my friends must be waiting anxiously to meet you."

Mr. Kapoor had six friends who had reserved one side of the bar where they were all waiting, and when Mr. Kapoor arrived with Vijay and Bharti, they all greeted them very warmly. Most of these friends were ex-officers in the army or air force. Mr. Kapoor introduced them one by one, and they all sat down to have a drink. General Kapoor (one of the friends of Mr. Kapoor) raised his glass and said, "Here is a toast to Vijay and Bharti and all the best in your new venture of married life, and may you have a successful, healthy, and happy life!"

Vijay and Bharti replied, "Thank you."

They discussed Vijay's career for a while, went to the dining room for dinner, and after dinner, Bharti and Vijay said, "We want to take your leave as we have to go to work early in the morning."

Mr. Kapoor suggested, "You can take my driver home, and he can come back and pick me up."

Bharti invited Vijay into her house and said, "How did you like my father's friends?"

"They are all fine, and it is good to have friends with a common interest, for example, they all have interests in golf and they were all talking about golf for a long time. At least, that way, your father doesn't have to discuss any business with them. He is very smart to keep the business and social circle separate."

"You're so right, Vijay. If he socializes with the business people in the evening too, he will never get away from business and will be tensed all the time."

"I want to go home, Bharti, what's on your mind?"

"It is only ten p.m. Can't you spend some time with me? Nobody's at home now, and Tara has gone for two days to the hospital for training."

"So who looks after the house and your people?"

"We have three other servants, one chef and two others, who live on-site in the quarters at the back of the house, and if you need them, we just go to the kitchen, ring the bell, and they will be here in five minutes."

"So you have provided accommodation for them? Do you charge them any rent?"

"No, of course not, the quarters go with the job. They get salary, and they get the flat to live in it."

"What does the flat consist of?"

"It consists of one family room, two bedrooms, one kitchen, and one bathroom. It is a two-bedroom flat. Their wives also come and help in the daytime, like doing the dusting, cleaning, etc."

"That's a good arrangement. What do you want to do now?"

"We can go into my bedroom and listen to some old-time songs, or would you rather listen to some slow English music? I have a full selection in my bedroom."

In her bedroom, she switched on the tunes of old-time songs and Vijay started humming the tune. At that, Bharti remarked, "This tune is based on old-time waltz." She started dancing with him and said, "Hold me close."

They danced away for a while. He held her close and whispered, "I have been missing you every night and couldn't stop thinking of you."

"Same here, Vijay." They started kissing passionately, and Bharti whispered, "I'm waiting for my wedding and want to be with you day and night."

"Sweetheart, it won't be long now. I promise you I'm yours and only yours, not just in this life but in the next several lives to come."

"Make love to me."

He replied, "The pleasure will be all mine."

After making love, Bharti asked, "Do you want some coffee or tea?"

Vijay was admiring a painting in the room and remarked, "It was not there when I was here last time. Who is that guy in the background with you?"

"Very observant of you, my dear Watson, I had painted it few years back when I returned from India after meeting you and you were in my thoughts!"

"It is an exquisite piece of work, and why didn't you become an artist rather than a doctor!"

"Because you know the answer to that and we must go downstairs before my father arrives. Now tell me, do you want tea or coffee, my lord!"

Vijay said, "I wouldn't mind a lemon tea, but who will make it?"

"I will make it, of course. I have made it for you before, haven't I?"

They went downstairs to the family room, and Bharti put on some music before going to the kitchen.

Just at that time, Mr. Kapoor arrived and asked, "Bharti, where are you?"

Bharti replied, "Hi, Papa, I am in the kitchen making tea for Vijay," and thought, *what perfect timing. If he had come a little earlier, we would have been caught in the act. Maybe he did come but didn't want to be embarrassed.*

"There you are, Bharti. As you are making tea, I'll have one too today, and where is Vijay?"

Bharti was dumfounded and thought to herself that they would never take that chance again. She replied in a stuttering voice to the earlier question, "He . . . he's in the family room, and, Papa, when did you come?"

"I came when you were upstairs, showing Vijay your bedroom."

"Why didn't you come up?"

"Did you really want me to disturb your conversation? Besides, I had some work in the study."

Mr. Kapoor walked over to the family room and remarked, "Vijay, I thought you might be here as you were getting pretty bored with all that golf talk at the club."

"I don't play golf but want to learn, and I think it's a great game. Also, I know many big deals are clinched on the golf course."

"It is very true, but the main thing about golf is you walk in the fresh air early in the morning. You relax and get your mind away from the business, and it is healthy for you."

"Yes, I agree, and I want to take some lessons when I am settled in my job and in the house."

"You and Bharti could play golf together."

"Bharti knows how to play golf? She didn't tell me."

"Of course, she knows how to play golf. After her mother died, she used to go everywhere I went, and then she stopped when she started med school."

Just then, Bharti returned with tea, instructing them to add sugar to their own taste.

"You didn't tell me you could play golf, Bharti?" astonished Vijay asked.

"It never came up. I like to play golf, but I'm not a fanatic like some of Papa's friends. They play golf, live with golf, and talk about nothing but golf."

"Now, now, don't be so harsh on my friends. I know sometimes they go overboard."

Vijay remarked, "It is great to sit with the family and have tea."

"I'm glad you consider this your family, and that's what I expected from you. You have touched my heart today," Mr. Kapoor replied in an emotional tone.

"I've heard how you loved Bharti after her mother died and all the sacrifices you made. I have the highest regard for you, and if you don't mind from today onward, I am going to start calling you Papa."

For a minute, Mr. Kapoor was dumfounded as he became emotional and did not know what to say as he didn't expect that from Vijay. He got up, hugged Vijay, and said, "You are a much better and much more intelligent human being than I thought you were. You have surpassed all my expectations, and I know now why Bharti loves you so much. Today you've taken away all my worries as I know you are going to look after her, probably better than I can, and thank you."

Vijay became emotional too and replied, "Papa, I would never give you a chance to complain."

Seeing all that, Bharti also became emotional. Tears started to flow from her eyes to her rosy cheeks, and she went over to Vijay, hugged him, and whispered, "Thank you, both of you," as she put her arms around her papa.

They sat around for a while. Vijay got up and said, "I must leave. I have to be in my office early for a meeting at seven a.m."

Bharti went to the door to see him off.

CHAPTER 18

V IJAY WENT TO work in the morning but returned home early as he had handled in his project. After that, he went to pick up the invitation cards from his parents' house to deliver the same to the DCP and the district magistrate. As he was leaving, his mother reminded him, "Don't forget to take the sweets as there is a stack of boxes in your room."

He quickly picked up two boxes and left.

First, he went to the DCP's house and informed the security guard outside, "My name is Vijay Shastri, and I'm here to see the DCP." The guard sent a policeman inside, and in a couple of minutes, the policeman escorted Vijay in and told him to sit down and wait.

After a little while, the DCP arrived and said, "Hello, Vijay."

"Good evening, sir, I am here to invite you to attend my engagement and wedding, and here are invitation cards along with some sweets for the family. My family will be honored if you will spare the time for these two occasions."

"Thank you very much, but the sweets are not necessary."

"You know, sir, it is customary to present the sweets with the cards."

"Okay, just sit down, I want talk to you. Tell me what is happening in the slum."

"The hoods have successfully intimidated the slum dwellers and are having a field day with their illegal activities."

"Not for too long." And the DCP asked Vijay to follow him to his secure office in the house, then continued, "Nobody can listen in or disturb us in this office."

After sitting down, the DCP said, "I will come to the point that I have a special operation starting on Saturday, that is tomorrow, and what I need for this operation is the map of the slum and, if possible, a map of the whole area including your old colony, the slum, and all the roads leading to it. Can you help me with that?"

"Yes, sir, I can. We had downloaded the maps by satellite as a company called GPS has started a system, which provides road maps and directions to the drivers."

"That will be fantastic! How can I get that?"

"Ajay, my friend, has that map, and I can have that delivered to you tonight or tomorrow morning in an envelope marked Personal."

"Don't forget to mark on that map the areas where the illegal activities are going on, but tonight, I'm going out. How about if I can get it by nine a.m. tomorrow?"

"Yes, sir, you will have it by eight a.m. So what is this special operation?"

"I'm sorry, but you realize I cannot talk about it at this time."

"Yes, sir, and can I take your leave?"

"Very well, Vijay, and thank you very much."

Vijay left for the district magistrate's house.

He met the district magistrate and said, "I have brought my engagement and wedding cards, sir."

"Don't call me sir. Just call me Amit, and come in."

He greeted Amit's family and sat down.

"Did your father get the extension?"

"No, not yet."

"Very well. Keep me posted and stay for dinner as you will meet somebody very special here tonight."

"Sorry, sir, I cannot, I have a prior commitment, but who will I meet if I were to stay?"

"My friend, the DCP, is coming here for dinner."

"I just came from his house, but he didn't tell me that!"

"He won't tell you because he's a police officer."

"Okay, in that case, I must leave now as I don't want to embarrass him." And after a while, he left.

Vijay went straight to Ajay's house and asked him, "Do you have that satellite map of the colony including the surrounding area. You remember you showed it to me once?"

"Yes, I have several copies of that. In fact, I made a big copy of that and put it up on the wall in my office at the back of the Mother Dairy."

Vijay walked him out of the house so nobody could hear him and said, "Get a fresh copy of that, and mark up all the areas where the illegal activities are taking place. Can you deliver it to the DCP by eight a.m. tomorrow? And don't tell anybody about it."

"It will be done by eight tomorrow. But what's happening, Vijay?"

"I think the DCP is going to have some sort of a secret operation in the slum, but he didn't tell me the details."

"I heard the ACP has gone on vacation for at least two weeks as of today."

"I think the DCP does not want the ACP to be there as he knows he's corrupt. Ajay, can you show me that map and let us just mark it up together."

They went to Ajay's office. Vijay and Ajay both marked the map and put it in a plain envelope, and Vijay wrote down the DCP's address on the envelope.

Vijay said, "I must leave and will talk to you tomorrow."

Vijay went to his house, told his father that he had delivered the cards, and asked, "Is there anything else to do?"

"We would like to go shopping with Bharti tomorrow morning," said his mother.

Vijay called Bharti on her cell. "Hi, honey."

"Don't honey me, I've been waiting for you for the last three hours."

"You know how it is, you go to two places and you cannot leave without having tea and a little conversation. Our culture is such, whether you want to or not, you have to eat everywhere you go."

"Okay, I understand now, you're fed up of eating and people's hospitality. For tomorrow morning, I have nothing much planned. Either I can go shopping with Pooja and Mommy or I can go shopping with Raju's Mommy, I haven't decided yet. What are you doing tonight?"

"It is up to you. I am free now until Monday morning, except that I have to do a bit of work on Sunday, and how about you?"

"I have nothing to do till Monday. If you want me to come over, I can come tonight."

Vijay said, "That's fine, I will see you. Do you want to do anything special?"

"We could go to a disco near your house and have Chinese food."

"That sounds like a plan." Vijay told his mother, "Bharti can go shopping with you tomorrow morning, and what time would you want to go?"

"Say about ten thirty a.m. because the shops don't open till eleven."

"All right, I must leave now as I have to meet Bharti."

He said bye to his mother and Pooja and left.

When Bharti and Vijay met, the very first thing Bharti said was, "Something has been bothering me all night. Did you know that Papa was downstairs when we were making love upstairs?"

"You know, come to think of it. I heard him walking in when I was looking at your painting!"

"That takes a load off my mind! We mustn't take that chance again."

"I agree, let's go somewhere to make us forget that incident."

They went to a disco, had a good time, and came back to make love and sleep and in Vijay's condo.

CHAPTER 19

THE DEPUTY COMMISSIONER of police (DCP) was waiting for Rathore, a corrupt assistant commissioner of police in charge of the slum and the surrounding area, to go on vacation. At that time, the DCP arranged the deputation of two ACPs from the crime branch for a special cleanup operation to put an end to the illegal activities in the slum. On Saturday morning, two young officers arrived at the DCP's house and told the guard, "Inform the DCP that ACP Rakesh and ACP Samir have come to meet him."

A DCP has several precincts under his command, and each precinct is headed by one or two ACPs and several police stations. An SHO (station house officer) heads each police station.

The guard saluted them and informed the DCP of their arrival.

The DCP looked at them and saw two well-built, smart six-feet-tall men and asked them, "Are you fellows bodybuilders?"

"We try to keep fit, sir."

The DCP took them to his secure office and told them to sit down. Both the officers handed in their papers. The DCP started off by saying, "I know your reputation, and you come very highly recommended to me."

Each one of them remarked, "We know your reputation too, and it is our privilege to work with you, sir, and we hope to learn a lot from you."

"I have brought you two fine officers for a special operation to stop illegal activities in the slum and have arranged backup from another police station within one of my precincts. The police station of the slum in question doesn't know anything about it because there is a lot of corruption in that station and I believe they have the backing of some politicians. So it is going to take some time to clean up the police station, but first, we want to shut down all the illegal activities in the slum because they are affecting the normal life of the people living in the slum who are being subjected to extortion and violence," the DCP briefed.

"We are with you, sir, and it'll be our pleasure to shut down these operations."

"Here is a map of that slum. As you see, this is a school, and farther down is the Anand Colony. After that, the slum starts, and farther down into the slum, there is a ground, and all around the ground is the main slum. The slum is egg shaped. On the right side of the ground are the bigger plots, and on the left of the ground is a big cluster of jhuggies. Behind this cluster of jhuggies is the open space, which is the greenbelt area, and after the greenbelt is a road that leads to the industrial area. And through this greenbelt is a pathway, which the slum dwellers use for their commute to work by foot, cycle, or scooter. But the hoods use this pathway for the illegal activities as marked here and drive their cars and trucks through this pathway. Any questions?" asked the DCP.

"No, sir, it is crystal clear. What we would like to do is to get in the slum when it's getting dark, say, about five thirty p.m. We will scout the area and make our own way in. We are going in plain clothes, are we not, sir?"

"Yes, I think that will be the best, and I want you to take all the precautions and have your guns on hand."

"Yes, sir, and we have special small rapid fire guns."

"Excellent! I will be your backup, and we'll be listening to all your conversations through this small microphone, which you will attach to yourself, somewhere. It even sticks to your skin."

"We will secure it, and you can test it."

"How are you going to secure it?"

"Rakesh is an expert on fixing microphones," Samir said.

"Okay, how are you going to do this, Rakesh?"

"I'm going to sew a cloth on the shirt, thereby creating a small pocket. Then I'll put the microphone in that pocket and finish sewing all around it and hope that will work."

"That sounds very good, and here is my secure cell phone number. You can always call me on that, and one more thing, do you want me to send the plainclothes officers with you or just after you? I can assure you that these officers are very reliable. They are from a different police station but are still under my command, and they have worked with me on many occasions."

Samir said, "It's a good idea, but I think we would like to go in first and they can follow us in about one hour."

"Okay, I will call them here this afternoon and arrange a meeting between you two and the four of them."

"Very well, sir, what time do you want us to gather here?"

"Get yourself ready with the bulletproof vests and your gear and let us meet at four thirty p.m."

"But we don't have any bulletproof vests, sir."

"In that case, I will get them for you."

They met at four thirty. The DCP introduced the two ACPs to the four subinspectors.

He informed them, "Rakesh and Samir are going in at five thirty p.m., and I suggest you go at six thirty p.m. By this time, they would have scouted the slum."

They exchanged their cell phone numbers, tested the microphones, and Samir said, "I got in touch with a property dealer in the area and told him that we are interested to buy some property in which we can open a dyeing and a fabrication unit for exporters. He said he has a property, so I have fixed a time of five thirty with him. Do you know anybody that we can trust in the slum or the adjoining Anand Enclave, sir?"

"I met some people there, but I'm not sure if I can trust them, but I know a chap named Vijay who used to live in Anand Enclave and his father runs a school in that area," said the DCP.

"What is the name of the principal who runs the school?" Rakesh asked.

"He's known as Shastriji. He seems to be honest."

"Did they ever live in Lajpat Nagar?"

"I think so, but I'm not sure. You can inquire about it when you go there."

"Very well, sir. Now we'll take your leave."

"Good luck, boys, and don't forget I will be listening and recording every word you say, and don't forget to leave your cell phones on."

The DCP called SHO Rawat, the officer in charge of the police station of the area, and asked, "How many men and officers do you have on duty?"

Officer Rawat replied, "I can spare two subinspectors and twenty-five policemen."

"Very well then. Get them ready and wait for my orders to join us in the police action."

"Where are we going, sir?"

"We are going to several places, and I will let you know where to come."

"When do you want us, sir?"

"I want you to be ready to go at seven p.m. and wait for my phone call."

Rakesh and Samir left on motorbikes and went straight to Anand Enclave to meet the property dealer.

They chatted with him for about ten minutes, and the property dealer told them that he had two properties. One was right in the Anand Enclave, which could be transferred into their name, and a plot adjoining it was still unauthorized but would be authorized soon.

Samir asked, "Are there any booze shops in the slum?"

"Everything is available in the slum, depends on what you want."

"We work very hard, twelve to fourteen hours a day, and when we are tired, we need a little relaxation."

"I understand you need a couple of drinks and something to watch."

"We only drink beer. Do you have a beer bar with some entertainment in this slum?"

"Oh yes, we have."

"Let us see the properties first, and then we can go for a beer."

Rakesh and Samir started inventing the plans as to where they would put the fabrication unit and how much open space would be required for the dyeing plant.

"You could even bore a deep well for all the water you want," informed Babu, the property dealer.

"What about the electricity?"

"This single-story building for sale in Anand Enclave has an electricity connection, and you can use that for anything."

They both agreed that it was a good property and feigned interest to buy.

"Labor is available in abundance in this slum," informed Babu.

The price was settled pending scrutiny of the documents.

"I'll get the documents from the owners on Monday, and we can meet, and you can finalize the deal. Let's go and celebrate."

As they walked, they saw the Mother Dairy, and Samir remarked, "That's great you have a Mother Dairy in the adjoining colony. Let's go there."

It was a busy time as everybody was trying to get milk from the milk-vending machines. Ajay was outside trying to get everybody to form a queue.

Ajay saw Babu and asked, "What are you trying to sell now?"

"You know the house on the edge of your colony, which is lying vacant. These two gentlemen want to buy it."

Samir came close to Ajay and introduced himself, "My name is Samir, and this is my friend Rakesh. We want to buy that house to put up a fabrication unit."

"That's very good, you'll do well here. If there is anything I can do, my name is Ajay. My father and I own this Mother Dairy operation."

"Somebody was telling us that there is one Vijay here, maybe we are mistaken."

"No, you're not mistaken. There is a Vijay, but he doesn't live here anymore, and he's a very good friend of mine."

"Previously, did this Vijay live in Lajpat Nagar?"

"Yes, did you know him?"

"Is he a son of a teacher? If so, he was our classmate."

"What a small world!" Ajay said. "I will call him right now."

He called Vijay. "Hi, Vijay, I have two friends of yours here from Lajpat Nagar."

"What are their names?"

"Samir and Rakesh."

Vijay kept quiet for a while (Vijay guessed that they must be part of the operation that the DCP was planning) and said, "Yes, I know them, and please look after them as I'm in the middle of something. I will talk to you later."

Ajay said, "He remembers you, but he could not talk at this time as he was in the middle of something he was doing."

They said, "Can we leave our motorbikes here for a little while and we will pick them up later?"

"No problem."

The property dealer said, "Let us go around the slum."

Samir asked, "Will we be allowed to take our bags in the bar, or shall we keep them here with Ajay?"

"No problem about your bags, nobody checks anything. Anyway, I am with you, so don't worry about it."

"Just a minute, we want to bring our motorbikes to the Mother Dairy."

They brought their bikes and parked them close to the Mother Dairy. They told Ajay, "We are leaving our bikes here for a while till we are done walking around the slum."

They went with Babu, walked around, and found the slum to be exactly as it was shown on the map, then finally ended up in the beer bar on the left back of the slum. It was kind of hidden, and you could not tell from outside that it was a beer bar. Samir strolled off to the back of the bar and saw a door at the back, which had a Danger sign. Babu said to Rakesh, "Why is he going there? The front door is on this side."

At that Rakesh said, "He is a bit of a nervous kind and wants to know the escape route in case of police action. This is an illegal operation, isn't it?"

Babu said, "Don't worry about it. This operation is run by Shakti, the main honcho of the minister, with the blessing of the police."

"This is all a temporary structure with tin roof and tarpaulin walls like a big square tent," Rakesh said.

"Yes, even the tables are the folding type in case they have to move the operation," assured Babu.

They went inside. People were drinking, and a couple of girls were dancing on the stage with loud music in the background.

Babu ordered three beers, and they sat down.

Samir remarked, "It's quite an operation, that's wonderful, and can you pick up some girls here?"

"Absolutely, do you want one now?"

Rakesh noticed about five tables away, a couple of girls were smooching a fat man. "Samir, do you see that?" Rakesh said.

"Yes, I see it."

Rakesh asked Babu, "That fat man must be somebody rich?"

Babu replied, "Don't point any fingers that side, and please be quiet."

Samir asked, "Who is that person? Do you know him?"

"Yes, he is a police officer and his name is Tomar. Everybody is scared of him, and he'll shoot before he'll talk."

"So what is he doing here?"

"Every Saturday night, he is here with a couple of those girls and goes home drunk."

"Is there anybody with him?"

"He usually has a couple of policemen in uniform guarding outside. And if you don't bother him, he won't bother you."

"So where does he take the girls?"

"There are a couple of rooms adjacent to the bar."

Samir said, "I want to go and pee."

"Go out and pee in the open air," Babu said.

Samir went out and called the DCP on his cell phone. "Are you taping and listening to our conversation? There's an officer called Tomar here."

"Yes, we have been listening to everything you are conversing about, and taping too. Is he doing anything illegal?"

"Yes, sir, he's drinking and flirting with the women and it seems that he's going to take them to the back room."

"Very well, give him five minutes in the back room and then pick him up. The four plainclothes officers are on the way, and I'm on my way too. Give me fifteen minutes, and we'll have the whole place surrounded from the back. Do you have your bulletproof vests on, and do you have your firearms?"

"Yes, we do, sir, and we have extra ammunition in our bags."

"Very well, let us stick to the plan, just give me fifteen minutes."

"Yes, sir."

Samir came back; in the meantime, Rakesh was sizing up the situation.

Rakesh asked, "Do you know that guy standing at the bar?"

Babu said, "That's Shakti who runs this operation, and he is armed."

"See if he can get a girl here," Samir asked.

"That's easy," Babu said.

He went over and talked to a guy. In the meantime, Rakesh said to Samir, "There are four suspects here: one is Shakti standing at the bar, another one is sitting at the table close to the bar, the third one is close to the entrance, and then there's the fourth one talking to Babu."

"We have to take care of all of them."

They sat and waited; two policemen in uniform arrived as mentioned by Babu.

They came in, and they talked to one of the men near the entrance whom Rakesh had identified. And in a couple of minutes, they walked out with the man.

In the meantime, Tomar took one of the girls to the back room.

Babu struck a deal with the pimp he was talking to and brought him over to the table and sat down.

The music was very loud, and the drinkers were very rowdy. The girls were dancing, and nobody could hear anything as to what was happening in the bar.

Samir pulled out the gun from his boots and pointed toward the pimp and said very sternly, "I am ACP Samir, keep quiet, or I'll blow your head off."

Babu was dumfounded and sat there frozen with his mouth open. Rakesh also pulled out his gun and told Babu and the pimp, "Keep quiet, and you won't be hurt."

Samir went over to the bar and stood next to the bad guy Shakti, who seemed to be the toughest of them all. Samir put a gun to his stomach, dug it in, and said, "If you move, I will kill you."

Facing the bar, ACP Samir put his left arm around him, still sticking the gun in his stomach, and brought him over to their table and made him sit down. Rakesh said, "Sit down quietly and put your weapon on the table, or with this rapid fire gun, I'll put so many holes in you that I'll be able to see through you."

In the meantime, the four plainclothes officers arrived and came over to the table. Samir told them, "Sit down, and one of you pick up the weapon from the table. Rakesh is going with me. One of you take care of the man sitting on that table close to the bar. One of you go over and stand at the entrance, and the two of you take care of these boys. Don't let them move. If anybody moves, shoot to kill."

Samir and Rakesh went close to the room where Tomar had gone. The barman said, "You can't go in there."

They went over to the barman and said, "If you don't want to die, be quiet."

Samir pointed a gun at him and said, "I'm ACP Samir. Look at that table, and they are all police officers everywhere in this bar. So if you want to save yourself, be quiet." He looked at the plainclothes officer sitting at the table close to the bar and said, "Take care of the barman too."

Samir went to the other girl who was sitting with Tomar earlier. Before he could get to her, she tried to skip out of the back door. He went after her, grabbed her, and said, "I'm ACP Samir, and if you don't want to get arrested or killed, cooperate with me."

She got scared and said, "What do you want to know?"

"That room where ACP Tomar has gone with the girl, is that closed from the inside, and if so, is there any other way out of the room?"

"Yes, there is a side door."

"Tell me if you go through the bar, where is the bed?"

"It is a small room, and the bed is right in front of you as you enter from the bar side."

"When you're lying down on the bed, are you facing at the bar door?"

"No, he is facing the side door, but Tomar is always watching the door from the side."

"Does he have a gun?"

"Yes, he keeps the gun under the pillow, and mostly he has one hand on it."

"How many times have you had sex with him?"

"Many times, sometimes he takes me first, and other times an hour or so after."

"Show me the side door."

She took him over and did as he asked.

He asked her to come with him into the bar and took her over to the table where the other police officers were sitting and said, "Take care of her too."

He went back to Rakesh and said, "You go from the bar door, and I'll go from the side door. Start to count to twenty and then kick the door in, but don't go in."

Rakesh and Samir started the countdown. Samir went to the side door, and they both kicked the doors in at the same time, and Tomar fired at the bar door.

Samir went in from the side door and pointed the gun at Tomar. At this time, Rakesh, standing outside, pointed the gun at Tomar too and said, "Drop the gun on the floor in front of me. I'm ACP Rakesh."

"I am ACP Samir. Put your hands up."

He was all nude from the waist down. Samir took out a nylon tie from his pocket and tied Tomar's hands really tight. In the meantime, Rakesh tied the girl's hands.

Tomar said, "I am a police officer too, you will be sorry."

Samir said, "We will see who is sorry. You should be ashamed of yourself, and if you don't shut up, I will take you out nude."

In the meantime, everybody in the bar got scared as they heard a shot.

The plainclothes officers took charge. They pointed the guns and said, "Everybody lie down or you might be shot."

Rakesh stayed with Tomar, and Samir went out of the room.

Hearing the shot, the two corrupt policemen and the hood rushed back to the bar, but the plainclothes officer standing at the entrance stopped them and told them, "This is police action. You get inside and face the wall if you don't want to be shot."

Just at that time, the DCP entered with his police force and surrounded all the activities that were marked on the map.

Samir said, "You came just in time, sir. We have Tomar and the girl tied up in the back room."

"Well done, boys, you have arrested a partner in crime and the right-hand man of ACP Rathore. I will take it from here."

The DCP went over to the back room where Tomar was tied and said, "What a shame to see you in this condition."

Tomar had his hands tied in front and was trying to cover his private area.

"Okay, I am just going to take a picture of you for the records, and you can cover your dirty spot with your hands while I take the picture."

"No, sir, please don't do that. I am ashamed of what I did," pleaded Tomar.

The DCP took a picture anyway and said, "Put on your clothes."

The DCP called SHO Rawat. "Come to the slum in your area and bring a lot of handcuffs as you have to make the arrests and process them. How long will it take to come here with all your men armed?"

"Give us fifteen to twenty minutes, sir."

"Very well then, see you in fifteen minutes."

In the meantime, the DCP ordered to all the officers, "Secure the place, tie the criminals with nylon ties, and especially look after this king of the illegal activity here. I believe his name is Shakti. Put his hands behind his back and tie him. If he gives you any trouble, shoot him in the legs so that he can't run away."

"Very well, sir," replied the officers.

Samir and Rakesh stood around watching with their guns drawn. When the station house officer in charge showed up, they showed him all the criminals and the dancing girls as well as the prostitutes.

The DCP said, "Your work is done, Rakesh and Samir. You can leave now, and I will see you Monday morning at ten in my office."

"Thank you, sir."

The DCP said, "SHO, take charge of all the criminals, arrest everybody here, and take them back to the police station. Seal the area, take the bottles and narcotics and anything illegal you find. You know what to do. You are an old hand at it and have done it many times, Officer Rawat. Especially take care of Officer Tomar. Don't let him escape and don't let him off till the time I tell you personally, is that clear? I want to give you a little warning that if you botch up this operation, you will not retire in six months, which you are supposed to, but I will make sure that you are dismissed without a pension."

Rawat said, "Don't worry, sir, I will look after this, and believe me, I am just as much fed up of Tomar as you are."

"If you need me, I will be in my jeep for fifteen minutes, and then I will leave."

Rakesh and Samir went to Ajay, picked their motorbikes up, and said, "We will talk to you later, Ajay. It seems like it is going to rain."

CHAPTER 20

O N SATURDAY, WHILE the police operation was being carried out, Vijay and Bharti went to Vijay's parents' house. They had breakfast there, and then Bharti went shopping with Pooja, Chemeli, and Vijay's mother in a chauffeur-driven car. The ladies came back from shopping, and Bharti asked, "Did you eat anything, Vijay?"

He said, "We had a big breakfast, and did you have anything to eat?"

"Yes, we did, we had *papri chaat*, etc."

Chemeli said, "I prepared the food in the morning. I'll just warm it up and serve it."

Chemeli served the food for Vijay and his father. They started eating, and Bharti asked, "What did you do all this time?"

"I made the labels, and Papa got the invitation cards ready for the courier, and we got them all done, about three hundred of them," replied Vijay in between mouthfuls.

"Wow, that many!"

Vijay finished eating, and Bharti said, "I want to go home and rest, I'm very tired."

Vijay's mother said, "Bharti makes the decisions very quickly. I'm very pleased today. We got most of the clothing shopping done today, and the other day, we got all the jewelry shopping done."

"So you got everything done."

"No, we might have to go once again for knickknacks, but we will do the rest ourselves – between Chemeli, Pooja, and I. The chauffeur-driven car was a big help as there was a big problem with parking close to the shopping center and we just got out of the car and didn't have to worry about parking especially since it was raining."

Pooja said, "Let us show you all the clothes we bought."

Pooja and Chemeli showed all the things they bought to Vijay while his father and mother went to rest.

Even Bharti was excited and asked, "Vijay, how did you like my *lehenga* that I'm going to wear on the engagement night? Your mother said that I can wear my own *lehenga* before the engagement, and after the engagement, I can go up and change into this *lehenga*."

"So where will you go to change?"

"I will go up to the room which we are getting along with the hall for getting-ready purposes. Actually, my father and I are booking a suite upstairs as we are going to stay the night in the hotel, bearing in mind that a lot of my cousins and my father's friends are all staying for the night in the hotel. My father has also booked the hotel restaurant for breakfast, and you are coming too."

"I'm not sure if I can come for breakfast as we'll have our guests at home, but for you, it makes sense to spend the night in the hotel."

Bharti said, "Look at the time, it's four thirty already."

Chemeli brought the masala chai and samosas and asked everybody to come to the dining table.

Pooja said, "I'm starving as we didn't have any lunch, only snacks."

Their father and mother woke up and joined them when they were having chai, samosas, and sweets.

Bharti said, "I especially like this *chaina murgi* [small balls of sweet ricotta cheese coated with flavored sugar] that we bought from the sweetshop in GK 2."

"You went to the sweetshop in GK 2?" Vijay asked.

"Yes, we had to go there to pick up the boxes of sweets, which you are supposed to send with the cards."

"Oh, that's great! Now I don't have to go there tomorrow."

"It was Chemeli's idea to pick up the boxes of sweets as they had called earlier to inform us that the boxes were ready as Chemeli took the call."

Pooja said, "We readily agreed to that as the best *papri chaat* is available in that shop."

"Even Bharti Didi liked the idea of going there as it reminded her of her young days."

Bharti said, "I'm very tired, and I want to go home and just sleep."

Mother said, "I can understand that shopping is not easy, it is very tiring."

Bharti and Vijay left for Vijay's condo and went to sleep till the sound of a thundershower and lightning woke them up.

Bharti said, "What's happening?"

"It is pouring, and it seems like extended monsoons," Vijay said.

"I forgot to tell you that we were invited by one of my colleague's house for his housewarming," Bharti said.

"Do you want to go? It is after eight p.m. now."

"Look at the rain outside. It is coming down in buckets. It will be impossible to drive in this rain," Bharti remarked.

"Let's check the news and see how bad it is."

They put on a twenty-four-hour news channel, and the news reporter said, "We have freak rains in Delhi. There was a big cloudburst in the central area, and most of the low-lying areas are waterlogged. Rain and flooding continue in Maharashtra, Gujarat, Bengal, Orissa, Bihar, and UP. There are estimated to be seventy-five million people without homes because of flooding, and this is unusual for this time of the year. People are very upset. The government is promising aid, but nothing is reaching the affected areas. The politicians are carrying on their aerial surveys, which is of no help to the people. The prime minister and the chief ministers all are promising aid and claiming that the army has been called. To date, we have not seen any army personnel. People are helping each other, they have lost their livelihoods, and they have lost their shelter. To stop the spread of disease, we must tackle this on a war footing and must get freshwater, food, and supplies over to the people. This is a national emergency."

Bharti said, "We have an excuse now not to go. I will just inform her that we cannot come because of the rain."

"What do you want to do now?"

"We could hang out together here and enjoy the cool damp breeze coming from outside. It reminds me of the hills. I remember when I was a young girl and we were living in GK 2, I went to Nainital with my parents in the Dushehra holidays about this time of the year. There was a cool damp breeze blowing, the clouds were touching the road, and our heads were literally in the clouds! We had so much fun there, and the charbroiled corn on the cob tasted out of this world."

"You remember all that?" Vijay remarked.

"Yes, I do."

"You know Nainital is a hill station?"

"Yes, I know there is a lake, surrounded by the hills, and it is at approximately eight thousand feet above sea level. I remember we had to go on this very winding road and my father kept saying, 'Keep eating and you won't get sick.'"

"He was right. I have been there a couple of times too. The best thing I liked on the hill station was the horse riding. We used to gallop the horses on the little road between the lake and the mountain."

"I remember, we stayed in this old palace of a maharaja now converted into a hotel on the mountain. There were a lot of bonsai plants in the garden, and one could see the whole Naini Lake from up there. The view was breathtaking. The faint clouds were below and among us. Just imagine you are having an aerial view of the oval lake surrounded by the mountains on all sides with a little opening on the far side for cars to come through."

"Oh really, that must have been a fantastic experience," Vijay remarked.

"Yes, it was, and that's why I still remember it. I'm feeling cold with the thought of it," she said with a mischievous smile.

"Do you want a blanket?"

"No, dummy, I want you to wrap your arms around me. I am feeling so romantic today in this cold breeze."

Vijay came and wrapped his arms around her and said, "You had that weather in England all the time."

"Yes, but ever since I've come back, it has been so hot here. Besides, you don't appreciate too much of anything."

"We Indians, who live in India, go crazy in this weather, and we think it's the most romantic weather."

"So you think it is romantic too?" She had this naughty smile and a frown indicating, "What is holding you back?"

"Yes, I do." And he kissed her passionately again and again.

They went to the bedroom and made love.

Bharti said, "It is about ten p.m., and I'm hungry!"

"It's good that the rain has stopped. What kind of food do you want, and we can have it delivered."

"I feel like having soup and some Chinese food."

"Let me try if they would deliver."

Vijay phoned the Chinese restaurant, handed over the phone to Bharti, and asked her to order.

Bharti asked Vijay, "Are you okay with the hot stuff?"

He said, "Yes, I can handle it."

Bharti ordered hot-and-sour soup, chilly chicken, Chinese vegetables, noodles, and fried rice. The food arrived in half an hour, and they started eating.

"Do you like children," Bharti asked in between sips of soup.

"Yes, of course! Why do you ask?"

"Because I want to have a child right away after getting married."

"Right away? Did you say . . . ouch!"

"What happened?"

"I burnt my tongue . . . and you were saying?"

"I want children right away because I'm getting older. I will be thirty by the time I have the first one – that is, if I get pregnant right away. I want my child to be a professional – usually one is at least twenty-six years old. By then, I will be fifty-six and you will be fifty-eight. When will we have grandchildren?"

"I never thought of it that way, but let's wait for a couple of years so that I'm settled in my job."

"You don't need to get settled in your job as my father can take care of that."

"No, that's not what I want, and I don't want to be forced into working for your father. I feel I should have the option, and if I feel comfortable working for him, I will tell you so."

"I'm sorry, I did not mean it that way, but between the two of us, we're making enough money to raise children. People who have a lot less than us still manage to raise children."

"I'm not against children, so please don't misunderstand me, but let us have our fun for a year or so."

"Okay, I will go along with that," Bharti whispered, feeling sad.

The next morning, Vijay was up early and took some tea at nine to the bedroom and said, "Rise and shine, it is a beautiful day." He put the tea down then lay down next to her and hugged her.

She put her arms around him and whispered, "I hope you will always wake me up like this."

"I will always wake you up like this, will always love you, and be there for you."

"You stay here, I'll be back in a minute."

When she got back, he was pouring tea into the cup; she came and sat on his lap and kissed him in between sips of tea.

"You went to brush your teeth?"

"Yes, hygiene, my dear Watson!"

He kissed her all over the face, the neck, and the chest.

She said, "You are driving me crazy!" She got up from his lap and put her legs around his waist, kissed him passionately, and they made love.

Bharti said, "That tea must be stone-cold by now. Do you want regular tea or masala chai?"

"Whatever you prefer."

"I think I will make masala chai."

Vijay said, "I'll make breakfast."

She said, "It is a deal!"

Bharti went to make the chai, and Vijay called Ajay.

"Ajay, what's happening?"

"I was waiting for your call as I have a lot to tell you. Yesterday, there was one big police action in the slum. A number of those minister's hoods were arrested. The police removed all the illegal operations and took away all the evidence. Everybody in the slum was happy even though, due to the downpour and heavy winds, a lot of jhuggies were damaged last night."

"Their jhuggies were damaged, and they are happy?"

"They are happy about the hoods being arrested and shutting down of the illegal activities. Today, you see they are jubilant and helping each other in the rebuilding of their jhuggies," retorted Ajay. He went on, "I called you about some Rakesh and Samir, but your cell connection got cut off."

"The reason I cut you off was that I knew they were there and that there was some sort of police operation going on as you had delivered the satellite picture of the slum and your colony to the DCP."

"Samir said that he went to school with you. Do you remember any Samir?"

"Come to think of it, yes, there were these two boys who always hung out together and wanted to join the police force. I remember they even saved me once from getting beaten up after the soccer match. We must find out who they are. Did they give you a telephone number or a card?"

"No, they left in a hurry as it had started raining. Okay, I'll see you later for lunch."

"What do you mean by see you later for lunch?" Vijay asked.

"Just ask Bharti."

Bharti and Vijay finished their breakfast, and Bharti said, "I have some work with Ajay. Incidentally, he invited us for lunch, so I committed to him for lunch."

"You did that without asking me, and what is your work with Ajay?"

"I guess I should have talked to you. I'm sorry, but I wanted to give you a surprise."

"So what is the big surprise?"

"Do you remember we were planning to open a clinic in the spare room next to Ajay's house?"

"Yes, and what about it?"

"Well, my father asked Raju to order all the furniture and equipment for that clinic. The furniture and equipment is arriving today."

"Does Ajay know that?"

"Yes, I talked to him on Friday. Ajay was insisting that we have lunch with him on Sunday as we have not gone to him for the last two weeks and we have time, if you want, to go to your parents' house first as it is on the way."

"Okay, let's go there."

They went to his parents' house, and they found out that Vijay's parents were also going to Ajay's as it was Ajay's parents' anniversary.

"I'm dressed in jeans. Oh my god!" Bharti said.

Pooja said, "You can borrow my clothes."

Her mother said, "No, I'm not having my daughter-in-law wear old clothes. Pooja, give her one of your new suits that you bought."

"Okay, Mommy."

"Thanks, Mommy, and shouldn't we take something for Ajay's parents?" Bharti asked.

"That's okay, we'll give something from the entire family," Vijay's mother replied.

Vijay said, "If we hadn't come to the house, we would not have found out about their anniversary."

Pooja said, "I was just going to call you to find out whether you were going there or not."

Bharti changed into the suit that Pooja gave her and said, "It fits me perfectly!"

Pooja said, "It is looking much better on you, and, Bharti Didi, wear this small necklace with it too."

"Okay, I will try it on."

"You're looking fabulous, Bharti Didi, and it is yours, a little token of love from me to you."

"No, I cannot take it as it is not right."

"Why is it not right? I earn my own money, and I work hard for it. My father doesn't tell me where I should spend it and where I shouldn't. I bought this from my own money."

"I'm sorry, Pooja, as I did not mean it like that. I meant it looked so expensive to me and you bought this for yourself, and I didn't think it would be right for me to take it away from you."

"I just bought it because I liked it, and in fact, I was thinking about you when I bought this. I thought it was such a cheap necklace that you may not want to wear it, but the thought was there, and God knows everything that we think of sometimes comes true."

"Thank you very much, Pooja, and I like little necklaces like this. I think it is very pretty, and thank you very much for the thought. I'm going to keep it with me and remember your first gift to me." She hugged Pooja, and they hugged each other, feeling very emotional.

Vijay came in Pooja's room and said, "If you two are finished getting ready, we can go as we are getting late."

Bharti said, "I want to take my own car as I have to go somewhere on the way."

Vijay said, "Okay." And he told his parents to go ahead as he was going to come in Bharti's car.

Vijay asked in the car, "What is it that you want to buy?"

"I don't like going empty-handed on their wedding anniversary. The least I would like to take is a bouquet of flowers."

"Okay, I will take you to a florist, and it is practically on our way to Ajay's house."

"Thank you."

They went to the florist, and she picked a nice big bouquet of flowers and took it to Ajay's house and said, "We will give this from the Shastri family."

Vijay said, "It is a nice gesture, and thank you for considering yourself as one of the family members."

Just at that time, Ajay called and Bharti picked up the phone and said, "Hi, Ajay."

Ajay said, "There are a couple of trucks here with the furniture and equipment."

"Did you get that room painted and all the work done?"

"Yes, of course, Bharti, I got all the work done before I got it painted when you told me about the furniture and equipment."

"Very good, Ajay, we are five minutes away, so you can tell them to start unloading."

"Okay, see you soon."

Vijay was all quiet and looked upset.

Bharti said, "You are very quiet, and you seem incensed."

"To tell you the truth, I am a little upset. You tell me that I'm your partner, you want to share everything with me, and yet you go ahead and plan the whole office and clinic without me. You did not think even for once that I could be of any help to you in any way whatsoever. You also asked Ajay to undertake some work without even thinking that he will have to incur some expenses, without knowing their family's financial condition."

Listening to the long lecture, Bharti almost broke down and started crying. Vijay stopped the car on the roadside and put his hand around her to console her.

"You are right. I made a big mistake. I did not think properly. There is no justification for this blunder. I should have consulted you on every step of the way. Yes, you are my partner, and I agree I have made it difficult for you, and I'm sorry. This will never happen again." She gave him a kiss on the cheek and hugged him, crying all the time.

Vijay said, "That's okay. I will handle it." He kissed her back. "Don't worry, it may cause a bit of a problem handling the financial side of this. Ajay has a lot of financial burden on him, and they are under debt because of their Mother Dairy project and other family commitments. They will not accept any money from anybody, not even my father or me. Even an offer will be taken as an insult to them."

"Is that the reason why Geeta is not married yet?"

"Yes, partly."

"Do you know the boy?"

"Yes, and you know him too."

"I do! Who is he?"

"His name is Krishna."

"You mean that boy from the printing press."

"Yes, Krishna and Geeta love each other, and they have known each other from their childhood days. She even goes to help him out whenever he needs help, and they are a match made in heaven."

"Geeta is such a nice girl. She's always smiling and always willing to help."

"Yes, the whole family is like this."

"You're right, the whole family is so nice, and there aren't many people like that in the world."

Vijay started the car again, and they reached Ajay's house. Ajay was standing outside, getting the truck unloaded.

Bharti pulled out a blueprint of the layout of the room with the equipment and the furniture in the room.

"Who made this?"

"Ajay sent us the measurements of the room, and my father got this done before ordering the equipment and the furniture."

"That's very good."

"It is the same furniture and equipment I have in my clinic in our house."

"So he furnished that room for you too?"

"Yes, he did." She moved onto the room and gave the blueprint to Vijay and Ajay and said, "You can get it done." She took the flower bouquet inside, wished Ajay's father and mother a very happy anniversary, and said, "May God give you a long, healthy, and happy life."

They in turn hugged and kissed her on the forehead.

"I hope you don't mind me using your room for a clinic!" Bharti remarked.

"No, on the contrary, we will be so happy to see you here. You're just like our daughter."

"Thank you very much, and I feel very much at home with your family."

Geeta came out of the kitchen and said, "Hi, Bharti Didi, it is good to see you again."

"You'll be seeing me more often."

"The pleasure will be all ours."

Vijay's father, mother, Chemeli, and Pooja arrived; and they wished them a long happy married life, presented them a gift, and said, "This is from the Shastri family, including Bharti."

Ajay's mother said, "But we already had the gift from you. Bharti brought the flowers from all of you."

"That was very thoughtful of Bharti because we had forgotten flowers."

"Come and see, they are beautiful," informed Geeta.

Pooja praised Bharti and said, "Bharti Didi has a beautiful taste for things."

They all went inside, and Bharti said, "I have to go and see how the boys are setting up the clinic."

Vijay and Ajay were getting things put in place. Bharti appreciated their attention to details and asked, "How long is it going to be, guys?"

"I think it is going to be another hour, and I may have to get some electrical outlets installed afterward," Ajay informed.

"My father has an electrician on staff, and I can send him here for half day."

"Okay. We will talk about it later."

Geeta came and announced that lunch was ready. At that, Ajay told Bharti and Vijay to go inside as he would get the job done.

Geeta said, "Give these guys a break. I will send lunch for these guys too."

The trucker turned around and informed her, "We have to go somewhere else too. We don't have time for lunch."

Geeta asserted, "You are going to have lunch here first, and then you can go. You're not slaves. Every human being has to get time for lunch."

"Your thoughts are very noble. I wish the owners of the trucking company thought likewise."

"Do you know, Didi, the whole trucking industry is going on strike from tomorrow for this only reason that we are not treated like human beings. We are treated like animals – not only that we are overworked and underpaid, we work sixteen to twenty hours a day. And compared to the industry standards, we don't even get half the wages. Although the trucking industry is going through a boom, the poor laborers don't get enough money to feed their families and to put a shelter over their heads. Rich people are getting richer, and the poor are still there where they were twenty years ago."

"Well, nobody's going to treat you like animals here. In about ten minutes, I will send you lunch. You can sit in peace and eat," informed Geeta before going inside.

Pooja and Chemeli were setting up the dining table for a lunch buffet, and Geeta went inside to get lunch out for one driver and two laborers.

Vijay and Ajay came in, washed up, and had lunch with everybody. Just at that time, Krishna and his mother arrived. They exchanged the normal greetings and wished them a happy anniversary and gave a gift to Ajay's father and mother and hugged them.

Ajay's mother said, "Come join in for lunch." And they did.

After lunch, Ajay, Vijay, and Bharti went out, set everything in the right place. The clinic was ready and functional.

The truck driver said, "Thank you very much, sir and madam. It is always good to know that there are good human beings like you in this world, who have a heart."

They went inside, and a little while later, Mr. Kapoor arrived.

Bharti asked, "What are you doing here, Papa?"

He replied, "I was invited by Pehalwanji."

Pehalwanji met him and thanked him for coming.

Mr. Kapoor said, "The pleasure is all mine. I wanted to meet the strong man with a soft heart who follows Gandhian principles. I have the highest regard for you for the path you have chosen, one of nonviolence instead of violence, especially given that you are physically so strong."

Pehalwanji said, "Please don't humble me, come in and have lunch."

Mr. Kapoor replied, "I told you I had a luncheon appointment, but I saved some room for the anticipated lunch of Geeta's special *channa bhaturas!*"

Geeta said, "I will make fresh *bhaturas* for you."

"Thank you, beta."

"All my equipment and furniture has come," Bharti informed her father.

"Let's go and see how your clinic looks."

They went along with him, and Mr. Kapoor remarked, "It is very good. However, you might need a waiting room for people."

Pehalwanji said, "We can build an extension. We had the plans passed already for three rooms plus two washrooms."

"Let's go inside, and we'll discuss it," Mr. Kapoor said.

Mr. Kapoor asked, "What happened to the school extension, and did my lawyers send you the documents for the new trust structure?"

Mr. Shastri said, "I received the documents, read them, and passed them on to Vijay just today."

Vijay said, "I will read them in a day or two."

Mr. Kapoor asked, "What is happening on the extension front?"

"As far as the school extension is concerned, the DCP and the district magistrate handed in a favorable report to HUDA, and I believe it has gone for sanctioning to the chairman and is held there for the last one week."

"If you give me the details and the file number, my man is going there tomorrow for some of my work. He can check it out," Mr. Kapoor offered.

Mr. Shastri asked for paper and pen, Ajay brought it over, and Mr. Shastri wrote down the details of the file and handed it over to Mr. Kapoor.

Mr. Kapoor said, "I will call you tomorrow evening."

In the meantime, Geeta brought fresh *channa bhaturas* and asked, "Where do you want to eat, here or at the dining table?"

He said, "On the dining table, but I would like to go to wash my hands first."

Geeta served lunch and showed him the washroom. Vijay and Bharti went to give him company while he enjoyed his *channa bhaturas*.

"I have eaten twice today," Mr. Kapoor remarked.

"That's okay, Papa, no dinner for you tonight," Bharti said jokingly.

"Okay, in that case, what is for dessert?" Mr. Kapoor asked with a smile.

"It is *rasmalai*, your favorite," Geeta informed.

"Well, I think I'll have one, if Bharti allows me," Mr. Kapoor asked, looking at Bharti with an inquisitive look.

"That's okay, Papa, you can have one, but definitely no dinner."

He finished dessert and came to the living room and asked, "What about the extension of your house you want to build?"

"We don't have the money to build the complete sanctioned plan, but we can build one more room for Bharti."

"That's nice of you, but I don't want you to financially strain yourself. Here's my plan. Once the new trust is in place, we can build the whole extension as per your sanction plan if all the trustees agree, of course."

Mr. Shastri asked, "How will it work?"

"It can work in this way," Mr. Kapoor explained. "The trust will give an interest-free loan to the owner of the land, and once the building is made, the trust would take it on lease for a term to make a dispensary, and in the same term, the loan will be repaid by lease payment without interest or deduction. After the term, the building will be handed back to the owner of the land."

"Where would the dispensary go after the term of the lease?"

"By that time, I'm hoping we would have built a hospital in the slum."

"That seems like a very ambitious plan that may be unachievable," Mr. Shastri said.

"No, nothing is ambitious or unachievable. I have friends of mine in England and in India who want to help the indigent people in India by giving lots of money to charity as long as they can be assured that the money they donate is actually going to help the poor."

"As far as the house extension is concerned, Vijay and I can work out the details and let you know," Ajay said.

"That's fine, and I will call you tomorrow evening, Mr. Shastri. Now I must go as my friends are waiting for me in the club. Thank you, Geeta, for the fantastic *channa bhaturas* and *rasmalai*."

Mr. Kapoor hugged everybody and left.

Bharti said, "I will see you at home later tonight."

Ajay informed his father, "There is a big problem brewing in the transport industry. Even the driver who came to deliver Bharti's equipment was saying that they're going on strike tomorrow. That's going to affect us bringing the fruits and vegetables, and who knows, the wholesale market may shut down from the day after tomorrow."

"If they're going on strike tomorrow, it may shut down tomorrow itself," remarked Ajay's father.

"No, because all the fruits and vegetables for sale tomorrow will come in tonight in the trucks or they might have come a day before. God knows how for many days the strike will go on."

"There is only one thing to do, and that is to buy as much as you can tomorrow, bring it in your own tempo, and maybe you can employ the man who owns the tempo in the slum as he's very friendly with you. The strikers will not stop you if you're doing it for yourself, will they?"

"I agree, Papa. I will go and see the tempo man in the slum in the evening."

Vijay was listening, and he offered, "Can I help you with extra cash just for a few days?"

Ajay said, "Thanks, Vijay, but I will let you know."

"No, you have to let me know now because today is Sunday and the banks are closed. There's a limit on withdrawals from the banking machine, and I know one of my banks which is open till eight tonight. If we have to get some cash, we will have to go there now, and it is about twenty minutes away from here."

"Thanks all the same, but we can manage," Ajay asserted.

"It pays you to be nice to the workers because they are human beings like us. You see, the truck driver told us about the strike because we were nice to him, and now Ajay can plan," Bharti remarked.

"Usually, I come to know through my friends if anything like that is going to happen. I had a hint of that yesterday, but now the driver confirmed it, and you are right, I get a bit of time to plan ahead."

"It is four p.m., I would like to go home as I have to prepare for tomorrow's seminar that I'm delivering. You can get a ride with Ajay to your flat, and I will talk to you tomorrow," Bharti said.

Vijay went out with Bharti; there he hugged and kissed her and said, "I love you, and I will talk to you tomorrow."

The next day, Mr. Kapoor called Mr. Shastri and informed him, "My man went to HUDA and found out that your file is with the superintendent, waiting for final signature by the chairman. The superintendent wants fifty thousand rupees to get it done, and if he gets the money tomorrow morning, he will get the extension signed by the chairman tomorrow itself. He will hand it over to my man tomorrow afternoon, who will bring it to you by the evening. What do you think?"

Mr. Shastri said, "I don't like to bribe them, but in the interest of the school, what do you think?"

"I agree in the interest of the school, we should pay and get moving with the construction," Mr. Kapoor said.

"Very well then, and I will send you the money today."

"Please, Mr. Shastri, don't make me look so small. I'm going to be your partner in charity. I will handle it, don't worry about it. I just wanted to get your permission to give you all the respect. Please afford the same respect to me in return."

"I'm sorry, Mr. Kapoor, I really am very sorry. Please get it done and get a load off my mind. I will appreciate it very much, and from now on, I will treat you as my equal."

"Thank you, Mr. Shastri, and I need not mention this, but don't tell anybody about this, and the work will be done tomorrow."

"Thank you again and bye."

CHAPTER 21

ON MONDAY AFTERNOON, Bharti got a call from a woman identifying herself as Chhotu's sister. She questioned, "Dr. Sahib, do you remember Chhotu in Mumbai?"

"Yes, I do, and he told me about your son not being well. Tell me about him and what is wrong with him."

"He does not eat well and is weak. He always wants to lie down even at school and doesn't play any games. His growth is very slow. He looks like a four-year-old whereas he's six, and all the boys are always picking on him."

"Didn't you take him to any doctor?" Bharti asked.

"Yes, I did. I took him to a municipal dispensary. There the doctor said that he is weak. He needs to drink milk and needs vitamins."

"What happened then?"

"Nothing happened at all."

"Did the doctor do any blood tests?"

"Yes, he said something about he has a shortage of red cells, and he gave him some iron pills."

"What happened then?"

"He's been on iron pills for six months, and nothing has changed."

"Okay, you will have to bring him to my hospital."

"Dr. Sahib, I'm very poor, and I cannot afford a hospital."

"Don't worry, it will not cost you a penny. I will look after that as I want your son to be well."

"Oh, thank you, Dr. Sahib, you are an angel."

Bharti gave her the address of the hospital and told them to come on Wednesday morning.

Bharti called Vijay and told him about Chhotu's sister and the dilemma about her son.

Vijay asked, "What are you going to do about it?"

"I have called them to the hospital on Wednesday, and I will have to do some further tests."

"I had a busy day today, and how about you?" Vijay asked.

"I was very busy today, it is seven, and I've just come home."

"It is going to be a busy week for me as I have to do a lot of work. I have been coming home late every night, and my company wants me to start a new project of acquisition."

"It seems that we won't be seeing much of each other this week as I have to finish shopping too," Bharti said.

"We will talk to each other every evening and see if we can make a plan to meet."

"Okay, bye and love you, and just to let you know, I'm not going to Ajay's house tomorrow morning as I have work to do in the hospital."

"What were you going to do there anyway?"

"We have to set up a system of seeing the patients, etc."

"We can do it together on the weekend."

"I think that's a great idea, okay, bye for now and love you."

"Bye, honey, will talk to you tomorrow."

Jubilant, Vijay called Bharti on Tuesday evening and said, "I have good news for you."

"What's the good news?"

"My father received the sanction of the school extension plan."

"How did that happen?"

"All the credit goes to your father. Apparently, your father sent a man to HUDA who brought the sanction with him and delivered it to my father."

"Oh really, that's wonderful."

"My father also wants me to review the documents regarding forming of the trust. I'm sitting down and reading them now, and tomorrow morning, I will send them to your father's lawyers."

"So everything is happening all at once!"

"My father asked me if we could both go to the school on Friday afternoon as the annual school function is going on this week and all the prizes will be distributed to the students along with the new uniform and sweaters, etc. He also wants to announce the school extension and upgrading of the school to grade 12."

"I will certainly try to take Friday afternoon off but will let you know for sure."

"I think my project of acquisition will be finished by Thursday afternoon because of the Friday deadline."

"I caught the news a little bit that there was a police action in the slum and the criminals were remanded to police custody for five days for further questioning, but what happened to ACP Tomar?"

"I talked to Ajay earlier, and he told me that ACP Tomar has been suspended pending inquiry into his estate, criminal activity, and his links with Mafia operating the trade of women and children. He was told by the court to report to the police station everyday and not to indulge in any illegal or criminal activity whatsoever."

"That's good."

"Yes, for the time being, it will do, but let's see what happens next."

"Sweetheart, when are we going to get together? I can't sleep at night. I'm thinking of you all the time, and I just want to be with you all the time."

"Same here, honey, I cannot force my mind to work as I'm thinking of you all the time, but it won't be for long. We have to be practical. Let me finish my acquisition project on Thursday, and I will see you Thursday evening for sure, and I love you, sweetheart."

"Okay, darling, bye for now and love you."

On Thursday morning, Mr. Kapoor called Mr. Shastri and informed him, "My lawyers have gone through the documents that Vijay sent yesterday, and they say everything is fine pending signatures. My funds will be ready Friday morning."

Mr. Shastri said, "That's fantastic because I was just going to call you to invite you for Friday, the last day of the annual school function. If you're free and the documents are signed on Friday morning, I can announce the school extension to the children on Friday. And a little later at the time of the prize distribution, we will also announce your contribution to the school."

"I have a meeting first thing in the morning. I'll try to be there by noon."

"That would work well, so I will see you at noon, and maybe we can have lunch together."

"I remember I also have a luncheon meeting with somebody. If I come at one p.m., will that be okay?"

"Yes, that will be fine."

"Thanks, Mr. Shastri, and I will see you on Friday."

Mr. Shastri also called the DCP and the district magistrate to invite them for the final day of the annual school function.

On Thursday evening, Vijay called Bharti and said, "I have finished with the acquisition project, and I am home now. Do you want to get together?"

"I have the day off tomorrow, but I have to go back to work on Saturday. I can spend the night with you tonight."

"Wow! That's exciting, but what will you do tomorrow morning when I go to work?"

"Well, I can go shopping then come back and have lunch with you – that is, if you are coming back at lunchtime. And in the afternoon, we are planning to go to your father's school."

"I will only find that out in the morning, and then I will call you."

"What do you want to do tonight?"

"You tell me."

"I would like to go out for a candlelight dinner with you, come home, and sip some wine with you," Bharti said very softly.

"That sounds like a very romantic plan."

"Yes, I'm feeling very romantic and hungry too."

"Well then, get ready quickly and come over. I know just the place to go – in a five-star hotel close by. And in the meantime, I will go and buy some wine and beer for the weekend, so see you soon."

"I have to go home, shower, and collect clothes for the weekend, so that means the earliest I can get to you will be eight thirty."

"That's fine, see you then."

Bharti arrived at nine and sheepishly whispered, "I'm sorry, honey."

Vijay looked at her. She was looking stunningly beautiful, and he whispered back, "You are looking gorgeous, and you are aptly dressed up for our candlelight dinner."

"Let's go as I'm starving, and let us take my car as I left it outside. You drive, and I can talk to you about Chhotu's sister's son."

"You mean that Chhotu, the driver in Mumbai?"

Bharti said, "Yes, his nephew is a very sick little boy. I did his blood tests. The sodium level was low, potassium was high, and hemoglobin was a little low. So we took his blood again, and I sent it in for a cortisol level."

"How did that test result turn out?"

"Well, it came out the way I suspected. His cortisol level was very low, then I sent him home with a small sample bottle of hydrocortisone. I think he has a case of adrenal insufficiency, a rare condition where the glands do not produce enough cortisol required by the body."

"How did you suspect that he had low levels of cortisol?"

"Because the sodium level was low, potassium was high, and he was still feeling weak and lethargic all the time. He was not having enough food due to loss of appetite and, therefore, was a weak little boy, not looking his age at all."

"So is he all right now?"

"No, he will have to take hydrocortisone for the rest of his life, but he will be able to lead a normal life and grow up to be a strong boy."

Just at that time, Chhotu's sister called and said, "Dr. Sahib, my boy is running around, and he's eating well too."

Bharti explained, "He will have to take this medicine regularly for the rest of his life, but it is quite cheap, and if you go to your family doctor at the dispensary, tell him to call me. I will explain everything to him."

"Thank you, Dr. Sahib, and please let us know if my husband and I can be of any service to you."

"What does your husband do?"

"He is the general secretary of the hospital workers' union."

"He is a big shot. He could have taken your son to any doctor."

"Yes, but he is a very humble man. He asked a couple of doctors before, but they all came back with the same answer that our boy doesn't eat and he is weak, but when Chhotu told me about you, I thought I might try you too as you are a child specialist."

"Okay, don't forget to give him the medicine. This medicine is very essential for him, and he must not miss even one dose. And remember, don't stop the medicine even if he feels better. Otherwise, he will get sick again."

"Thank you, Dr. Sahib, you have saved my son's life!"

Vijay said, "We're almost there."

"Where is this place?" Bharti asked.

"It is an Italian restaurant in a five-star hotel that opened last year. One of my colleagues went to the restaurant last week with his friend, and he said it was an authentic Italian restaurant with good food and a three-man band straight from Italy."

"Swell! I will love to go to that place tonight."

"We will be there in about five minutes. It is very close to the international airport, and I will tell you the good news once we are seated in comfort in the restaurant."

After reaching the hotel lobby, Vijay gave the car keys to a valet to park the car. They went to the restaurant, and the hostess gave them a nice table near the dance floor.

The restaurant was elegantly decorated with huge wall posters of Roman Era all around. On one wall was the Leaning Tower of Pisa. On the other wall were Romans dressed in their traditional costumes, sitting in the Colloseum. And on the third wall were the farmers harvesting the grapes. In front was the band with a backdrop of Pavarotti's huge poster, playing Pavarotti's and Dean Martin's tunes of love songs!

As soon as they sat down, a waiter approached and asked, "Would you like to drink something, sir and madam?"

"Yes, we will start off with a beer and give us the wine list as we might like a nice Italian wine with our dinner," Bharti said.

Vijay started off and said, "The good news is that next week, I'll be getting a fully furnished four-bedroom condo that I am entitled to, but I have to move in to it a week after next Saturday as they need my existing flat for a junior man they have hired, and he's part of my team. He's coming from Chennai with his wife."

"I guess that takes care of the next weekend, and do you want my help?"

"If you want to help and if you are free, you're most welcome to."

"No no no! It does not work like that. What you should be saying is that 'I expect you to help me since you're going to be my life partner.' You should have confidence and be able to assert your right with me. Let us switch the roles. What will you do if I told you I have to move?"

"I will ask you when and how I can help."

"Well, that's good enough."

The waiter brought the beer and the menu.

Vijay said, "Cheers!"

"Cheers!" Bharti said. "When do you start moving in, next Friday or Saturday?" she asked.

"I think probably the next Saturday as I have some work to do on Friday morning."

"I'm free on next Friday afternoon, and I can come whenever you want me to."

"Please come as soon as you can as you have the key of the flat anyway. Sweetie, you can start packing my clothes in the suitcases. How do you like that?"

"Yes, I like that. I'll be there as soon as I can, probably after lunch, and shall I bring somebody with me to help?"

"No, next Saturday morning, my company is actually providing me with the movers. There will be a truck with four men, and I suspect it will take them a couple of hours as I am only moving down the road and I don't have much stuff."

Bharti said, "That really is wonderful news, and maybe we can have a little honeymoon that weekend."

"We certainly can."

Vijay asked, "Do you believe in astrology?"

"Not really! One of the astrologers told my mother that she will have a long life and will play with her grandchildren. None of that came true, and my mother died the very next year."

"Was he a renowned astrologer?"

"Yes, he is quite well-known in England."

"Something very funny happened to me in my office this morning. One of our old accountants came to sort out my benefits and allowances, and he started staring at me. I asked him why he was staring at me. He said he was getting a vision about me, and when I insisted, he told me that the next three months are going to be difficult for me, but after that, everything would be okay and I'll have a beautiful daughter because he could see the mother, the daughter, and me playing in the park."

"If he saw a vision, he might be right, but I will not let anything happen to you. I believe in God, and he would not let me down as I have not done any harm to anybody. On the contrary, I have tried to do good as much as I could."

"He's a bit weird, but he has been with the company for the last twenty years, and everybody says he is a bit cuckoo, but he's a brilliant man." He paused for a minute and then continued, "Do you believe that people get visions?"

"I've been getting visions and premonitions since childhood. When I was very young, I used to know exactly what my mother was going to tell me. When my mother became sick with cancer, I had a vision in which I saw that my mother was lying dead and that came true. So do you think I'm weird too?"

"No, I don't think you're weird, but I'll have to be careful what I think when I'm around you."

"Just ignore it, and let's enjoy the evening."

The waiter brought a basket of fresh bread and freshly crushed garlic with olive oil in a plate and said, "Enjoy, and are you ready to order?"

"No, not quite, what is your special dish in chicken or pasta?" Bharti asked.

"We have chicken fettuccine: fresh grilled chicken breast with sun-dried tomatoes and spinach in a cream tomato sauce on fettuccine pasta. I would suggest a red wine with that. Another good one is chicken marsala: sautéed fresh chicken breast topped with marsala mushroom sauce, served with linguine pasta, with cream sauce and fresh vegetables. With this, I would suggest a white wine. And would you like another drink, madam?" asked the waiter.

"No, we will have a bottle of wine with dinner," Bharti said.

"I suggest a nice bottle of red wine, and we have a house special, Campofiorin Masi Veneto."

"What do you think, Vijay?"

"I would like chicken fettuccine and maybe a glass of red wine."

Bharti said, "I will have the same, and we'll have a bottle of Masi and two glasses."

"Thank you," said the waiter.

Vijay said, "Something is weighing heavy on my mind from the other day's conversation. You wanted to have a baby right away, but I said maybe we should wait for a year. Well, I want to apologize for that and want to reverse my opinion and say that if you want to have a baby right away, we will go ahead with that."

"Why did you change your mind?"

"I remembered a conversation between Ali's father and Ali in which he said that the children are God's gift to us and it is the woman's decision when to have them. Afterward, I found out that there is a lady in my office who was trying to have a baby for the last eight years, and she told me that when she got married, she was not ready for a baby and had an abortion as she was only twenty-two years old. Now she has gone to all the fertility clinics, and they say nothing is wrong with her, and yet she cannot have a baby."

"God has his ways. I'm glad that you have made that decision because that was bothering me all this time too," Bharti said. "Let us dance, I love this music, especially Dean Martin's love songs they are playing."

Vijay said, "Let us, and even I like the music."

They danced away for a while, cheek to cheek and holding each other close. When the music ended, the waiter came to the dance floor and said, "I am sorry to disturb you, sir, but your food is ready."

The waiter served their food as soon as they got back to the table.

Bharti said, "The food is excellent."

Vijay agreed and said, "This is the best place I've been to."

"We might do it again."

"I understand there is an Indian restaurant in this five-star hotel that serves excellent *tandoori* [clay oven] dishes."

"Okay, we'll try that next time as I love *tandoori* food."

They finished their dinner, and Vijay said, "It is time for us to go as it is midnight already, and I have work to do in the morning."

Bharti said, "Let's go." She gave the signal for the waiter to bring the bill.

The waiter came and asked, "Would you like some dessert and coffee?"

"No, thank you, just get the bill."

"Yes, ma'am."

Bharti took out her credit card, but Vijay said, "It is my treat, and after we get married, we will have a joint account, so we won't have to worry about this." He paid the bill.

They picked up the car, and on the way, Vijay said, "The day after tomorrow, on Saturday, when you go to work, Bharti, I will visit my parents and then I'm going to visit Ajay, Ali, and Joy to find out how things are in the slum, also to get the news from Joy as to what is happening in the Communist Party."

"Actually, I might be free Saturday afternoon. If you want, we could go together or I can meet you there at your parents' house, and then we could go together to the slum because I want to sort out the logistics of seeing the patients there."

"That's a good idea. In that case, I will see you at my parents' house on Saturday afternoon."

They got home, and Vijay asked, "Would you like a drink, Bharti?"

"Not really."

"In that case, we should go to bed as I have to go to work in the morning," Vijay remarked.

"Yes, you do, but I have other things on my mind," Bharti whispered with a smirk.

"What is that?"

"I want to make love to you, dummy!"

"I am game, let's do it."

Bharti couldn't wait and got on top of him after taking off her clothes and made love to him passionately.

Next morning, Vijay got up bright and early while Bharti was still sleeping. Vijay made tea, brought it to Bharti, and softly said, "Good morning, rise and shine."

Bharti got up and asked, "What time is it?"

Vijay replied, "It is seven thirty, and I should be leaving in half an hour."

"Okay, honey, I'll just quickly wash and brush and be out to make breakfast."

"The breakfast is all ready, you just have to come and eat it."

After their morning chores, they sat down to have breakfast and Vijay said, "I love you, honey."

"We will talk on the phone, and I'll meet you either at the school or here, whichever is more convenient for you."

Vijay said, "That's fine." And he left.

Bharti took her time getting ready and left to go shopping. Vijay called at noon and asked, "Bharti, what is the plan?"

"Whatever you say, I'm done with my shopping for the day."

"In that case, I will pick you up at the condo at twelve thirty."

"See you at twelve thirty, and love you."

They both went to Vijay's father's school for the Annual Day function that was being held at the vacant plot next to the grounds.

The volunteers knew Vijay, and they gave them seats in the VIP row in the front. Finals of track and field were going on in front of them; and at the back a little farther away, long jump, high jump, and shot put were also taking place at the same time. In a little while, Mr. Kapoor arrived, followed by the district magistrate. The volunteers also seated them in the VIP row. Mr. Shastri came over and greeted Mr. Kapoor and introduced Mr. Kapoor to the district magistrate. In about half an hour, all the events finished and the prize distribution started.

The principal of the school started his speech, "This function is to appreciate your hard work and your talent in sports, games, and academics. In a few minutes, we'll start the prize distribution for achievements in various categories of sports, drama, and of course, the studies. But first, I have to make an announcement, and that is we are expanding our school from grade 10 to grade 12 from the next school year, and I want to give all the credit to Mr. Shastri, the founder of the school. Now I request Mr. Shastri to say a few words to encourage and appreciate your hard work as I do." The ground roared with applause.

Mr. Shastri came on the stage and said, "Boys and girls, you are the future of the country, you are the Lal Bahadur Shastri, you are the Nehru and Naidu, this is your school, and this is your day. You are the most important asset of the school, and we are here to guide you. I don't want to take too much of your time as this is your function, but I'm very pleased to tell you that we are building an extension of the school on this plot on which we are holding this Annual Day. You will have a lot more facilities for drama and cultural activities as there will be a hall and, of course, the principal has already announced that the school will be upgraded to grade 12. This has all been possible due to three individuals, and they are the DCP, the district magistrate who helped us to get the plans sanctioned for the new building, and last but not least, Mr. Kapoor for his generosity of donating one hundred million rupees for the new building."

Everybody applauded and gave a standing ovation to Mr. Shastri. He stood there waving his hands up and down to stop applauding, and he finally said, "Thank you, please stop clapping, and I want to call Mr. Kapoor to the stage to say a few words of encouragement to you."

Mr. Kapoor was overwhelmed and said, "This is" – he showed a check – "an investment in the future of our country, and I want our students to be as good as any in the world. I want you to work hard and show this world that five thousand years ago, we were the most advanced culture in the world and we will be again. I want to give you all the latest tools such as computers, science labs, and world-class sports equipment, but you children have to work hard to show the world that you are the best. Thank you very much, Mr. Shastri, for giving me the opportunity to be a part of this noble cause."

He presented the one-hundred-million-rupee check to Mr. Shastri, and everybody applauded and didn't want to stop.

The prize distribution was carried on by the principal, and he called upon Mr. Shastri and the district magistrate to hand over the prizes to the children. The principal announced that every child would get a package containing a new school uniform, one sweater, and some sweets to take home and they should collect that on the way out.

The principal invited Mr. Shasti, Mr. Kapoor, the district magistrate, Vijay, Bharti, and other dignitaries, who had come to attend the annual school function, to join him for tea and snacks.

Mr. Kapoor said to Mr. Shastri, "I've to leave to attend a very important meeting. Please excuse me, and I would appreciate if you would sign the trust documents and give them to Vijay."

Mr. Shastri said, "Vijay is coming over to our house tonight and tomorrow. He will give you the signed trust documents."

Mr. Kapoor said, "That's fine." And he left.

They had tea and snacks. Vijay introduced Bharti to the district magistrate Amit Malik.

After a little chat, Bharti said, "I have to leave as I have work tomorrow."

Vijay said, "Papa, you have your car, so I'll go with Bharti, and we'll see you tonight."

Mr. Shastri said, "That's fine."

Vijay said to Bharti, "Take me to my condo, and I will pick up my car and then go to my parents unless you want to stay the night with me and go early in the morning to your work."

Bharti had to work at nine a.m., so she decided to stay the night at Vijay's condo and said, "You have to get me out of your condo at eight."

Vijay said, "That's not a problem, I will just pick you up and throw you out."

"You promise, all the way down from the ninth floor."

"No, sweetheart, I love you too much to do that."

"I have to go to my parents to get the trust documents signed. Other than that, the evening is ours."

"I will go with you, meet Mommy and Pooja, and maybe we can have dinner there. Besides, I have not had home-cooked food for a long time. What do you think?"

"I think it is a fantastic idea, and I think my parents would love that."

"Let us give them a surprise, and I want to take some flowers for Mommy!"

Vijay said, "Let us take some *rasmalai*, and I know a place where you can get really good *rasmalai*."

"So you also like *rasmalai*, like my father?"

"Yes, as long as it is not too sweet."

With flowers and *rasmalai* in their hand, they gave Vijay's parents a surprise visit.

Vijay's mother said, "I had a feeling that you're going to show up today, so I told Chemeli and Pooja to cook something special. So they cooked *rajma* [red kidney beans] and rice."

Vijay and Bharti both said, "We love *rajma* and rice."

In a while, Mr. Shastri arrived. They all had food together, laughed, and joked. It seemed like such a happy family.

Earlier, Bharti had put the *rasmalai* in the fridge, and nobody saw her. She brought out the *rasmalai* and said, "Surprise! You are all going to get a treat, but not more than one *rasmalai* each."

Vijay remarked, "Spoken like a doctor."

"Yes, we must have control over what and how much we eat," advised Bharti.

They all burst out laughing.

They finished eating the dessert; Mr. Shastri, Vijay, and Bharti went into the living room to sign the documents. When they finished signing the documents, Pooja and Chemeli brought the masala chai.

Mr. Shastri was very happy and said to Bharti, "Your father has made my dream come true, and I cannot thank him enough, and I'm so glad you came today."

Vijay said, "It was all her idea to come today and to have dinner together."

Vijay's mother said, "I consider her my older daughter and not my daughter-in-law."

Mr. Shastri, in a very unusual mood, got up and hugged Bharti and said, "She's my daughter too."

Bharti was overcome with emotions, and tears started flowing down her cheeks.

Vijay's mother asked, "Why are you crying, Bharti? Come close to me." And she hugged her.

Bharti, still in an emotional state, murmured, "You reminded me of my mother, you are a wonderful family, I'm glad to be a part of it, and I love you, Mommy and Papa."

Pooja said, "How about me?"

Bharti hugged Pooja. "I love you the most, silly."

After staying for a while, Bharti said, "I have to go to work in the morning. I will go to Vijay's house, and Vijay will drive me home."

Vijay and Bharti started off for home, and Bharti said, "Can you please take me home as I'm not feeling too well. Anyway, I still have to prepare more for the seminar that I'm giving tomorrow."

Vijay asked, "Anything serious?"

"No, just the regular stuff."

"What about me, how will I get home?"

Bharti said, "I'll get one of the drivers to drop you home."

Vijay took her home and said, "I hope you'll be feeling better tomorrow. You know we had planned to go to Ajay tomorrow afternoon."

"I know. I'll call tomorrow after my seminar."

"Okay, I love you, hope you get better soon, and please give these trust documents to your father."

One of the drivers took Vijay home.

CHAPTER 22

T HE NEXT DAY at noon, Vijay went over to Ajay's house and announced, "I'm here to have lunch."

"You are most welcome, bhaiya, and how is Bharti Didi?" asked Geeta.

"She has gone to the hospital to deliver a seminar and will call me later. Where is Ajay?"

"He is in bed. You know, bhaiya, he went to the fruit-and-vegetable *mundi* and returned about an hour ago."

"How come he came so late?"

"We still have the transport strike, so he borrowed somebody's truck to bring the fruits and vegetables himself."

"Oh, dear, I wish he had told me and I would have gone with him this morning."

"You know he's very independent."

"How is everybody at home?"

"Papa is at the Mother Dairy. You met Mommy, and she is feeling better now that she is taking Bharti Didi's prescribed medicines regularly."

"I'll just go to the slum to say hi to Ali and Joy."

Vijay went over to Ali's house. He paid his respects to Hakim Saab. Listening to Vijay's voice, Ali came out and asked, "What is the rich man doing in the poor man's house?"

"Don't be nasty or you will get beaten up." And he hugged him.

"I think he needs a good thrashing, and the only person who can give him one is you, Vijay," Hakim Saab joked.

"No, Uncle, I cannot thrash him as I have too much affection for him." And he hugged Ali again.

Ali said, "I'm seeing you after ages, Vijay."

"I have been very busy at work and the school extension. You heard about that, didn't you?"

"Yes, of course, I went to the Annual Day function at the school and noticed you and Bharti Bhabhi [sister-in-law] sitting in the VIP row."

"Why didn't you come and sit with us?"

"I was enjoying it in the back and didn't want to disturb anybody."

"Have you seen Joy or Mohan lately?" inquired Vijay.

"Yes, I saw them both this morning. Why, do you want to meet them?"

"Yes, of course. It'll be nice if Joy, Mohan, and you can come over to Ajay's place later this afternoon. We'll have a chat. Besides, I have not met them for a while."

"Okay, I will go in the afternoon and ask them."

"What are they doing anyway?"

"Mohan is not doing much, except that he is very involved with the RSS and the *shakha*."

"How is he making a living?"

"He has taken a small place in the village close to the industrial area and is making *paneer* and *khoya* [an ingredient used in making Indian sweets] as the Diwali season is coming. He was also saying that he wants to start off a factory for English and other types of cheese such as cheddar and mozzarella, but there is a lot of money involved and he's trying to find a partner to start the business. He wants to do everything legal and aboveboard so that nobody can harass him. While his earlier business was also legal, it is just that his dairy farm was in the way of the metro and the government acquired it. It is a separate matter that he did not get what the minister promised him. He should have got something in writing from the minister."

"What is Joy up to these days?"

"I don't know very much really because he doesn't talk to me very much."

"Okay, if you can get them over this afternoon, we'll all get together, so see you later."

He shook hands with Ali and went back to Ajay's house.

Ajay was waiting outside his house, and as soon as Vijay arrived, Ajay remarked, "I haven't seen you for a while, big fellow!"

Vijay got out of the car, hugged him, and said, "Same here, and how are you keeping?"

"I'm fine, just too busy trying to get the fruits and vegetables in the morning. It is becoming a big hassle. I'm thinking of changing the business into a grocery type of store, and I will give a small stall on lease to a fruit-and-vegetable vendor."

"It is a very good idea, but don't give it on lease, rather make a percentage agreement. If you want, I will draft one for you when you're ready. At least that way, the guy running the fruit-and-vegetable business will have no right on your property."

Geeta came out and announced, "Food is served, come and get it."

Between mouthfuls, Vijay said, "We were talking about Bharti running a clinic here."

"I thought about it too, but I see a problem that everybody is going to come and would want to see her. They only know one thing, that she is a doctor. They don't know she's a child specialist. There will be a big crowd outside her clinic, so who will control the crowd?" Ajay asked.

Pehalwanji was also sitting at the table, eating food with them. He asserted, "Ajay is right, I can see the problem, but I tell you boys, where God closes one door, he opens another."

"What do you mean?" both Vijay and Ajay asked at once.

"Do you remember one Dr. Khanna, who has a big house about a block away from here?"

"It is all locked up, we heard that he went away to America," Ajay informed.

"That's right, he went to live with his son whom he had sent to study in America. Apparently, the son is settled in America for the last ten or so years. He married an Indian girl and has two sons, who are now eight and ten years old," Pehalwanji explained.

"So what happened?"

"Well, he has come back, and he said it is for good."

"Did he come to see you?"

"Yes, of course, he's an old friend. We used to go for walks together in the morning. He used to run a clinic here, and when you were young, you had gone to see him many times."

"I remember him, Papa, and I remember his son too. He was very frail and would not come out to play with us."

"He was very good in studies," said Ajay's father. He continued after a pause, "And you wanted to play all the time."

"So what happened to him?"

"Dr. Khanna and his wife packed up everything and went to America to live with his son."

"Why did they come back?"

"From what I can make out, in the first year, they were really happy. Their daughter-in-law was not working, and the children were going to school. They had a maid to clean the house, and the mother and the daughter-in-law took care of the cooking. They travelled all over America. When the son and the daughter-in-law wanted to go out in the evening, they would take care of the children."

"So what went wrong?" Vijay asked.

"The problem came in the second year when the daughter-in-law started working. The children would come home from school and start watching TV. When they were told to do their homework by their grandparents, they simply refused. Earlier, they were getting good grades. Later, their grades started sliding. When the school reports came at the end of year, their son and the daughter-in-law got very upset at the children and also blamed the grandparents for not looking after them properly."

"What happened then?" Ajay asked.

"Then the daughter-in-law had to leave her job. She was always upset at the children and taunting the grandmother. Finally, one day, Dr. and Mrs. Khanna got so upset that they quietly decided to move back to India. When they confronted their son, they were told that they did not know how well-off they were and that there will be nobody in India to look after them. They came back anyway."

"Is Bharti coming today?" Ajay asked.

"Yes, she is coming later."

"Maybe you and Bharti can go over and talk to him?" Pehalwanji said.

"In fact, I'm going to ask my father if he wants to invite them for our engagement and the wedding. I'm sure he knows my father."

"Yes, of course, it is a good idea. Why don't you ask your father?"

Vijay called his father and asked, "Did you know one Dr. Khanna?"

"Yes, of course, he went away to America to his son."

"Yes, he is back now and wants to start his practice in Anand Enclave. Do you want to invite him for our engagement and wedding?"

"Yes, of course, he is a good friend of mine, but why do you ask? Do you want to see him today?"

"Yes, but I don't have an invitation card."

"It doesn't matter, you can invite him in person, and then we can send a card to him in the mail."

"That's a great idea, Papa."

"Where are you now?"

"I'm sitting with Ajay and his father."

"Give my regards to Pehalwanji."

"Papa sends his regards."

"Very well then, it is all settled. Bharti and I will go to him later this afternoon. I would appreciate it if you would call him and ask him as to what is a good time for him to see me?"

"Sure." Pehalwanji called Dr. Khanna and asked, "Do you remember Mr. Shastri?"

"Of course, I do, who can forget him?"

"Well, his son, Vijay, is here, and he along his fiancée wants to come over to invite you for their engagement and wedding."

"He can come. It will be more convenient at about four p.m."

"He will come to you at four then."

"You and Bharti can go at four, talk to him about opening the clinic and whatever else you want to propose."

After eating, Ajay and Vijay went to Ajay's room.

In a little while, Bharti called and said, "How are you, sweetheart?"

"The question is how you are. It is two o'clock now, did you finish your seminar, and did you have a chance to eat anything?" inquired Vijay.

"Yes, honey, I had food at the hotel where I was giving the seminar. And in about half an hour, I'm coming over, just tell me where you are."

"I am at Ajay's house. We just finished eating, and I have a good news for you."

"What is that?"

"I will tell you all about it when you get here, but to tell you in short, we have a family doctor in Ajay's colony who can also work."

"Great, my main worry was that everybody in the slum and Anand Enclave will come to see me for all their medical problems."

"That is exactly what we have been discussing, and now we have a solution for you."

"Very good, I will see you about three thirty."

"Make sure you are here by four because we have to go and see Dr. Khanna at four."

"Okay, sweetheart, bye for now."

"I went to see Ali earlier on, and he said he will come after lunch."

"He should be coming soon," asserted Ajay.

Just that time, Joy, Mohan, and Ali arrived; and each one said, "It is good to see you, Vijay."

"It is good to see you too," Vijay said, and he went over and hugged them all.

"How are things with you, Mohan?" Vijay asked.

"Diwali season is coming. I have taken a place in the adjoining village to start the production of *paneer* and *khoya*."

"That's very interesting, have you actually started production?" Vijay asked.

"Yes, we did the trial runs last week, and I hope to be ready for production next week. I have also joined the RSS and am actively attending the *shakha* and teaching Indian martial arts as I know them well."

"That's interesting." And he asked Joy, "What's happening on your end?"

"Not much." He paused and then continued, "Except for teaching music to children."

"I mean on the political scene."

"Communist Party hierarchy is still talking about a revolution. They are saying that the poor are becoming poorer and the rich are becoming richer. There is no equal distribution of wealth. Look at all the problems in Maharashtra, Gujarat, Bihar, Bengal, and all the eastern states, which have been suffering from floods. The government has been promising them food, water, and compensation. To date, nothing has been given to them, people are getting very frustrated, and unless something is done soon, they will resort to violence. The first to feel the brunt of violence will be the politicians and the very rich."

"Do they have any plans?" Vijay asked.

"I heard something that they are training a number of people and they are searching around for more volunteers, or you can say the vulnerable that have suffered and have nothing more to lose."

"Ali, what do you say, what is happening in your community?"

"My community and your community are the wrong words. All the communities are pawns in the hands of the politicians. We have to change the politicians who are corrupt and have no scruples. They incite racial riots and get people killed for their own gain, just to retain their *chair* and power."

"Yes, it is all very wrong."

Just at that time, Bharti arrived and said, "Hello, everybody." She hugged them all and went on, "I haven't seen you all for a long time."

"Same here, and it is good to see you again," all of them replied at the same time.

"You're all coming to the engagement party, aren't you?"

"Of course, we are, and we will all dance and celebrate."

"Bharti and I have to go regarding setting up another medical clinic. Ajay will explain it to you in detail."

Bharti and Vijay went to see Dr. Khanna. He opened the door and asked, "I was expecting you, Vijay, but who is this beautiful young lady?"

"This is Dr. Bharti, my fiancée, and we're getting engaged on Saturday, the fifth of October, and getting married on Saturday, the ninth of November. Uncle, please keep those dates free. My father will send the invitation card to you."

"For now, all my dates are free, and did you say that this young lady's name is Dr. Bharti."

"Yes, and she is a pediatrician."

"Oh. A child specialist, and where do you practice, Bharti?"

"I don't have a private practice. I work out of a hospital and have a clinic there. I'm starting a clinic at Pehalwanji's house on a part-time basis. It will be every Tuesday and Friday from four to seven p.m."

"That will be very good for this colony and also for the slum."

"Yes, and I was wondering if you are going to start your practice again?"

"I was thinking about it, but I don't have all the equipment now."

"My father has a friend who deals with medical equipment. Maybe we can help you out from my father's trust. That is if you open a free clinic for the slum dwellers."

"Yes, I was thinking about that. In fact, what I thought was that I will open the clinic for two hours in the morning for our colony and the rich surrounding colonies. I'll charge them a fee of one hundred rupees per patient, will also run a clinic for the poor in the evening from four thirty to seven, and charge a nominal fee of twenty rupees per patient, just to cover the salary of my assistant. In addition, I will also give some medicines free."

"That sounds like a very good plan."

"For the poor people, I need some cards printed. Last time, Krishna did the printing for me."

"He will do it again, Uncle," Vijay said.

"It is all settled then. Give me a list of the equipment you need, and I will see what I can do," Bharti said.

"Where did you do your medical studies?"

"I did my MD and my specialization in England. I heard you went to America. Didn't you try to pass the exams to get an American license to practice there?"

"No, we went to our son as we thought we would retire, but it was not to be. It is better to be self-sufficient and live alone rather than being dependent on others. You know, you lose your self-respect, and now I have decided to work till I die."

"You had your son and your grandchildren there. Were you not happy being with them?"

Just at that time, Mrs. Khanna came in the room and said, "I heard him talking to some strangers."

Vijay said, "I'm no stranger, I am Vijay, son of Mr. Shastri, and she's my fiancée, Bharti."

"It's nice to meet you, Bharti."

Dr. Khanna said, "They have come to invite us for their engagement and wedding."

"That is nice, and how is your mother, Vijay?"

"She is fine and would be glad to know that you are back as she often talks about you."

"Yes, we used to go to your new house to meet them."

"Auntie, why did you come back from the USA?" Bharti asked.

"I think more than I, Dr. Khanna wanted to come back."

"Don't blame me, Prem, you were very upset at your daughter-in-law taunting you for your grandsons not getting the grades, especially that you were a teacher and were a principal of a school in India."

"Yes, but I liked being with my son and grandchildren. However, you're right, we're better off here."

"You know we were housebound the whole day. In the summer, we could go out for walks, but during the winter months, we couldn't go out anywhere. We were both working people in India. It is difficult to sit at home all day," explained Dr. Khanna.

"I agree with you, you have a lot of company here. You can go for walks in the morning and have a social life," Bharti remarked.

"That's true. I am part of the Morning Walkers Club already. I'm used to getting up at five thirty a.m. You know when your father was in this colony, I used to go for walks with him. In America, I didn't know what to do, I couldn't go out for a walk."

"I agree, at this age, it is very difficult to adjust in the foreign countries. On top of that, the children are brought up in the American way. They do not have the same respect for their elders. In most of the families, they call their father, mother, uncles, and the neighbors by their first name," Vijay said.

Mrs. Khanna said, "It is time for tea." She called her maid and asked her to make some tea.

"Do you want regular tea or ginger tea?" asked the maid.

"We'll have chai with ginger as we had enough of regular tea with a bag in America."

"What you've asked are all small things, and you left your family and grandchildren for that?" Bharti asked.

"When you think about it, they seem quite trivial, but when you're going through it, they are very discomforting. To top it all, the children were getting out of hand and they were not listening to us. They were making remarks like we were stupid. Whenever we told our son or daughter-in-law, they either just ignored us or said we were over-reacting," replied Mrs. Khanna.

"Was there any major incident that happened that made you leave?"

"Drop by drop, the bucket gets filled, so we were upset with all the little problems. On top of that, we didn't have any money to spend, could not go out to buy anything. In the summertime, sometimes we used to walk to the Indian grocery store and buy some Indian groceries, but if we wanted to buy something extra, we didn't have any money. Every time we asked our daughter-in-law for money, she would say she had to get it from the bank. The final straw that broke the donkey's back was when the children's reports came at the end of the school year. My son and daughter-in-law became very upset and started shouting at us, saying that we did not look after our grandchildren, that it would have been better if we had stayed in India and not come over to America. At that, I lost my temper and said we will be happy in India and told him to book our tickets as soon as possible," Dr. Khanna said with tears in his eyes.

"What happened then?" Vijay asked.

"It was summertime, my son tried to make it up to us. He took us to Disneyland, we had some fun, but I was determined not to spend another winter in America."

"Didn't your son try to stop you and to talk you out of it?"

"Yes, he did, my son and I had long walks and talks. Finally, we came to the conclusion that it will be for the best for us to come back to India, and we left on good terms."

"Oh, that's good that you left on good terms. Have you talked to them ever since you have come back?"

"Oh yes, the telephone is so cheap. We talk practically every other day," replied Mrs. Khanna.

Vijay and Bharti had the tea and snacks and left.

After reaching Ajay's house, Vijay said, "It is all set. Dr. Khanna is going to start his medical practice again and will hold a clinic for the slum dwellers in the evening from four thirty to seven p.m. every day, except Sunday."

"That's really good, it will take away the crowd from Bharti Bhabhi."

"Bharti and I are leaving, and we will talk later."

"Okay, bye for now."

Bharti and Vijay went to Vijay's condo in separate cars, and Vijay asked, "What do you want to do tonight, and what are your plans for tomorrow?"

"My plan for tonight is," Bharti paused for a while and then continued, "to be with you and only you, and for tomorrow, I would like to get home in the afternoon as my papa wants to talk to me about all the people who are coming from abroad to attend our engagement. He also wants to talk to me about taking them around to show them some parts of India like the Taj Mahal and Rajasthan."

"Do you want to go out tonight?" Vijay asked.

"It is just after six now. I suppose we could go out to see a movie, have dinner, and come home early."

"That sounds really good as I haven't seen a movie for a while."

"I will quickly get ready, and then we can catch the earlier show."

"I don't even know what's on. While you are getting ready, I will find out from the movie Web site."

"Okay, that's fine."

Vijay logged on to the movie Web site and said, "There's a good English movie starting at seven at one of the theaters in the mall, and there are couple of nice restaurants in that mall too."

"That's good, let's go there, the movie would finish before nine. And after eating dinner, we could be home at eleven o'clock at the latest."

After the movie, Bharti said, "I don't feel like eating in the food court in the mall. Let's just get a takeout, and we will eat at home."

"That's fine by me. What kind of food do you want: Indian, Chinese, or Continental?"

"I had Chinese food for lunch."

"There is a good Indian take-out place. His *tandoori* dishes and *nans* [flatbread baked in clay oven] are very good."

"Let's go for that," Bharti said.

They went and ordered Indian food at a take-out place.

The person at the order desk said, "It will be fifteen to twenty minutes."

Vijay said, "That's fine." And he asked, "Is there a bar in this mall?"

The person at the order desk replied, "Yes, there is, sir, just around the corner."

Vijay said, "We will be back in half an hour, and here's my telephone number. Just call me when the food is ready. Only make sure it is fresh and good."

"Yes, sir."

Bharti and Vijay went to the bar and ordered two beers.

The bartender said, "Would you like draft beer or bottled beer?"

"Draft beer, please," Bharti said.

After a couple sips of beer, Bharti said, "From Monday, the sixteenth of September, onward, there is a conference of pediatricians starting, and I will be very busy in that conference. I've been told to deliver the opening speech. The conference will last for four days till Thursday afternoon. Doctors are coming from England, Canada, America, Australia, and the rest of the world."

"Do you know anybody from England?"

"I will know next week. I'm sure a couple of my colleagues must be coming."

"What is happening tomorrow at your house?"

"Papa has called Raju and me to discuss the arrangements for accommodation and travel for the people coming from abroad."

"Do they have the final list of all the people coming?"

"Maybe Raju has it. I haven't seen it as his name was on the RSVP."

After a few seconds, Bharti asked, "What's happening with your company?"

"Not much, except that they are quite keen on buying a company in Canada."

"Does that mean you have to go there?"

"No, not immediately, I told them that I'm getting engaged and getting married soon. I have invited my boss and a few other people from the office."

"Are you still moving in to the new condo next Friday afternoon?"

"Yes, that's for sure because they have booked the movers for Saturday early morning. Are you still coming Friday afternoon?"

"Yes, silly, I will be coming for sure at about two. I've told my senior doctor and my secretary."

They finished their beer and paid the bill and walked over to the Indian take-out place.

Vijay said, "It is over half an hour, but you didn't call me?"

"Your order is ready, sir, I was just about to call you. I just thought you must have been enjoying your beer, so I thought I might as well put another urgent order for delivery through, ahead of you."

"So you deliver too?" Vijay asked.

"Yes, we do, sir, within eight kilometers from here."

"Give me your menu."

Bharti asked, "Do you have any wine at home?"

"I think I do, but I can't be sure."

"Is there a wine store close by?"

"Yes, there is one, and we can pick a couple of bottles on our way."

They picked up a couple of bottles of wine and went home. As soon as they got home, Bharti grabbed Vijay, hugged him, and said, "I've been missing you all week."

Vijay hugged and kissed her back. "I have been missing you too."

They kept hugging and kissing and made love.

After making love, Bharti said, "I am starving."

"Do you want a glass of wine?"

"Yes, please, and I will go and warm up the food."

Vijay poured a glass of wine and went over to the kitchen, put the glass down on the side counter, grabbed her from the back and kissed her on the neck, and said, "I will give you a hand."

She turned around, gave him a hug and a kiss, and asserted, "Thank you for the wine, but I don't need a hand, you go and set the table."

After having dinner, they chatted for a while and went to bed.

Next day, they got up, had breakfast, and made love.

"I'm becoming very impatient as I want to be together with you all the time."

"Same here, Bharti, it is only a matter of a few weeks."

"Okay," she said with a sad face. She paused, then continued, "All next week, I'm going to be very busy looking after the arrangements for all the people attending the conference as my hospital is hosting the conference. I have to leave now, love you, and miss you."

"Very well then, keep in touch, if you need anything, I will be here, love you, and I will miss you."

CHAPTER 23

T HE WHOLE WEEK, Bharti was very busy at work, overseeing the arrangements for the conference, going through the list of people attending the conference, and making sure that the travel company had arranged their accommodation. On top of that, she had some very sick children from slum colonies with jaundice in the hospital.

During the week, she phoned Vijay every day just to tell him that she loved him and missed him.

On Friday, September 14 at 4:00 p.m., she reached Vijay's condo unannounced, to find out that he had already moved out and the gate security didn't know his new address. She called Vijay's cell, but there was no answer.

She sat in her car, wondering what happened to him. After about ten minutes, Vijay called. "Where are you, honey?"

"Don't honey me. I'm mad at you as you didn't tell me about moving today."

"You were supposed to come at two p.m."

"I was stuck in a traffic jam, and I've been trying to call you ever since."

"The movers came in at one p.m. My phone was dead, so I couldn't call you, and then they started moving quickly as they said they had to finish moving my stuff by the evening. Tomorrow they have to move a new family into my condo as their stuff is already here from Chennai, South India. I'll give you the address of my new condo, or do you want me to come and get you?"

"Just give me the address and the directions. I will be there soon."

"It is not very far, only five to seven minutes by car."

Vijay gave the address and directions. Then he went down to wait for her outside the condo building.

She arrived in ten minutes, got out, hugged and kissed him as if she had not seen him for a year, and whispered, "I thought I had lost you."

"How will you bear it if I really get lost or something happens to me?"

"I don't know. I would die, and don't ever say that again! When I lost my mother, I was totally heartbroken. Because of that, I never got close to anybody for the fear of losing them. But somehow you slipped into my heart without my even knowing it."

"Yes, it was not easy. It took three long years, but I got in your heart. The place is a little cramped, but it is very cozy, tender, and thoughtful, full of consideration and love for others and, of course, for me," Vijay whispered gently.

Feeling very emotional, Bharti hugged and kissed him and whispered, "I love you, sweetheart, but I'm not fully in your heart yet, am I?"

"Yes, you are, but you don't know that you were there the first day I met you. However, I couldn't tell you that for the fear of losing you."

"Okay, let's go and see your new condo."

"It is on the eleventh floor with a beautiful view of parks and a golf course. Your father would love it."

Outside the condo entrance, Vijay proposed, "Let me carry you into your new home."

"Leave the carrying for the wedding night. Let's go arm in arm as we will live here together after we are married." As she walked through, she exclaimed, "Wow, it is really elegantly furnished!"

The condo entrance faced north, and after the entrance was a lobby, which led into the dining area with a carved rosewood six seating dining room set. A little farther and you were in the living room with two sets of designer leather sofas. In front on the south side was the walk-out balcony through a set of sliding doors, and the view from the balcony was breathtaking. On the east side were two bedrooms with attached bathrooms that were still unfurnished, and on the west side adjoining the living room was the master bedroom suite with a sauna, and in the corner was one bedroom with a bathroom attached.

"This is our executive suite. Living, dining, and two bedrooms are completely furnished. It has all the appliances, including a washing machine. I still have a budget of two hundred thousand rupees to furnish this condo as we choose to. There is also a scheme which is called rent-to-own. If I opt for the scheme, the rent, which is taken out of my salary, will go toward purchase of the condo."

Next they went to the master bedroom, and Bharti remarked, "It really is tastefully furnished and decorated. I must say your company is very generous."

"Starting next week, I will get a chauffeur-driven car as well."

"Congratulations, my sweetheart, I hope the success will always be with you." She gave him a tight hug and a kiss.

"Thank you, sweetheart." He hugged and kissed Bharti and said, "It is all your luck and your good wishes."

"Let's get you settled in."

And they started putting his things in place. Vijay noticed that Bharti was trying to reach the upper part of the closet to put away an empty bag. He went over and grabbed her from the back and gave her a kiss while she was still holding the bag up.

Bharti threw the bag down, grabbed and kissed him, and said, "So you can be naughty too! I will teach you a lesson."

In a second, with a judo technique, she threw him on the bed, and she landed on top of him and started kissing him passionately. Vijay didn't know what hit him.

In about a minute, Vijay asked, "What happened, where am I?"

"You are on the bed, and I'm taking advantage of you, my sweetie."

"Where did you learn this?"

"This is called judo. I learned it at school. They taught us to defend ourselves. Now be quiet and make love to me."

After making love, they finished off all the unpacking, and Vijay said, "This is our master bedroom, and you can pick any closet you want to put your clothes in."

"I've already picked one." And she opened the closet door to show her clothing brought from his old condo.

"That's what I like about you. You know exactly what you're doing and what you want."

"What are we doing tonight? I can be with you tonight and tomorrow. On Sunday, starting at eleven a.m., we are registering the people attending the conference, followed by a light lunch. And on Sunday night, we are having a formal cocktail party and a dinner for them."

"Can anybody attend the conference?"

"No, most of them are doctors, and they were invited officially."

"It is almost eight, what do you want to do?"

"I want to celebrate your success and getting the condo."

"Where do you want to go?"

"I brought a suitcase full of clothes. First, I want to bring it up, take a shower, and get ready."

"I want to do the same, but where do you want to go?"

"Let's go to a disco because we can afford to be late tonight. But tomorrow night, we will go for a nice, quiet dinner, if that's okay with you?"

"That's fine with me, except that maybe we can invite my family over for lunch tomorrow," Vijay suggested.

"I think that's a brilliant idea, but what would we make for lunch? I know your papa and mommy don't like to eat from outside."

"Oh yes, they do, but it has to be vegetarian."

"Why don't you give them a call and find out what they're doing tomorrow? I feel we have to give them a bit of time and not invite them at the last minute."

"You're absolutely right." Vijay called them up and said, "Hi, Pooja. I'm calling from my new condo."

"Already? I thought you were moving tomorrow!"

"That was the plan, but my company changed the plan. The movers came in today and moved us already."

"Who else is there?"

"Bharti, of course, and she wants to talk to you."

"When did you come, Bharti Bhabhi?"

"I went to his old condo today to give him a hand in packing. He was nowhere to be found. Finally, after two hours, I got here. We were thinking, why don't you three come for lunch tomorrow and see his new condo?"

"Let me ask Mommy and Papa, just hold for a minute." After couple of minutes, she came back. "How will you make lunch there? You have nothing there, but I have a suggestion. Why don't we make lunch and bring it over?"

"We can get food delivered from outside, and we have all the plates and cutlery that we brought from the old condo."

"Mommy said we can talk in the morning and we will decide. Maybe we will do a potluck."

"Let me talk to Mommy." In a few seconds, Bharti said, "*Namaste*, Mommyji. Congratulations for your son's success, and how are you feeling?"

"Hi, *beti*, congratulations to you too, and I know it is your good luck that is bringing him success."

"Mommyji, we'll see you tomorrow."

"Yes, we'll definitely come, but we'll talk about lunch in the morning. God bless you, my *beti*."

Bharti and Vijay brought Bharti's bag from the car. They got ready and went out to a disco.

While dancing, they were approached by a rough-looking tall man who said, "May I?" And he tried to grab Bharti to dance, pushing Vijay aside.

Vijay thought for a minute that he knew her, but Bharti resisted and said, "I don't want to dance with you."

Hearing that, Vijay tried to intervene. Just then, the ruffian's two other friends tried to grab Vijay; but Vijay pushed them back while Bharti, using her judo technique, flipped the man grabbing her, and he landed on the dance floor. There was a big commotion in the dance hall, and the bouncers intervened between Vijay and the other two guys. In the meantime, the man got up from the floor and asked, "Don't you remember me, Bharti? I am Dave, whom your father sent to England, and I met you about six years ago."

Bharti replied, "I remember you, loser. You are the same Dave who was sent for training to England, but you disappeared and became an illegal immigrant. I didn't want to have anything to do with you then, and I don't want to have anything to do with you now, so get lost."

Vijay shouted, "Get lost, or I'll rip your head off from your body."

As the bouncers grabbed them, Dave boasted, "You don't know who you are tackling. My uncle is a minister, and I'll have this place locked up."

Just at that time, two police officers in plain clothes showed up and introduced themselves as ACP Samir and ACP Rakesh and asked, "What seems to be the trouble?"

Vijay pointed toward the men held by the bouncers and said, "These jokers tried to be fresh with my fiancée. Anyway, it is nice to meet you both. My name is Vijay Shastri, and this is my fiancée, Bharti."

Samir and Rakesh shook hands with both and said, "It is nice to meet you both. And, Vijay, we were in school together."

"Yes, I remember the last time also you tried to save me from getting beaten up at the soccer game."

"Those drunken ruffians couldn't beat you up as you are looking very tough and in fighting fit," Samir remarked.

"After that incident at school, I learned my lesson and built up my body," Vijay replied.

Rakesh instructed the bouncers, "Take away those troublemakers and hand them to the local police, and I'll phone the SHO of your precinct."

The bouncers took away the three men and apologized, "We are sorry, madam and sir, please have a drink. Enjoy yourselves on the house, and please don't worry about the three ruffians as they will be handed over to police as instructed by ACP Rakesh."

Bharti and Vijay chatted with Rakesh and Samir for a while, and after inviting them to their engagement and wedding, they went to a restaurant to have dinner.

They came back to the condo, and Bharti said, "I am ready to hit the bed."

"Out of curiosity, who was that ruffian Dave?"

"Just some guy who was sent for training by my father, but that idiot ran away and became an illegal immigrant. He tried to contact me a couple times, but I reported him to the police, and he never bothered me again."

"That was a fantastic move. I like the way you threw him on the floor."

"I know how to protect myself, so don't try anything with me now," Bharti remarked jokingly.

Vijay grabbed Bharti and whispered, "You are not in a loving mood tonight, are you?"

"Yes, I am, and I want to cuddle up with you in bed and flip you over."

Next morning, Vijay got up early as usual. He did his regular routine of yoga exercises, made masala chai and brought it over to Bharti, put the chai down on the table, kissed Bharti, and whispered, "Rise and shine, my sweetheart, tea is served."

While having tea, Bharti asked, "What are we doing for lunch?"

"There are a couple of options. Either we can cook something here or we can get something from outside. But can you cook something?"

"I'm not really that good at any Indian dishes. I can make an omelet, rice pilaf, salad, and some English desserts. That's about all."

"Why don't we call up Pooja and ask what she has in mind?"

"I think that's a good idea."

Vijay called Pooja. "What's happening, and what do you want for lunch?"

"We were thinking of making lunch here and bringing it over."

"Bharti can make a nice rice pilaf. You can make some vegetable curry of your choice. We can get some *channas* and *nans* delivered to us."

"That's fine, you get the *channa* and *nans*, and we have enough yogurt. We will make the *raita* [yogurt mixed with chopped cucumbers, onions, and tomatoes] when we get there."

"Okay, I will also get all the salad ingredients, and when will you be here?"

Pooja went to Mommy and Daddy, and she came back and said, "We will be there by one."

Bharti said to Vijay, "If you can get all the ingredients, I can make a trifle for dessert."

"You mean the three-layered dessert with cake, jelly, and custard? That'll be great, and it'll be a surprise for them. Just make a list of all the things you need, and I'll try to get them delivered here."

Bharti made a list and gave it to Vijay. He ordered the groceries from his old contact. They said it was a little farther now, but for him they would deliver it. After a while, all the groceries were delivered to them. Bharti got busy with cooking and said to Vijay, "You can help me get all the ingredients ready by cutting up the fruit for the jelly."

While Vijay was cutting the fruits, Bharti asked, "I hope you got me the cake mix without eggs?"

"Whatever you wrote was delivered. Just check on the packet."

Bharti checked the packet and found it to be correct; she baked the cake and got the food ready by twelve thirty. Vijay had placed the order for *channas* and *nan*; they were also delivered.

Bharti said, "You have a nice table with six chairs. Just lay the table for six people."

In a little while, Vijay got a call from the entrance security guard. "Mr. Shastri and family are here to see you, sir."

Vijay said, "Please let them in and show them my parking spots."

Bharti asked, "How many parking spots do you have?"

"We have three parking spots with this condo."

"That's really great!"

Vijay opened the door and waited in the hallway for his mommy, papa, Pooja, and Chemeli to arrive. When they arrived, he said, "Welcome." And they hugged each other. Bharti also came out of the condo, hugged everybody, and asked them to come in.

They came inside the condo, all carrying containers of food. Bharti led them to the kitchen and took care of their containers.

Mrs. Shastri said, "Bharti, show us the condo."

Bharti took them around the condo. They praised it and said it was very beautiful. Pooja asked, "What are you going to do with the other two bedrooms, which are not furnished?"

"When you get married, you can come and stay in them. We'd have them furnished by then."

Vijay's father said, "Normally we should have done a *havan*. However, we must do a little *puja* [prayer to the Almighty God] before we sit down for lunch."

Bharti said, "It's a very good idea, and what do you need, Papa?"

"We brought all the stuff with us. Let us sit down on the floor, and let us start praying."

Bharti and Vijay moved the furniture to make room in the middle; Bharti brought a bedcover and put it down on the carpet.

They all sat down, Mr. and Mrs. Shastri sang a *bhajan* (a hymn), and the rest of the family joined in. After the *bhajan*, Mr. Shastri requested everybody to pray to God and meditate for two minutes to bless Vijay and Bharti for their long lives, good health, and happiness in this new condo.

Bharti remarked, "You brought so many dishes, Pooja!"

"No, Bharti Bhabhi, we made three vegetable dishes and one *paneer* dish. And Mommy made some *halwa* for Prasad [a dessert dish usually distributed in a temple after prayers]."

Everybody ate together and appreciated the food, especially the rice pilaf made by Bharti. After lunch, Bharti informed them, "I have a little surprise." And she went into the kitchen and brought out the trifle.

They all said, "Wow, what is that?"

Bharti replied, "It is called trifle, and I made it myself. I hope you'll like it."

Mr. Shastri said, "Looks like a cake base. I hope it doesn't have eggs in it."

Bharti said, "I made sure of that, and I've got the packet to prove it."

"No, that's fine, I believe you. And I appreciate your thoughtfulness and that you are concerned to honor other people's beliefs, which may be different than yours."

"Thank you, Papa, and I would never let you down," Bharti said.

They all appreciated Bharti's cooking. Chemeli and Pooja helped to clear the table.

While Vijay and Bharti loaded dishes into the dishwasher, they all sat around in the living room and chatted for a while. Mr. Shastri said, "It is time for us to take a rest, so we will go."

Vijay suggested, "You can rest in one of the bedrooms here."

"No, thank you, son, but I'd rather go home now. I have some work to do as well."

"Okay, Papa." They hugged each other and said bye.

"I have to call Ajay as he called me earlier, but I couldn't talk to him."

"I am very tired. And also, I'm not feeling too well."

"I can understand. You have been working very hard. Just go and lie down."

Vijay called up Ajay. "What's up, man?"

"Just wanted you to know that all the hoods are out on bail. They came to the slum yesterday evening to show their faces despite one of the conditions of their bail being that they will not go within one kilometer of the slum."

"These people don't have any respect for the law. I understand that Nandita Basu and some selected newspaper reporters were called to the minister's office."

Ajay said, "That's correct. They were given a briefing that the toilets and showers issue has been resolved and that he has authorized the local municipality to connect the showers and the toilets to the main sewer."

"Did he also give a time line?"

"No, not at all, but Nandita is going to follow it up with the local municipality and then print it in the newspaper."

"That's very good. Nandita is very thorough, and she's doing a great job."

Ajay said, "Bye, and I will keep you posted."

After a while, Bharti got up and asked, "Vijay, who were you talking to?"

Vijay told her that he was talking to Ajay and filled her in on what Ajay said.

"Is Nandita going to follow it up?"

"Yes, of course, she's very thorough."

"Is Nandita going to get married to Joy?"

"I think so, they've been friends since schooltime, you know."

Just at that time, Vijay got a call from Joy. "Hi, Vijay, did I disturb you?"

"No, not at all."

"Is it a convenient time to talk?"

"Yes, only Bharti and I are here."

"Actually, Nandita has some information she would like to discuss with you personally. When is it convenient for you to meet us?"

"Come over to my new condo and have tea with us."

"Okay, that will be great. We will see you at about five p.m."

Vijay gave him the address and directions.

Bharti remarked, "Isn't that strange that we were just talking about them?"

"Yes, I think we get vibes. I'm sure there is a system of communication that we human beings don't know about."

"Are Joy and Nandita coming over?"

"I have invited him for tea, and they are coming over at five."

"Do we have to make some arrangements for tea?"

"Yes, we can get some samosas and sweets delivered."

"There is also a pastry shop close by, but I don't know if they would deliver."

Vijay called the sweet and the pastry shop and placed an order for delivery.

"Just curious, why do Nandita and Joy want to visit us out of the blue?"

"They want to discuss something serious. I thought it'll be nice to invite them to our new condo too."

"Absolutely, it'll be nice to meet them. In fact, I wanted to meet Joy's mother as she's a music teacher. Maybe I can learn something from her."

"Sure, it is a good idea."

"What are we doing tonight?" Bharti asked.

"I was thinking of calling your father, and if he wants to come over in the evening, then maybe we can go out for dinner together."

"He'll be very happy to hear that you have such a nice condo. It is kind of short notice. However, there is no harm in trying. Do you want to call him?"

Vijay called Bharti's father and said, "This is Vijay, is it a good time to talk to you?"

"For you, my son, any time is a good time," Bharti's father replied.

"Papa, we moved in to our new condo, and I know it is short notice, but would you like to come and see it and have dinner with us tonight?"

"Congratulations, may God bless you with all the success, happiness, and good health. I had a prior dinner engagement, but I can definitely come and see you in the evening. Please give me the directions, I will see you around six p.m., and I'll try to get out of the dinner appointment."

"Was it an important dinner appointment?"

"No, a bunch of my friends want to talk about the school and the trust we have formed."

"I think you should go, Papa."

"Maybe you two can join me?"

Vijay said, "It's fine with me, but you can ask Bharti."

Vijay handed over his cell phone to Bharti.

"Hi, beta, how are you? Congratulations, do you want to join me for dinner with some friends of mine? We're discussing the school project and the trust we have started."

"Sure, Papa, it'll be our pleasure, but then are you going to come to see us before?"

"Yes, of course, I'll see you at six, and then you can follow me or come over later to my friend's house in Vasant Vihar."

"Okay, Papa, Vijay will give you the address and the directions. Bye and love you."

"You know Nandita and Joy are coming at five. Does it matter if they meet each other?"

"No, not at all, Papa will be glad to meet them."

Bharti and Vijay went to take a shower and got ready, the samosas and sweets were delivered, and he got the table ready for tea.

Just before five, Joy and Nandita arrived at the security gate.

Vijay told the guard to show them the visitors' parking and send them up to condo number 1112.

Vijay opened the door and said, "Welcome!"

"It is good to see you again."

"It is good to see you too," both Nandita and Joy said at once.

"What's up?" Vijay asked.

"The minister of urban affairs told me that he has signed the papers and has handed over the issue of toilets and showers in the slum to the municipality concerned," Nandita said.

"Did he?" Vijay asked.

"Yes, he did, but he told his PA to hold the file. He has been intentionally delaying and causing unnecessary suffering to the poor people of the slum. I told his personal assistant that if the file doesn't get released, I will have to print this story in the newspaper."

"So what happened then?"

"The PA sent the file right away to the municipality."

"That is really great."

"Something else happened. I had gone to cover a story in the neighborhood of the minister's farmhouse. My photographer zoomed the camera to see what was happening at the farmhouse. He found that the minister was drinking and laughing with the hoods who were released on bail, and he decided to take some pictures."

"That is totally amazing!" exclaimed Bharti.

"Yes, it is, so I decided I should ask for Vijay's advice whether I should publish these pictures or not."

Vijay said, "There could be complications. I think this is not the time to publish them because if you do, he is going to send his hoods after you. As he is a criminal, we have to think about this carefully."

"Do you want to keep the pictures in case you want to consult somebody?"

"Yes, that will be a good idea, but you keep the negatives in a safe place."

Bharti interrupted, "Sorry for the interruption. Are you ready for tea?"

Joy said, "Anytime you want."

"If we wait for fifteen minutes, my father will be here, and we can all have tea together."

"Yes, of course, it will be our pleasure to meet your father."

"Would you like to discuss this in front of Bharti's father as well?" inquired Vijay.

"I don't see any harm, I'm sure we can trust him," Nandita said.

"I know you can trust him, if anything, he will give you good advice," Bharti informed.

"The election is coming. I think you should publish the pictures at the time of the election after the DCP has taken care of the hoods," Vijay said.

"Are you going to show these pictures to the DCP?" asked Nandita.

"We can trust him. If you want, I can go and see him and show him the pictures."

"Okay, let us get his input."

Bharti said, "I want to talk about music to Joy."

"I understand you're a very good singer yourself, Bharti," remarked Joy.

"I don't know about being a very good singer. I understand your mother is a teacher, and I would like to meet her to see if I can continue my learning of music."

"My mother knows about you, and she would be very pleased to meet you. Anytime you want to come over, just call me and we can arrange a time for you."

The security guard called and said, "Mr. Kapoor is here to see you."

Bharti and Vijay opened the door for him, hugged him, and brought him into the condo.

Mr. Kapoor appreciated Vijay, "This is the result of your hard work. Please give me a tour of the condo."

"Papa, I want you to meet our friends. This is Nandita Basu, and this is Joy."

"Pleased to meet you," Mr. Kapoor said.

Bharti gave the tour of the condo, Nandita and Joy joined in, and they all appreciated the condo.

In the meantime, Vijay went to make the masala chai.

In between sips of tea, Mr. Kapoor asked, "What do you do, Nandita?"

"I am a journalist and an investigative reporter with a national newspaper."

"So you're the one fighting for the cause of the slum dwellers whom Vijay and Bharti were talking about?"

"I try to help the poor people as they have nobody on their side. I understand you're doing a great job too, Mr. Kapoor, by helping to build a school for the poor. I was there at the school function when they announced that you had donated a very large sum of money. I became a fan of yours then. I hope more people will follow your example."

"No no, please don't build me up so much."

"I understand you have also helped in getting the school project sanctioned."

"I will tell you the inside story because you are an honest reporter. There are corrupt people everywhere in the government right from the minister to the peon. Sometimes I feel the whole system is corrupt, and I've had to go along with that even though I am a nonresident Indian. Luckily, a few weeks ago, I met Amar Bedi, a DCP with the CBI, on the golf course. When my assistant who normally deals with the government departments went to the HUDA office and found out that they were demanding a bribe to release the sanction of the school, I contacted Amar Bedi. He suggested giving the money using marked bills so that he could catch the culprits red-handed instead of making a complaint to the CBI. So he sent a CBI officer in plain clothes with my man, they gave the marked bills, and the CBI officer got both the superintendent and the PA of the chairman of HUDA. But Amar Bedi let them go with a warning. He said he will keep an eye on the whole department as he wants to see if the chairman is also involved."

Bharti was amazed to hear that and asked, "So what happened to the fifty thousand rupees?"

"They were returned, of course, and I called Vijay's father today to give him the news."

Nandita said, "That is one good story. I would like to follow it up."

Mr. Kapoor advised, "Have patience, and I will keep you informed."

"I want to consult you on one more issue." She showed the photographs to Mr. Kapoor and asked, "What shall I do now?"

Mr. Kapoor asked, "Vijay, what is your opinion as a lawyer?"

"I think the minister has not committed any crime, so I have advised Nandita to wait and publish them possibly at the election time."

"I agree with Vijay," Mr. Kapoor said.

Nandita said, "I must go as I have a lot of work to do. It was very nice meeting you, Mr. Kapoor, and I will see you at their engagement."

"The pleasure was all mine, and at any time you need advice, I am available for you."

Nandita and Joy left after hugging Vijay and Bharti.

"Bharti, we should leave too. You and Vijay can come with me, and my driver can drop you home at night. That way, you don't have to take your car."

Bharti agreed, "I think that's a good idea. I'm not coming back here tonight as I have a lot of work to do in the morning. The driver can leave Vijay at night. Just give me a few minutes to get ready."

They all left to go for dinner at the house of Mr. Kapoor's friend in Vasant Vihar (a very posh colony in New Delhi). It was an exclusive dinner, and cocktails were served by waiters. Mr. Kapoor's friends were all appreciative of Vijay's achievements in his career and his efforts to help the poor.

They wanted to contribute toward the help for the poor. They asked Mr. Kapoor to work out a plan to further utilize the trust he had formed with Mr. Shastri. They committed to contribute more than five hundred million rupees ($10,000,000) collectively. They realized that the gap between the poor was becoming bigger and somebody had to help the poor as the government certainly was not. The friends suggested adopting that cluster of jhuggies where Bharti and Vijay had been helping. If that could be done, they committed to contribute ten million dollars by Diwali.

Mr. Kapoor promised his friends that he would form a financial infrastructure by Diwali so that they could build houses for the poor in the slum where Bharti had a clinic now.

All the friends enjoyed their drinks and dinner and finished off with a toast. "A toast to Vijay and Bharti for their coming adventure as they begin their new married life together."

Bharti and Vijay hugged and said bye to each other feeling sad. "So I will not see you for a whole week as you'll be busy with the conference."

"Yes, darling, it cannot be avoided. However, if we were living together, we could be together, at least, at night."

"Before you make a decision like that, sweetheart, you have to consider many factors such as the society you are living in and the norms thereof, our belief in the institution of marriage, and finally, our belief that we get married for life. Don't be impatient, honey. I will miss you as much as you will miss me, if not more."

"You're right, sweetheart. I believe in all that what you believe in. I'm just being impatient."

"I want to be with you all the time and, at least, when I come home from work. Somebody said, 'Patience is a virtue.' I guess we just have to wait, but we will talk on the phone every day."

CHAPTER 24

O N SUNDAY, BHARTI became busy with administrating the registration of all the attendees; and in the evening, during dinner, she delivered a welcome speech.

The conference went on till Thursday afternoon. At five o'clock, Bharti called Vijay. "Hi, honey, are you at work? I'm sorry I've not been able to talk to you for the last two days as I was very busy at the conference right from eight a.m. to eleven p.m."

"That's okay, honey. I'm at work, just getting ready to go home. I'm missing you. I've been thinking of you all the time and could not sleep for the last two nights!"

"Same here, honey, I've been absentminded thinking of you. Anyway, there is an opportunity to meet tonight. There are cocktails followed by dinner, and I can invite you for that. The only thing is you might get bored at dinner as there are a couple of speeches and an awards ceremony."

"I'd love to come. For you, I'll go anywhere and listen to anything. At least, we'll be together. Tell me the time, the venue, the dress code, and I will be there."

"The time is seven p.m., the venue is the hotel, and the dress code is formal."

"Okay, honey, see you soon."

Just that morning, Vijay received his new car and a chauffeur to go with it.

Vijay asked the chauffeur, "Can you stay in the evening as I have to attend a dinner?"

The chauffeur replied, "No problem, sir, I can stay until midnight. If I could park my scooter at your condo, then at night when we come back, I'll just pick up my scooter and go home."

"That's fine. I'll drive to the condo, and you can bring your scooter there."

Vijay arrived home in his new car, put on a nice black suit, and was waiting for the chauffeur to arrive when he finally received a call from the gate security that his chauffeur, Rahul, was there with the scooter.

Vijay told the gate man, "Show him the visitor's parking lot and send him up."

Vijay asked him, "What took you so long?"

"I had my dinner and came as quickly as I could."

"Let me pay you for dinner." "No, the company will take care of it. I will hand in an expense account report on Monday."

"But this is for my personal use."

"From what I understand, you are allowed to keep me for four evenings a month on the company account."

"Oh really, that's awesome, let's go."

They got to the hotel lobby, and Vijay said, "Park the car, and I'll call you on your cell phone when I'm ready to leave."

Vijay went inside and noticed Bharti chatting with some people in the lobby.

"Hi, Vijay, nice to see you." She gave him a hug and a kiss and said, "Meet my friends from England, John Turner and Audrey Westwood. We did our specialization together, and this is Vijay Shastri, my fiancé."

They chatted about England and how Bharti was so dedicated to her work. John asked Vijay, "Have you ever been to England?"

Vijay replied, "Yes, for a short time. It was very nice, but it was a bit wet while I was there."

"We English are used to the rain. It is part of our life."

Vijay asked, "Have you been to India before?"

"No, this is my first time."

"What about you, Audrey?"

"This is my first time too. Last Saturday, the first thing we did was visit the Taj Mahal."

"How did you like the Taj Mahal?"

"It was stunningly beautiful, the inlaid work was awesome, and the architecture was unbelievable."

"So what is on your agenda?"

"We want to visit Jaipur and Khajuraho temples. I'm afraid we don't have very much time as we are flying back a week next Saturday evening."

"Are you visiting all the important sites of old Delhi and the new malls?"

"Bharti has planned something for us," said Audrey.

Bharti informed, "Yes, I'm sending a driver with John and Audrey to see all the sights of Old and New Delhi tomorrow. On Saturday, they are going to Jaipur with a group and coming back on Sunday night. On Tuesday, they fly to Khajuraho for two days."

"I see you're making all your plans together. Are you just friends, or are you married?"

"Friends for sure. We are just living together for now, but have plans to get married next year. We're not as fortunate as Bharti, hailing from a rich family. We both come from very poor families and are saving to have a nice house before we get married."

"There is nothing wrong with that. You have your moral standards of your society, and as long as you are within the norms of your moral standards, you are okay."

"The West has become more liberal because of their needs. Anyway, we are not saying that you should be doing that here. It certainly wouldn't fly here," remarked Audrey.

"It is time to go to the conference hall," Bharti suggested.

They sat on their preassigned seats; Bharti went to the podium and delivered a small speech, thanking everybody for attending the conference, and called upon the head of the Pediatrics of her hospital to say a few words. He praised Bharti for doing such a fantastic job of organizing the conference and announced an award for the best paper presented on diabetic children. A few other awards were presented to various doctors from abroad.

Finally, Bharti announced the end of the conference and thanked everybody again for contributing and coming to the conference and announced, "The bar will stay open till midnight. Have a drink, dance, and enjoy the evening."

Bharti came back to her assigned seat with Vijay, John, Audrey, and a few other doctors on her table.

Bharti said, "Don't forget that you guys are invited for dinner at the golf club tomorrow evening."

"Of course, we're looking forward to that," affirmed one of the other doctors, quite well-known to Bharti.

After dinner, they all asked Bharti for a dance.

Bharti said, "Let us all dance together."

Bharti and her friends all danced together to the Punjabi Bhangra tunes; they had fun dancing to all kinds of music.

They all thanked Bharti for such a wonderful evening and said good night to each other and left. Bharti and Vijay went out together, and Vijay asked Bharti, "So what is your plan for tonight?"

"It is past midnight. I'm very tired and have not slept too well for the last four days. Can we meet tomorrow evening? You can come over to my house, and from there, we will go to the golf club."

"Okay, sweetheart, can I just give you a ride home tonight?"

Bharti's car came first, and she told the driver, "You go home, and I'll come with Vijay Sir."

Vijay's car arrived; Rahul came out of the car and said, "Good morning, sir."

Vijay and Bharti sat in the backseat of the car, and Rahul drove off.

Vijay introduced Rahul, his new driver, to Bharti.

Bharti said, "It's a beautiful car, congratulations for that. But you surprised me, and now we will have to celebrate. Would you please tell Rahul that we are going to Golf Links to my house?"

Vijay instructed Rahul, "Please take us to Golf Links first to drop off Bharti Ma'am."

"So, Bharti, will you be free after tomorrow?"

"Yes, relatively, but I'll be busy with last-minute shopping and the arrangements for all the guests coming for our engagement."

"For that matter, I'll be busy too, but we can meet, can't we?"

"We'll meet tomorrow. You are coming to the party at the golf club, aren't you?"

"Yes, of course, and I'll come early to your house."

Rahul stopped the car in front of Bharti's house, and Bharti said, "Take it inside and she instructed the gate man to open it.

Rahul stopped the car and opened the door for Bharti to get out. Vijay came out from the side, hugged Bharti, and whispered, "I love you and will see you tomorrow."

Vijay went over to his parents' house in the morning, and they planned the stay of their guests and various logistics of picking them up from the railway station, etc.

Vijay then went to Bharti's at five. They met like they hadn't met for years, hugging and kissing each other. Bharti invited him, "Come upstairs to my room."

Vijay asked, "Where is your maid, Tara?"

"She has gone to do some shopping with my driver and should be returning home at about six."

"Where is your father?"

"He has gone to the golf club, and while he's there, he'll organize our dinner as I have invited quite a few people."

"So it's going to be a big party!"

"I would say about twenty people, and we booked a party room. Come on, honey, don't waste time. I'm just dying to make love to you as we have met after so long. You don't know how I've been living without you."

Vijay replied, "Same here." And he grabbed her, kissed her passionately, took her clothes off, and they made love passionately.

After making love, Bharti asked, "After the engagement, do you think we can live together?"

"As long as our fathers do not mind, I think we can be clever about it and not tell anybody that we are living together. You could come and stay a few days a week with me depending upon your schedule."

"I think that will be nice and workable."

Vijay said, "Can I take a shower?"

"I'm going to take one. You might as well take it with me."

They both got in the shower, kissing each other and enjoying the shower.

Bharti strongly asserted, "It is almost six. Let's get ready as Tara might be coming soon, and we have to reach the golf club by seven to welcome the guests."

They quickly got dressed, and just at that time, Tara knocked on the door.

"Bharti Didi, are you there?"

Bharti opened the door and said, "Tara, did you get all the grocery shopping done?"

"Yes, Bharti Didi."

"Great, can you please make some masala chai for Vijay Sir and me?"

"Of course, ma'am."

They came downstairs, had some chai, and left for the golf club.

Most of the invitees were doctors known to Bharti from the UK, Canada, and Australia. The party was in full swing. Bharti introduced everybody to Vijay and vice versa.

After the usual conversation, a group of people from the UK and Australia started talking to Vijay, and one of them made a remark that India was progressing so much and yet there was so much poverty, and then there was the hygiene issue.

Vijay quickly retorted, "As far as the poverty is concerned, the government is not doing enough. It has lots of money available now, and they should be paying more attention to the poor. As far as the second issue of hygiene is concerned, that comes with education and money. As people get educated and they can afford to have houses with washrooms and toilets and have the money to spend on hygiene products, the hygiene issue can be eliminated, but it will take time. People want to live well, but the corrupt politicians want to keep them down. Let's hope that it is not too late for our politicians to wake up and do something about it."

While having a drink, one of the doctors from England remarked, "Somehow, I perceive that this is part of your culture."

"Tell me what England was like after the Second World War. Were people not living in appalling conditions? In fact, just a couple years ago, I was in England and some of the people were still going to community baths and taking a bath only once a week. Some of the houses had toilets outside in the backyard. Would you attribute that to your culture or to poverty?"

The doctor replied, "I'm sorry about my remark. Yes, I agree I would attribute that to poverty and illiteracy."

Bharti said, "Dinner is served. Please come and enjoy dinner and look at the better side of India, rather than the poor and the undeveloped side. Look at the glorious past, the monuments, music and culture, the art and the architecture, and finally, the respect and hospitality of the people of India. In a few years, India will be one of the top economical powers. The poverty and illiteracy will be eradicated, and India will be a sought-after place as it was in the past."

Everybody started clapping, and one of the doctors remarked, "I'm sure India will be all right as its strength is its people, like you, Bharti, and your fiancé, Vijay."

They all enjoyed dinner, had a good time, and went home.

Vijay asked Bharti, "Do you want to come over to my place tonight?"

"Yes, of course. I was planning to, and with that thought in my mind, I got my night bag ready."

"You must have an extrasensory perception. You can read my mind, and it can be dangerous for me," Vijay gently remarked with a smile.

"No, I just love you and want to be with you all the time. I'm going to be busy at work from Monday onward. I got behind in my work because of the conference. Now I have to catch up."

"Does that mean you won't meet me?"

"No, it means I'll not be able to meet you even if I want to, which I do."

"Why don't you bring some of your clothes with you and keep them at the condo? That way, whenever you want to come over, you can without worrying about your clothes and your night bag."

"That's a good idea. For example, if I'm going to my clinic at Ajay's house on Tuesday, then I can stay the night with you on Monday."

"So you could bring some clothes on Monday night from home."

"Can you please drop me home tomorrow night?"

"Of course, I'm at your service anytime."

They got home, and Vijay said, "For tonight, I have chilled a special white wine for you."

"But you know I like red wine."

"I have a Spanish red wine and an Australian white wine, whichever you prefer."

Bharti said, "I love Spanish red wine."

Vijay and Bharti were madly in love with each other. Last week's separation proved the proverb that "absence makes the heart grow fonder."

They had some wine, made love, and started making plans for their honeymoon.

Bharti said, "I've not been to Australia."

Vijay said, "Neither have I."

"Let's go to Australia."

Vijay said, "That's fine."

"Do you know anybody in Australia?"

"We don't have to know anybody for our honeymoon, but I do know a few doctors in Sydney who moved from England. In fact, one of the doctors came for the conference, and you met him. I also have an aunt living in Australia. Raju was sending the invitation card to her. We'll see if she comes."

"Yes, I remember him. With regard to our honeymoon, I'm going to keep you with me in the room twenty-four hours a day for the first nine days, so we might as well save money staying in the condo for the first nine days," Vijay remarked.

"Why only nine days?"

"In the Indian culture, they say, 'Nine days for the new bride.' After that, she's not new anymore."

"Oh, I'm going to last for nine months, if not, nine years."

"It is your positive attitude that makes me love you even more, sweetheart."

This love saga of Bharti and Vijay went on as they spent days and nights waiting to be engaged and finally married.

CHAPTER 25

THE WAITING PERIOD was over as the engagement was on the next day. Guests of both families had arrived from out of town and abroad.

The celebrations started five days before the actual engagement when the relative arrived. A party atmosphere prevailed in both the families. Every evening, the ladies sat down and started the *dholak* (a kind of bongo, which is played with both the hands) and sang folk songs, sometimes in verses competing with the verses sung by the menfolk.

In the Shastri house, officially, there were no drinks; however, the boys went and drank in Vijay's room, where he had a small bar stashed with beer and scotch. Many vegetarian dishes like samosas, *pakoras*, nuts, and appetizers were being served. Nobody drank hard liquor in front of Mr. Shastri, out of respect. Singing and dancing went on nonstop. It was a joyous occasion, and everybody was happy.

In Mr. Kapoor's house, there was an open bar served by a bartender; and to tantalize the guests' appetite, all kinds of nonvegetarian and vegetarian appetizers were being served. Music was playing; guests were singing, dancing, and chatting. The atmosphere was one of celebration and ecstasy. Many people were meeting for the first time after years.

Both families were having a ball and enjoying to the fullest.

Finally, that much-awaited day had come when, in the evening, they were having the engagement ceremony and a party in a hotel.

Members of both the families were getting ready; some of the ladies and the girls had gone to the beauty salons to have their hair and makeup done.

In Mr. Shastri's family, the boys were ready. Everybody was waiting for the ladies, the atmosphere was tense, and the cars and buses were waiting to head out to the hotel. Finally, the ladies and the girls arrived; they were told to get ready and leave quickly.

Mr. Kapoor and Raju left early to see to the arrangements in the hotel. The rest of the people followed in cars.

Mr. Shastri's family and their guests were finally ready, and an entourage of cars and buses left Mr. Shastri's house to reach the hotel.

The engagement ceremony is between a man and woman, but Hindus believe that before the ceremony, both the families must be united spiritually. It is the responsibility of the Hindu priest to unite the families spiritually. Usually, the oldest members of each family come together first, and they garland each other while the Hindu priest chants some mantras (prayers to God) to unite the families in this holy ceremony. The father of the groom-to-be and that of the bride-to-be must be united spiritually as well first before the ceremony takes place. Since Bharti didn't have a mother, there was no further ceremony for the mothers before the actual engagement ceremony.

After the initial *mini* ceremony, the entourage from Vijay's side entered the hall.

The hall was beautifully decorated with a chandelier in the middle and strings made of white jasmine flowers and roses wrapped around with a golden thread extended from the chandelier to all around the hall. The whole hall was glittering and filled with the fragrance of jasmine, and it looked like there was a huge umbrella of white and red and gold flowers covering the hall.

As one entered, in the middle of the hall was a passage leading to the stage with two thrones on the stage. In the passage, there were two photographers and two cameramen filming the guests and the whole event using a digital movie camera on wheels. Tables and *chairs* draped with red, white, and gold covers were placed on both sides of the middle passage. And behind was an open space on each side, and then behind the open space were two bars.

Mr. Kapoor was wearing a long golden *sherwani* (a long Nehru-style coat) and was looking very handsome, and on the other side, Mr. Shastri was wearing a white *sherwani* with golden trim.

As the Shastri family entered the hall, lightbulbs flashed and the cameras rolled as they were welcomed by the Kapoor family. Vijay, also wearing a gold *sherwani*, entered the hall, looking majestic; and he sat down on the golden throne on the stage. Mr. Kapoor welcomed Vijay, and the guests went to their assigned tables. A short time later, Bharti entered the hall, looking like a princess, wearing a red, white, and gold *lehenga* with a trail, held by two girls behind her. She had her hair in an updo and looked stunningly beautiful with the diamond necklace she adorned.

Bharti, looking gracious and beautiful, reached the stage; and Vijay got up. The Hindu pundit chanted some mantras and told Vijay to place a ring on Bharti's finger, and then the pundit told Bharti to place a ring on Vijay's finger.

The hall resounded with applauses.

With both Vijay and Bharti seated on their thrones on the stage, the guests lined up to congratulate them and to present them with a gift or an envelope of money. (Usually, the bride's side of the family gives the money to the bridegroom, and the groom's side of the family gives money to the bride.)

The bartenders in both bars were busy serving drinks as most of the activity was around the bars. The guests met each other from both the families, the music started, waiters started serving snacks and appetizers, and everybody, while enjoying, praised Mr. Kapoor for the excellent arrangements he had made.

The whole evening was a fun-filled affair with wining, dining, and dancing. There were no speeches, except for one, when Mr. Kapoor went over to the disk jockey and took the microphone to deliver a short welcome speech, "I welcome the Shastri family and urge the Kapoor family to mingle with the Shastri family, get to know each other, have fun, dance together, and enjoy."

Both families went home so happy that they talked about the event for days to come.

The next day, Vijay came over to Bharti's house to help Bharti take some of her clothes over to the condo. As Bharti entered the condo, he took off his jacket, laid it down on the floor, and said in a very English manner, "Welcome, lady of the house."

Before entering, Bharti picked up the jacket and said, "There is no need for that. I am entering my own house yet, it is only a love den."

Over the next few weeks, Bharti held her clinic at Ajay's house on Tuesday and Friday afternoons and treated the sick children of the slum complex. Dr. Khanna also opened up the clinic in his house with all the new equipment sent by Mr. Kapoor, and it worked out very well between the two of them.

CHAPTER 26

O CTOBER 14 WAS the day of Dushehra celebrations when Lord Rama killed the evil king Ravana.

Vijay and Bharti both decided to go to the slum complex to witness the celebration of Dushehra.

At the open end of the ground where the slum ended, three very large effigies of Ravana, Kumbhakarna, and Megnath stood on the ground.

People wearing new clothes were celebrating the victory of good over evil. That is what Dushehra represents. *Ram Leela* (a stage play of the epic story of Lord Rama) was being enacted; kids were very happy and were waiting for Lord Rama to kill Ravana in battle so that the fireworks could start.

The ground in front of the effigies was filled with thousands of men, women, and children. An atmosphere of celebration and happiness prevailed. The children were ecstatically running around, busy buying balloons and candy floss on one side, while on the other side, they were lining up to go on the rides. Suddenly, people shouted out all at once, "Bhagwan Ram ki jai ho" (Victory to Lord Rama).

It was obvious that in the enactment, Lord Rama had killed the evil king Ravana. Fire-tipped arrows were fired at the effigies, which stood ninety feet high and were made of paper, wood, and firecrackers. When the arrows hit the effigies, they caught fire and burst into flames with fireworks coming out of them in all directions.

Kids and adults alike loved this show of firecrackers and flames. Also watching from a distance were all the residents of Anand Enclave, including Vijay, Ajay, Bharti, Ali, Joy, and Nandita Basu.

After a little while, the show was over. Men and women and children started returning home, talking about the show. The children especially were so excited that they didn't want to go home, pleading with their parents to stay a little longer.

Suddenly, a fire broke out in the slum, starting from the south end. It spread through the slum complex very quickly as the wind was from the south. The whole atmosphere changed from one of happiness to panic; everybody was running to save their family and their home. There was complete chaos with people running in all directions. This turned into a stampede, and of course, women and children were the ones who suffered the most. The lights went out, which threw the whole complex into darkness except for the light from the flames of fire.

You could hear the shrieks of women and children. "I'm burning, please save me," shouted one. The other was crying, "My house is burnt, and everything is lost." The fire engulfed the whole complex.

Vijay, Ajay, Joy, and Ali ran to help save lives after telling Nandita and Bharti to call the fire department.

People were grabbing buckets, pots, pans, and whatever they could lay their hands on to get water to extinguish the fire. There was hardly any water in the slum complex, and the fire was spreading throughout the complex rapidly. Joy jumped into the fire and brought one child out of the fire. Ajay and Ali were helping the others to extinguish the fire. People from Anand Enclave joined in to help put out the fire by providing water through plastic garden hoses attached to electric pumps. Some houses close to the slum switched on their floodlights.

Vijay met Mohan and exclaimed, "This fire is deliberate. Let's go and investigate. It seemed like the fire was started intentionally at various points, keeping in mind the direction of the wind."

They went around the whole slum complex and could smell gasoline at various points around the complex. Suddenly, they saw two men on motorcycles with jerricans. Vijay and Mohan ran after the motorcycles. Mohan leaped in the air onto one motorcycle, grabbed the rider, and the gasoline jerrican fell on the ground. Vijay went after the other rider and caught him. They then beat them up and threw them on the ground.

Vijay called Ajay and informed him, "We have a couple of bad guys who set the fire. Come quickly with a rope!" And he gave his location. Ajay arrived in a few minutes with a couple of other guys and a rope; they tied up the bad guys and took them away to where Nandita and Bharti were.

On the way, Vijay heard a child's cry, "Uncle, save me. Vijay Uncle, save me."

Vijay turned around and saw a child trapped in a burning jhuggie; he rushed inside and grabbed the child. As he tried to run out of the jhuggie, a burning wooden beam fell on him, setting him on fire. He rolled on the ground, which put the fire out, but he became unconscious due to smoke inhalation. The child was safe and ran out calling people to help Vijay Uncle, but nobody listened to him as there was total chaos. The whole complex was burning, resulting in devastation and mayhem all around. Bodies were lying all over with some people half-burnt; you could hear the cries and shrieks from everywhere.

Nandita called the fire department again and inquired, "Where are the fire trucks? I called a half an hour ago as there is a fire raging here."

"We're sorry, madam, we have limited resources, and today, because of Dushehra, there are so many fires. We have asked for help from New Delhi, and they know about the problem. The fire trucks should be reaching there any minute. We have asked ambulances to be sent there, and we have also called the emergency task force. Please, madam, bear with us."

In the meantime, Nandita and Bharti started helping the people who were burnt, wounded, or had fainted due to smoke inhalation.

Nandita also called the police and informed them of the two arsonists that were caught and said, "They are lying here, tied up."

Finally, a couple of fire trucks arrived. On handheld loudspeakers, they told the people to clear the area so that firemen could do their work. The firemen went to work by taking water from Anand Enclave adjoining the slum complex on the north side.

The police also arrived; they took charge of the arsonists, and the ACP in charge called for more policemen to come to the scene to control the crowd.

When the fire marshal saw the massive fire covering over ten thousand jhuggies, he called for more fire trucks and emergency services like ambulances and trucks carrying electric generators and floodlights. He instructed them to approach from the south side as there was easy access and they could get water from the industrial area on that side.

Nandita called her office and asked for the camera crew to come to her location to shoot the massive fire in the slum.

Several more fire trucks arrived from the south side along with the necessary equipment, and the firemen went to work. They had the fire under control within two to three hours; now came the hard task of saving lives and treating the injured.

Soon, the ambulances arrived along with a fully equipped van having four doctors and six paramedics to treat the injured with minor burns; however, serious cases were sent to the various hospitals right away after giving them first aid treatment.

The doctor in charge phoned the director of emergency medical services and informed him, "This should be declared a disaster area as hundreds, if not thousands, are dead. Thousands are injured and burnt, and the army medical services should be called in."

The director replied, "I'll deal with the matter in the morning as it is four a.m. now and everybody is sleeping."

"It will be too late in the morning. You will be responsible for extra deaths for lack of first aid," replied the doctor sternly.

"I will do what I can, but in the meantime, I'll try to send more ambulances."

"We need vans to carry the dead, more ambulances to carry the critically injured with third-degree burns. We also need buses to carry people with minor injuries and burns."

"I'll do my best, considering it is a holiday, we are short-staffed."

Firemen, doctors, paramedics, and other workers worked throughout the night. In the morning, people living in Anand Enclave brought tea, biscuits, bread, cakes, and whatever they could lay their hands on to feed the workers.

Bharti and all of Vijay's friends were frantically looking for Vijay, but he was nowhere to be found; they tried his cell phone, but even that was not working.

They were approached by a little boy who said, "Come and save Vijay Uncle who got hurt and burnt while saving me."

They went to the jhuggie with him but couldn't find Vijay; they found his burnt cell phone in the debris.

Bharti came over to meet the doctor in charge and said, "I am Dr. Bharti Kapoor."

The doctor in charge said, "I'm Dr. Sheila Gupta, and are you the Dr. Bharti Kapoor, pediatrician, who presented a research paper a couple of weeks ago on diabetic children at the world conference that you organized?"

Bharti said, "Yes, call me Bharti, and right now, can you help me locate my fiancé, Vijay! One little boy who was saved by Vijay said that he got badly burnt and injured while saving him. When we searched for him, he was not there in that jhuggie, only his burnt cell phone."

"We sent the critically injured to various hospitals after recording their names and address before sedating them."

"Can you show me your list, please?"

"Of course, here is the list in my laptop."

Bharti looked at the list, and Vijay's name was not on the list.

Bharti told Dr. Gupta about her clinic near the slum and talked about how they can help these poor people, and Sheila promised to see her after this was all over.

Bharti and her friends went through the jhuggies, helping people and hoping to find Vijay.

Nandita Basu had her full crew with her, and she was reporting while the cameraman was filming the scene.

Nandita reported, "This is a national disaster of a magnitude equal to any major disaster where thousands of people are dead, injured, burnt, and homeless. There is not a family which is not affected. There were over ten thousand homes here that have been destroyed. There is pain and suffering everywhere. People have lost their livelihood and everything they had. There is no water to drink here, nor is there any food. Look at these pictures, what do they tell us? They tell us we should be ashamed of ourselves to see people living in such deplorable conditions while we and the politicians live in palaces. We should be ashamed of calling ourselves an advanced society and a major economic power to reckon with."

Nandita paused for a while, wiped her tears, and continued, "Our economy is growing at 11 percent, and yet some of our people are earning mere three dollars a day. We have 1.1 billion people, of them, 20 percent live in slums like this, 25 percent live below the national poverty line, and almost 75 percent live below the international poverty line. The firemen did a great job of extinguishing the fire, and the doctors are working hard, but we don't have enough of them. There are no vans to take the dead and not enough ambulances to take the critically injured to the hospitals. This is Nandita Basu reporting live at six a.m. on this sad day of the disaster."

A new day had dawned, the sun was up, but it was a bleak day for Bharti, her friends, along with thousands of other people who were homeless.

All the friends gathered at Ali's house, which was on the northern edge of the slum but inside Anand Enclave.

Vijay was nowhere to be found; the inference was that he must have been taken in an ambulance as he was on the south side where he was trying to save the life of a boy. The fire was most devastating on the south side as if it first started from there, and the wind was also blowing from south to north, propagating the fire.

Ajay said, "Bharti, you must rest, come to my place, and Geeta will look after you."

She whispered while crying, "Where is he and what condition is he in? I hope he's all right."

Ajay said, "I insist, please go to my house and rest for a while, and then we'll go through the list again. All you boys have been working all night, and you must rest for a while too. There are many more doctors here now, and they'll take charge of the situation. Rest for a while, and we will meet at my house in a couple of hours."

Bharti was crying, and Geeta asked, "What happened, Bharti Bhabhi?"

"Vijay is missing, we don't know where he is. Last we know is that he was hurt trying to save a little boy, and we found his cell phone, but he's nowhere to be found!"

"They must have taken him to a hospital."

"But his name is not on any of the lists."

"Come and lie down for a while and try to get some sleep. We will go together and look at the lists again."

Bharti lay down in Geeta's bed but couldn't sleep. She was having all sorts of thoughts like they took him to the morgue without identification. And the next minute, she thought he could be helping the other guys in the hospitals; if so, he should have called her. She said to herself to think logically like a doctor. She came to two logical conclusions: One, she must check the list of the injured once more. Two, it is possible that he fainted; in which case, they would send him to the hospital without knowing his name, so she must go right away and inquire from the doctors.

Bharti called Geeta and said, "I must go to speak to the doctors to find out what happened to Vijay."

Geeta said, "Why don't you rest for a while?"

Bharti said, "I must go before the doctors change their shift."

Geeta called Ajay, who was also resting as he had not slept all night. Pehalwanji came over and said, "I will go with Bharti."

Bharti started crying and hugged Pehalwanji. They walked through the burnt and devastated slum. Sounds of people crying and shrieking were still coming from all over; it looked like a war zone, and the brick walls were all but left of the jhuggies. Everything else was burnt to the ground, and a stench of burnt flesh filled the air. Water, ashes, and smoke covered the pathway through the slum.

They reached the middle ground where the doctors had brought their vans to administer first aid.

Bharti talked to the doctors and asked, "Did you have any patient at the far end of slum who was unconscious, and you couldn't get his name?"

One of the doctors responded, "Yes, there were a couple of cases like that. Are you looking for anybody in particular?"

Bharti said, "I'm looking for my fiancé. We came to know that he was hurt while saving a boy in the far end of the slum."

The doctor informed her, "Yes, I came across one case like that. He seemed to be dressed quite nicely but was unconscious. We gave him a shot of morphine and sent him in the ambulance to one of the hospitals."

"How tall was he?" Bharti asked.

"He was about at least six feet tall, was burnt chest up, and his face was partly burnt too, and he was wearing jeans and a half-burnt T-shirt."

"Do you know which hospital you sent him to?"

After looking at the list, she replied, "In the first part of the list, there are three such cases and they were each sent to different hospitals. One was sent to All India Institute of Medical Sciences, the second was sent to Safdarjang Hospital, and the third one was sent to a military hospital in Delhi cantonment."

"Do you have the list of the dead?" Bharti asked.

The doctor in charge came over and said, "Hi, Dr. Bharti, I had photographs of all the dead. They were downloaded onto a disc, and the disc has been sent to the central morgue in New Delhi with the dead."

"In that case, you must still have it on your laptop."

"No, I deleted it as my laptop was starting to freeze on me being a small laptop with very little memory."

"Okay, thank you very much, Doctor."

"Wish you all the luck, I hope you find him. I'm sorry, I would like to help more, but you see the situation here, we are totally swamped with patients."

"No, I understand, thank you for helping me. Can I do something to help you?"

"You are a pediatrician, aren't you?"

"Yes, should you have any cases of children that you need my help with, please call me on my cell phone." Bharti gave her the cell number.

Pehalwanji asked, "Can I offer some tea or food for your staff?"

"Some freshwater and tea for the workers would be really nice," replied the doctor.

"With all the smoke and dirt around, it will be difficult to send for water. My suggestion is that you send the workers and the doctors one by one to our house across from the Mother Dairy. They'll be able to wash up and freshen up too."

The doctor in charge agreed and said, "I will send them one by one to your house starting in about thirty minutes, and thank you very much for your help."

They walked back to the house, covering their faces with handkerchiefs.

"Nandita Basu reporting at nine a.m. from the slum. There was a devastating fire here, the people have become homeless, hundreds are dead, and thousands injured and burnt. There is no sign of any politician, and there is no word from any level of government for help. However, there are a lot more emergency workers going through the rubble, looking for bodies and badly injured or burnt people. Ambulances are still coming and taking away the injured. The doctors have two vans in the middle of the slum, treating the injured and providing first aid. The seriously injured are being sent to the hospitals, and those with minor injuries or with burns are treated and released. People are in a state of shock, and the whole slum looks devastated as if a tornado has gone through it, and they are searching through the rubble looking for their belongings which are not burnt or damaged. Now I hear some sirens, looks like a motorcade is coming toward the slum complex from the Anand Enclave side. It is the home minister surrounded by his Black Cat Commandos coming out of the car. People are rushing and crying for help."

Nandita Basu went over to the minister and introduced herself, "Sir, I am a national reporter and am reporting live. You are on TV live, do you have anything to say to console the people?"

The home minister said, "This is a tragedy, which should not have happened. I believe that they have caught some culprits, a couple of arsonists. I will not leave any stones unturned to find out who's behind this. This is a futile loss of many lives, and it has caused such grief to the innocent people. I cannot undo the situation – if I could, I would. However, I declare that from the prime minister's fund, the following compensation will be paid immediately: Rupees one hundred thousand for each jhuggie lost, rupees five hundred thousand each life lost, rupees two hundred thousand as compensation for pain and suffering of those badly burnt or injured, and rupees twenty-five thousand to one hundred thousand for other injuries, depending upon the nature of the injuries. On top of that, free medical treatment for all."

Nandita asked, "Sir, who will decide about the injuries, and what will somebody get who is slightly burnt or injured?"

The home minister replied, "Twenty-five thousand rupees is the base if they are slightly burnt or injured. The doctors will have to decide what one should get as I think they're competent people and highly professional and they will not be challenged by any bureaucrat."

"When will this compensation be paid?" asked Nandita.

"I will release the fund as soon as I get back to my office, but the money will be paid to people as soon as the lists are made and verified by my office, and that may take about a week."

"There are a couple more issues, sir, and they are about the toilets, baths, water, and electricity for the slum, which have been pending for a long time."

"What about those issues?" asked the home minister.

"Sir, did you know that the contractor did not join the main sewers to the toilets and the baths? The local minister promised to get that done right away, but we have seen nothing so far."

"I will look into all these issues as soon as I get back to my office."

"Thank you, sir, and when shall I follow up with you on those issues?"

"Give me about a week," said the home minister.

"Very well, sir, and thank you very much for coming here," Nandita said.

Nandita got away from the crowd and continued her coverage by saying, "Many a minister has come here, and many promises have been made and broken. Let us hope that the home minister of the country keeps his promise. The local politicians have not taken any interest in this, and yet the home minister has spared time to come here, and we thank him for that. This is Nandita Basu reporting, and I will be back with more news in a few hours."

Bharti called her father and asked, "Where are you, Papa?"

"I am in the car going to my new corporate head office. Why, what is the matter? You don't sound so good!"

Bharti broke down and started crying and sobbing as she said, "Vijay is missing."

"How is he missing? Where was he?"

"Do you know there was a fire at the slum? He was trying to save one little boy. In the process, he got hurt, and now he's missing. We found his cell phone, all burnt."

"Yes, I heard about the fire on the radio, and where are you?"

"I'm at Ajay's house."

"You wait right there, I'm coming."

By the time Mr. Kapoor reached Ajay's house, the whole household was up and consoling Bharti. Everybody was telling her not to worry as Vijay would be found.

Ajay said, "I will leave no stone unturned to find him. My heart says Vijay is alive in a hospital somewhere."

Mr. Kapoor came into the house; Bharti ran over and hugged him and started crying uncontrollably like a child who meets his mother after a day's separation!

She complained, "Why does this always happen to me?"

She spoke to her father while crying, "Papa, first I loved my mother and I lost her. Now I'm afraid of losing Vijay too because I love him and he is the only love of my life."

"Beta, go with your heart, do you really think he's dead?"

"I don't know what to think, all I know is he's not here. He's always trying to help other people. That was his nature, and that's the way God made him."

"Come on, sweetheart, I will take you home."

Ajay and Geeta said at the same time, "Uncle, have some tea before you leave."

Ajay said, "Please, Uncle, sit down and relax, we will find Vijay, all my friends will be here soon. Our first task and the only task from now will be to find Vijay. Let us work out a logical strategy to find Vijay."

Mr. Kapoor sat down with his arm around Bharti and said, "Okay, I'll have the famous masala chai Geeta makes."

"Uncle, would you have something to eat with it?"

"No, I had my breakfast."

"But you know, Bharti Bhabhi has not eaten anything since last night. I doubt if she even had dinner last night!" Geeta said.

"Oh really! Let's all get together, tie her hands with a rope, and feed her!" Mr. Kapoor said and laughed.

"Let us do it," Geeta said.

Bharti had a slight smile on her face.

"Tickle, tickle, Bharti Bhabhi is smiling," Geeta said.

"It is an old joke when Bharti was small. After Bharti's mother passed away, every time she would not eat, I would tell her that I would tie her hands and then feed her."

He asked, "Bharti, what do you want to eat?"

"I'm not hungry."

"That I know is a sure sign that you are."

He went on to say, "Geeta, can you make her *aloo paratha* [a stuffed roti with potatoes]? She'll have it with yogurt."

"Yes, Uncle, in fact, we were going to have that for breakfast."

"Make it with lots of butter, she likes it with lots of butter," Mr. Kapoor said.

Bharti spoke out, "I don't like it with butter, and instead, I like it with butter on the side."

"My *gudia* [doll] knows how to speak too."

Ajay asked, "Seriously, Bharti, what does your heart tell you?"

She composed herself and said, "My heart says he's alive and he cannot be dead."

"Then instead of crying, let's put all our efforts into searching for him. It is obvious to me that he has been taken to some hospital without recording his name as he was unconscious or burnt on the face so that he could not speak," Ajay said.

"That is the obvious deduction," Mr. Kapoor said.

"The doctors are still going through the list of patients injured or burnt they had on their computer, and I think by the afternoon, we should be able to get some information."

"I don't think we are going to get any information as I checked the lists already. We have physically gone through the slum crowd and asked everybody if they have seen Vijay anywhere. The last I know as per the little boy is that he was lying unconscious in a jhuggie," Bharti said.

"Are there beams in the jhuggies?" Mr. Kapoor asked.

"Some of the jhuggies are built with bricks, and the roof has a wooden beam to support the plastic sheet which serves as the roof, which is then covered with the tarp on top and tied down to give it strength and insulation from heat," Ajay said.

"So Vijay was hurt trying to save the boy from the jhuggie, and the burning wooden beam fell on him," summarized Mr. Kapoor.

"That's correct, and his cell phone was lying there burnt."

"How much would a jhuggie with brick walls, a couple of windows, and a tin roof supported by a steel beam cost?"

"Depending upon the size, between one hundred thousand to two hundred thousand rupees. Why do you ask?" Ajay asked.

"I saw the news that the home minister is going to give one hundred thousand rupees for each jhuggie destroyed by the fire. I was thinking of helping them out to rebuild the slum so that this kind of disaster doesn't happen again. A lot of my friends are interested to help too."

"That would really be wonderful. The slum dwellers are good people, they are honest and are interested in giving the best possible education to their children, and finally, they are all hardworking. You will see, within days, they'll have their life back to near normal with whatever they have left. They will be going to work, and their children would be going to school with half-burnt or torn clothing."

Listening to Ajay, tears welled up in Mr. Kapoor's eyes, and he said in a sad tone, "We will have to do something, and we will have to do it fast."

Bharti was feeling a little better; they all had breakfast and masala chai. After breakfast, Mr. Kapoor said bye and thanks to everybody for their help and left with Bharti.

"Papa, what am I going to do now?" Bharti said in the car while going home.

"You will carry on with your life the way you did before and not give up hope. I'm sure Vijay is alive and thinking about you somewhere out there."

"I also feel that he's calling me, and sometimes I think I am imagining it."

"First, we must go to the morgue to eliminate the possibility that he is dead."

"When can we go?"

"Let us go right now." Mr. Kapoor told the driver to take them to the central morgue in New Delhi.

It was about noontime, and what they saw at the morgue was disgusting and appalling as bodies were lying around unattended; they got very upset and called the doctor in charge.

The doctor in charge informed them, "So many bodies have been sent to us, and we do not have the staff to handle them all at once."

Mr. Kapoor inquired, "What would you do in case of a national disaster? These bodies are of human beings and not of animals."

Bharti asserted, "I am a doctor, and I was taught to respect human beings, dead or alive. What was your education, Doctor?"

The doctor apologized and asked, "What can I do for you?"

"We want to go through the list of the bodies you have, and as I understand it, Dr. Gupta sent a disc with the bodies containing their pictures."

He showed them the list and said, "We have not printed the pictures yet. Anyway, some of them are burnt so badly that you can hardly recognize them in a photo. The best will be to go through the bodies. Here are some of the bodies that have been put in the freezer, and the other bodies are lying unattended."

Mr. Kapoor asked, "Are these all the bodies?"

"Yes, for now, there are about one hundred and eighty-nine so far."

"Do you know if more are coming from that slum complex fire?" Bharti asked.

"I understand some of them were critically injured and were sent to the hospitals, out of which, one or two have died there, and I believe they will be coming here soon."

"Can you tell us the names of those?" Mr. Kapoor asked.

"Yes, I have just been sent names via e-mail from the doctor in charge at the hospital." And he showed and told them the names.

"Thank you very much," Mr. Kapoor said.

Bharti and her father left satisfied that Vijay was not dead.

It was already three o'clock, so Mr. Kapoor said, "Let's go home, have some food, and, Bharti, you'll need to rest. You have a long struggle ahead of you."

Bharti and her father went home, had lunch, and after that, Bharti went to her bedroom. She lay down on her bed, started weeping, and finally went off to sleep.

At 9:00 p.m., Mr. Kapoor went into Bharti's room and whispered, "Come and have dinner."

Bharti, half-asleep, asked, "What time is it, Papa?"

"It is nine p.m., and dinner is served downstairs. Please wash up and come down."

"I'm really not hungry."

"But staying hungry or going without food is not going to bring him back. You need the energy to search for him. You can only do that when you are fit and healthy yourself. You have a long road ahead of you. You might have to take care of him for a while as it seems that he is critically injured and lying somewhere unconscious without a name. Come on, don't lose heart, have dinner with me, and then we will plan how to find him. It is a challenge, and you've always accepted the challenges in your life."

"Okay, Papa, I'll be down at the dinner table soon, and thank you."

Bharti came down and saw Raju sitting there, "What are you doing here, Raju Bhaiya?" Bharti asked.

"Papa called me and told me about Vijay being missing."

She hugged him and started crying.

Raju said, "Don't worry, we will find him. He's just playing hide-and-seek with us the way we used to when we were young."

"This is not the time to joke, something very serious has happened to him. Obviously, he's badly hurt and burnt."

Raju became all serious and consoled her, "Don't worry, we will find him. From tomorrow morning, I am assigning my own driver, Ranbir, to you. He will be looking after you on a full-time basis. He is not just a driver, but like a friend to me. He will be helpful in getting things done."

They had dinner and retired into the family room. Raju left, and Mr. Kapoor asked, "What do you want to do, Bharti? Do you want to listen to music, or do you want to see a movie?"

"First of all, I want to see the news. Can you please put on the news channel?"

"Yes, of course."

"The latest report from the slum complex fire is that there are over two hundred dead, thousands were burnt or injured, and over fifty thousand are homeless now. The fire spread so fast because of the high winds that the whole complex was burnt to the ground within hours. The slum dwellers were in a frenzy to save their jhuggies and belongings. The critically injured have been sent to various hospitals in Delhi and Gurgaon. We will keep you updated with that news," said one reporter.

Mr. Kapoor switched off the TV and asked, "Would you like to listen to some music, Bharti?"

"Yes, Papa, you know when I'm sad, I like to listen to the yesteryears songs."

While listening to music in an emotional state of mind, she saw a vision in which Vijay was calling her, lying solitary and motionless on a bed all bandaged up.

Bharti suddenly yelled out, "Papa, I hear him calling me!"

"Yes, beta, this is the proof that he's alive. It is a voice from one soul to another. In the scientific expression, don't they call it extrasensory perception?"

"Yes, they do, but it is more than that. I'm sure now that he's alive somewhere and he is calling me."

"Sleep well, eat well, and stay healthy, and believe me he will need you when we find him."

"Papa, it is difficult to pass time, what can I do? Please help me."

"For now, practice your music. Music will give you solace and peace of mind. Tomorrow, I'll go with you to the three hospitals where the unnamed patients were sent, and we'll leave no stone unturned to find him."

"Thank you, Papa, and good night."

"Good night, beta, and try to sleep."

CHAPTER 27

IN THE MORNING, Bharti and her father went to three hospitals where the burnt unidentified patients were taken. The staff at all the hospitals was most cooperative and showed them the list of all the patients admitted. Alas, they had no luck.

Bharti told her father to attend to his business as he had some foreign clients to attend to. She had a strong conviction that Vijay was alive; so every morning, for the next two weeks, she went with a driver and visited all the hospitals where patients were taken from the slum fire.

Nearly two weeks had passed by, and she visited each and every hospital possible, but there was no sign of Vijay despite her vision earlier that he was still alive. She was starting to believe that he may be dead. Sadness instilled in her life; she didn't talk to anybody very much, and she had forgotten how to smile. Her personality had totally changed, and she was no longer the fun-loving person she was before losing Vijay.

The slum dwellers complained but repaired their burnt jhuggies; however, life had become near normal in the slum. When anybody talked to Bharti about Vijay, tears rolled down her cheeks, unstoppable at times.

One evening, two weeks after the fire, Bharti was sitting down with her father in their family room when he came over to her, put his hand on her back, and softy said with tears in his eyes, "Beta, I cannot see you withering away as I saw your mother. Please take a hold of yourself and try to get busy with your work as those children in the slum need you to take care of them, especially after the fire, or if you like, we can go back to England where all your friends are and leave everything to God Almighty!"

She got up and hugged him and whispered with tears trickling down her cheeks, "I am sorry, Papa, I am causing you pain. I promise you, I'll try to go back to work to help those poor children." She did not want to give up on Vijay but thought if she helps others, perhaps God will bless her and reunite her with Vijay.

Nandita Basu kept on reporting, keeping track of the people injured in the slum fire and following up on the compensation promises made by the minister.

"This is Nandita Basu reporting today live at the National Network exactly two weeks after the huge fire at the slum complex where it is believed that two hundred and ten people died and thousands were injured. Whereas the home minister had promised to pay compensation to all the injured and the families of the deceased, not a penny has been paid so far. The lists have been made and completed except for some minor discrepancies, but most are clear-cut cases. They have been submitted to the home minister's office, but no action has been taken."

She paused and then continued, "People are living in appalling conditions, and nothing has been done about the toilets and the showers. The home minister said he would look into it, but we have heard nothing about it. People are becoming very frustrated and talking about taking the law in their own hands. Now I will take you to those hospitals where the injured and the burnt are being treated. This video was shot over the past two days. In this Burns Ward, there are about fifty patients critically injured or burnt, still recovering from the devastating fire."

She showed a video of the patients; one of them seemed to be calling the cameraman toward him, and his name was shown as B. J. Khatri.

The same evening, Vijay's mother was watching that video on the news as she liked watching all the stories reported by Nandita Basu.

Suddenly she shouted, "That's my Vijay!" She called up Bharti and said, "Bharti, I think I saw Vijay in one of the video clips Nandita showed on the six p.m. news!"

"But, Mommy, I have visited every hospital and gone through every patient," replied Bharti.

"I don't know the hospital that patient was in, but I remember the name on the bed. It was B. J. Khatri. Also, he seemed to be saying something and calling Nandita and the cameraman. His hands were in bandages, and his face was covered with a net tent."

"Okay, Mommy, I will call Nandita and find out."

Bharti called Nandita and said, "Vijay's mother claims that she saw Vijay in your last report, which was just flashed on the six p.m. news. Vijay's mother believes that the patient named B. J. Khatri seemed to be Vijay. Can you please look it up and let me know which hospital that patient is in?"

"I seem to remember that patient. He was trying to call the cameraman toward him. I'll call you back in about half an hour."

"Thanks, Nandita."

"You're welcome, anything I can do."

Bharti was very anxious and started praying to God.

In a few minutes, Mr. Kapoor arrived, and she ran up to him and said, "Vijay's Mommy called and thought she saw Vijay in one of the clips Nandita Basu showed on the six o'clock news today."

"Did you call Nandita?"

"Yes, I did, Papa, and she said she'll call me back soon. I'm anxiously awaiting her call."

"I will quickly freshen up. In the meantime, you tell Tara to make me a cup of tea."

"Okay, Papa."

"Tara, Vijay's mother thinks she has seen Vijay on TV, in a hospital."

"Oh really, that's fantastic news."

"We don't know for sure, but we will find out soon. You make the tea."

"Okay, Didi."

Mr. Kapoor came down; they had tea and were waiting for Nandita's call.

Bharti said, "It has been over an hour, but Nandita has not called, it's not like her."

"She might have gotten busy, why don't you call her?"

Bharti called Nandita and asked, "What happened, you didn't call me?"

"I'm going to that hospital with Joy. I was going to call you after confirming so that you don't get disappointed."

"That's very considerate of you, Nandita, but I'm very anxious, so please tell me which hospital you are going to?"

"I'm going to the All India Institute of Medical Sciences, and that patient was in the Burns Department."

"Okay, I'm coming there too."

Mr. Kapoor consoled her and said, "Let's go."

They went to the hospital, but the hospital staff stopped them as no visitors were allowed at night.

Bharti asserted, "I'm not a visitor, I'm a doctor." And she flashed her ID card.

They went to the Burns Ward and were looking for the patient marked B. J. Khatri.

Nandita and Joy were already in the ward and were looking for that patient too. They met each other, and they all went to that patient's bed.

Vijay jumped up seeing Bharti. Mr. Kapoor and Bharti both started crying; the ward nurse came and told everybody to be calm and said, "You are disturbing the patients."

Bharti started crying and, with her hand on his shoulder, whispered, "Thank God I have found you, and now I'm going to take care of you. I missed you so much."

Mr. Kapoor and Nandita held Bharti's hands and assured her, "Now that you've found him, calm down and be happy."

Bharti asked the nurse, "What is this? There are no facilities here for visitors to sit down."

The nurse replied, "This is a general ward for the poor."

Bharti asked, "Can I see the doctor on duty?"

The nurse pointed toward the end of the ward. "There is his office. You can go and see him there."

Bharti went to the doctor and introduced herself.

The doctor said, "I remember seeing your picture in the paper."

Bharti asked, "Please tell me about the patient named B. J. Khatri."

The doctor looked at his charts and informed her, "He has first- and second-degree burns on his face below the nose, on the mouth, specifically on his lips and on his chin. Second-degree burns on his neck, chest, and both his hands. Both his hands are bandaged as the burns are a little deeper. His face is in the tent. When he arrived here, he was unconscious, and because he had first- and second-degree burns on his face and hands, he was sedated, and after a week, he said his name was B. J. Khatri, but he couldn't speak too well. He kept calling for Aarti again and again."

"How is he now, and what are his chances of recovery?"

"He's doing very well on his lips, his face has almost recovered, but his chest is going to take a little longer."

"Is this a general ward for the poor?"

"Yes, it is."

"We would like to move him into a private room, and we will pay for it, if there is a room available."

"You will have to do that tomorrow morning. Patients don't get moved at night."

"What are your visiting hours?" Bharti asked.

"Visiting hours are three p.m. to six p.m., and it is posted in the main lobby. But you can come in the morning and arrange a private room or whatever is available with the doctor in charge of the Burns Ward."

"Thank you very much, Doctor. He's my fiancé. If you have any problems or if you need anything, please call me." And she gave her cell phone number to him.

"Yes, of course, Doctor, we'll take good care of him."

She went back to Vijay and said to him, "I love you, the last fifteen days were like fifteen years. Don't say anything, and I will take care of you. Tomorrow morning, we will move you out of here to a private room or to another hospital."

Bharti praised Nandita, "Nandita, you are doing a fantastic job!" And she hugged her and Joy.

Nandita replied, "I'm only doing my job, we're so glad we've found Vijay." And she had tears in her eyes.

Joy also had tears in his eyes and said, "God is great, we have got our friend back."

The next morning, Bharti woke up at seven and went to her father's room and asked, "Papa, I couldn't sleep all night. Are we going to the hospital, or do you have some important work to do?"

"None of my work is more important than your happiness, and we will do everything possible to look after Vijay, and that's my priority number one."

Bharti and her father went to the hospital and talked to the doctor in charge of the Burns Ward.

Mr. Kapoor said to the doctor, "We are interested to move one of your patients to a private room, and we will pay the cost, whatever it may be."

The doctor asked, "Which patient?"

Bharti said, "The patient named B. J. Khatri, but his real name is Vijay Shastri."

"How did we get the name wrong?"

"Because he could not speak too well as he has burns on his face, lips, neck, and hands."

"Can he speak now?"

"Maybe, he can a little."

"Okay, we can go over to him, but your face looks very familiar to me."

"I'm a pediatrician, and my name is Dr. Bharti Kapoor."

"I remember now, I saw a picture in the newspaper, in an article about the world conference of pediatricians."

"That's correct, and Vijay is my fiancé."

"We'll see what we can do for you, Doctor."

They went over to Vijay and asked him, "If your name is Vijay Shastri, just nod your head."

He nodded his head and said, "Bharti, I love you."

Bharti replied, "I love you too, and don't speak anymore."

"I'm satisfied." He picked up his report, changed the name to Vijay Shastri, and continued, "He's recovering very well, but he might need some plastic surgery. It is best to leave him in this hospital rather than moving him out to another hospital, and I will see if I can arrange a private room for him."

Mr. Kapoor remarked, "That will be very good. In fact, it would be good for the poor people too. You will we be able to give the bed to another poor patient."

"Oh yes, there are patients lying in the corridors, and we have an acute shortage of beds in this ward for the poor people. This shortage has been created because of the thousands of people who got burnt in the slum fire and other fires, which is common at this time of Dushehra celebrations."

"Can I stay with him?" Bharti asked.

"Yes, when Vijay has a private room, you can come and go as you please. This is a General Burns Ward, and we have a lot of patients in this ward. We don't allow anybody to stay with the patients here."

"Very well, when is he expected to be moved to a private room?"

"Let's go to my office and check what's available."

They went to the doctor's office, and they found one VIP room available.

The doctor said, "I cannot give you that room as it is reserved for VIPs, in case anybody comes."

"Who can give us this room?"

"The administrator of the hospital has to release this room to us."

Bharti and her father went to meet the administrator and requested him to release the room. He said to Mr. Kapoor, "I know you very well. You may not remember me, but I met you in England and you looked after me."

"Yes, I remember, you were attending a conference and Bharti and I both met you."

"I also remember Dr. Bharti. She was finishing her specialization in pediatrics as she told me then."

"Are you a pediatrician too?"

"Yes, I am, but I am now working as an administrator of this hospital. Although that private room is reserved for VIPs, I'll give it to you as you are as good a VIP as anybody who comes with the minister's letter. May I ask who do you need the room for?"

Bharti informed, "For my fiancé who was burnt in the slum fire near Gurgaon."

"Oh, what a tragedy that was!" the doctor said with a heavy voice.

A tear trickled down Bharti's cheek.

"No please, we will look after him. We have the best Burns Department in the country. The head of our Burns Department is a plastic surgeon who is highly educated and acclaimed from America."

"Oh really, I didn't know that," Bharti said.

"Thank you very much, Doctor. If I remember right, you play golf, don't you?" Mr. Kapoor asked.

"Yes, I do."

"How about a game of golf with me? I am a member of the Delhi Golf Club."

"It will be my pleasure."

"I will arrange it and get back to you soon," Mr. Kapoor said.

Mr. Kapoor and Bharti got back to the office of the doctor in charge of the ward and said, "We have arranged everything with the administrator."

"Yes, I know, he just called me and has released the VIP room to me, and I have asked my staff to move Vijay into that room as soon as possible."

"Just to tell you that Vijay's father and his family are here to see him, and they are over there with Vijay now."

"I was a student of Mr. Shastri, and I have a lot of respect for him."

"I understand that you are a plastic surgeon?" Bharti asked.

"Yes, I am. I moved from America to be in my own country and to look after my old parents."

"That is commendable," praised Mr. Kapoor.

"There are some Indians in America who call their parents over there and then treat them like babysitters and servants," Bharti remarked.

"Yes, I know, it is a shame, their values have changed. Anyway, you can come back in about two hours and see him in the private room."

"Thank you very much, Doctor."

They went to Vijay's bed, and the whole Shastri family was there along with Pehalwanji and Ajay. After greeting everybody, Bharti said to Mrs. Shastri, "Mommy, we have arranged a private room for Vijay. Let's go to my house, and we'll come back in two hours."

They all went to Bharti's house as it was very close.

Mr. Kapoor was in the process of welcoming the Shastris to his house when just at that time, Bharti got a phone call from Nandita.

She said, "I have news for you, four men have been shot at point-blank range in the slum!"

"How did that happen?" Bharti asked.

"You know the arsonists who were caught by Vijay and Ali were set free on bail last Friday. On Sunday, they came to the slum with two other hoods and tried to grab some land from a couple of the widows, who lost their husbands in the slum fire. Do you remember that man whose horses were injured in the fire? Well, he shot the hoods at point-blank range."

"Yes, his name is Badal. What happened to him?"

"He was very upset because two of his horses were partially burnt in the slum fire. He had to put them to sleep. He loved his horses and has only one horse left now. Apparently, he acquired a gun and was waiting for the hoods to come back. The hoods were trying to grab the land very close to his stable. He took this opportunity, went over there, and shot all four hoods at point-blank range. They didn't have a chance."

"What happened to Badal?"

"He has disappeared. The police are investigating, and nobody's telling the police who shot the hoods."

"Thanks, Nandita, and Vijay will be moved to a private room today."

"That's really great, bye for now."

Bharti came back and asked Tara to get breakfast ready.

Mr. Kapoor said, "I have already instructed the chef to prepare some stuffed *parathas*. Maybe you can get some other things made to go with breakfast."

"Okay, Papa, I will take care of it."

Mrs. Shastri said, "We had some breakfast in the morning, and we don't want too much."

Bharti said, "Let's have some brunch. We will be going to the hospital, and I don't think we'll get lunch anywhere. Would you like to have some milk, tea, or coffee?"

"Masala chai will be fine. In fact, if you get that made first, it will really be appreciated."

"Of course, Mommy, I will get that made right away."

Mr. Kapoor sat down with them in the living room and said, "She's so glad that we have found Vijay. He will be all right."

"Given the circumstances, do you think we should postpone the wedding?" Mr. Shastri asked.

"Let us take Bharti's opinion."

When Bharti came back, Mr. Kapoor asked, "Bharti, do you want to postpone the wedding plans, given that Vijay is not fully recovered?"

"In my opinion, Vijay should be better within a few days, but I have not seen his neck, chest, and hands. So once I see them and discuss it with the doctor, I should be able to evaluate his recovery period."

"I think we should not postpone the wedding, yet," Mr. Kapoor said.

"I would rather get married and look after him after getting married as in my mind, I'm married to him already."

"As long as you can live with his scars, I have no problem," Mr. Shastri replied.

"Papa, I just said, I'm married to him through my mind, body, and soul. I don't care about his superficial looks. It is the person behind the mask that matters. A face is just a mask, hiding the real personality of his person, and it is his soul that is united with mine." Tears flowed down her cheeks while speaking.

Mr. and Mrs. Shastri were overwhelmed. Mrs. Shastri got up, hugged Bharti, and asserted, "I know how you feel, and I know you love my son very dearly, so we will do exactly what you want to do. Don't worry, I will make sure that your wishes are fulfilled."

Bharti hugged Mrs. Shastri very tightly and said, "I love you, Mommy." And still crying, she went on to say, "I lost my mommy earlier, but I have now found another." And she hugged her again.

Tara brought tea and biscuits and said, "Breakfast will be served in ten minutes."

While eating breakfast, Ajay said, "You have put out quite a spread, Tara."

The table was laden with dishes like stuffed paranthas, yogurt, fresh fruit, *poori alu* (a kind of bread and potato curry), hot milk, tea, coffee, cereals, dates and nuts, and sweets.

"We just wanted a simple breakfast. Who is going to eat all that?" Mrs. Shastri said.

"Bharti is going to eat all that as she has not eaten for the last two weeks, ever since Vijay was lost. The rest of you eat whatever you like," joked Mr. Kapoor.

"Yes, Papa, I'm going to eat all that today, and I will take some paranthas and yogurt for Vijay too."

"I'm going to eat the paranthas. They look so good, and the flavor is so appetizing," Ajay said.

"Just go for it. You've come to my house for the first time, and I have had food at your house many times."

"I wish Pehalwanji had come too, rather than going back to his house from the hospital."

"He had some work to do," Ajay replied.

They finished eating and went to the hospital. They found that Vijay had been transferred to a private room; they went to his room and found to their delight that he didn't have the tent on his face anymore.

"I love you, and you are looking great. How do you feel?" Bharti softly asked.

"I feel great, now that you have come," replied Vijay.

Mr. and Mrs. Shastri were overwhelmed to see him; tears came out of their eyes. Mr. Shastri said, "Be strong and you will be all right."

Bharti took the paranthas and yogurt for Vijay and asked, "Do you want to have some paranthas?"

"I was on a liquid diet till yesterday. The nurses have been feeding me through a tube. Only this morning, I had some custard by mouth. I will try a parantha."

Bharti fed him the parantha and said, "You look wonderful, and I love you."

"Now that you're here, I will get better very soon. Tell me the truth, how do my face and lips look as I have not seen a mirror in the last two weeks?"

"They look fine. Now tell us, how did you get burnt?"

"We were going through the slum complex and helping people put out the fires when I heard a little boy calling my name. He was trapped in his house and was calling for help. I went inside the jhuggie. He was surrounded by fire, so I leaped in, pulled him out, and told him to run out. As I started to run out, a burning wooden beam fell on me. I put my hands up and tried to push it away as I was trying to save my head. It was too heavy for me to hold, and I fell down with the beam on my chest. I pushed the beam up with my hands and slid out from underneath. I was overwhelmed by the smoke. At that point in time, the beam was still burning furiously. I must have fainted with smoke inhalation. Next I knew was that I was in the hospital with bandages on my hands and chest and they were asking my name."

There was a silence for a couple of minutes, and then Vijay broke the silence and asked, "May I ask you something, Bharti?"

"Yes, of course, ask me anything."

"How come nobody came to see me for two weeks?"

"It is very simple, we didn't know where you were! They had the wrong name on your chart. Do you think we didn't look for you? There was not a single moment when I wasn't thinking about you. For the last two weeks, all I have done is to go from one hospital to another hospital looking for you. Finally, it was your mother who spotted you on the television in one of the reports televised by Nandita. Everybody was looking for you. We didn't leave any stone unturned in your search. Do you know I have not slept for the last two weeks, ever since you went missing?" Bharti got it off her chest all at once and started crying.

"How could that happen? I told them my name," Vijay said.

Bharti spoke while sobbing and crying, "When you were brought to the hospital, you were unconscious, your lips and chin were burnt, you could not speak too well, and they got your name wrong. They wrote down your name as B. J. Khatri."

"I'm sorry, please forgive me, come over and give me a hug. Lying in bed, I kept wondering as to what had gone wrong. I kept calling your name, but they wouldn't let me move or get out of bed. One day, I saw Nandita and the cameraman. I tried to call her to come over to me, but she did not pay any attention," Vijay said while holding Bharti.

"It was all a big misunderstanding. God has tested our love, and now we are going to be together forever."

"You know, you've lost weight, what's left of you is only skin and bones."

"I didn't feel hungry, I couldn't care less about eating, and all I wanted to do was to find you. Now that I have found you, I'm going to eat like crazy and grow to be a big fat mommy."

Vijay laughed.

"It's good to see you laughing." And they all left except Bharti who stayed till the night and left after kissing him on the cheek with a promise to come in the morning. In the morning, Bharti hugged him lightly and asked, "How are you feeling, my darling?"

"I'm fine, and get me out of this hospital as soon as you can. It seems I have been locked up in this place forever."

"Don't worry, I am here with you now, and I will take good care of you."

"What is my condition? These doctors don't tell me anything."

"Your lips and chin have healed quite well. Your hands and chest have slightly deeper burns. The plastic surgeon is coming to see you today. We will know better once he has made his assessment."

"You are a doctor, can't you tell?"

"I'm a pediatrician. My field of specialization is children's diseases and not dermatology or plastic surgery."

"When is Diwali?"

"Today is Tuesday, and Diwali is next Sunday."

"Can you please ask the doctor when I can go home?"

"I certainly will, and I'll tell him that I want him to release you, in my care."

"So where will you take me?"

"Where would you want to go?"

"I want to go to my parents' house as I want to be close to my mother."

"It is understandable, your mother has the greatest right on you. We'll do as per your mother's wishes."

"By the way, when are my parents coming to see me, did they say?"

"I think about noontime. Your mother wants to bring some food for you."

"Oh, fantastic, I'm dying to have some home-cooked food."

Just at that time, the doctor in charge of the Burns Department arrived along with a nurse and three interns.

"How are you feeling, Mr. Vijay Shastri, alias B. J. Khatri?" the doctor asked.

"I'm feeling much better, now that Bharti is here."

"Very well, let's examine you."

The nurse opened the bandages on his hand and asked Bharti, "I'm going to take off his bandages from the chest. Do you want to watch this as this may be disturbing to you?"

"No, nurse, it will not be disturbing to me. I am a doctor, so you go right ahead and take off his bandages."

"Yes, Doctor." And she took off the bandages from the chest.

The doctor and the interns examined him, and Bharti also had a good look at the wounds.

The doctor said, "He has recovered quite well on his lips, face, and the chin and has almost healed in most areas whereas the chest and the hands need further recovery. The chest will have to be bandaged. However, his hands need not be bandaged anymore, but, Vijay, you will have to be very careful while using your hands for some time."

"When can I go home?" Vijay asked.

"In a couple of days, I will examine you again, and hopefully, we can discharge you at that time. That is, if Dr. Bharti takes responsibility for looking after you."

Bharti jokingly remarked, "I don't know about that. Sometimes he doesn't listen to me and can be a pretty bad boy."

"I promise, I will be a good boy," assured Vijay.

The doctor instructed the nurse to bandage him up again with new dressings on his chest only, and then he left with his interns.

The nurse said, "I will be back soon with the new dressings. In the meantime, leave your chest uncovered."

The nurse returned in about five minutes and put on the medication and the new bandages on his chest and left.

"So where will you take me?"

"I suggest you come to my place for a day or two. In case something goes wrong with you, this hospital is very close to my house. In any case, I have my clinic in the house, which will be quite handy. I have a lot of medicines and will order some more painkillers, etc., as per your needs."

"That's fine. Maybe my mother and Pooja can come to stay there too."

"Who will look after your father? He needs your mother. Maybe Pooja can come and stay with us. Then we can go to your house for a couple of days, and finally we will move to your condo."

"That's a good plan."

"What's happening with Ajay and the boys?"

"They have all been worrying about you, and ever since they found out that you're feeling better, they are all very happy and will come to see you today, later in the afternoon."

"How is the slum complex, any improvements?"

"For the last two weeks, I've been holding my clinic there. Some construction is going on, but the whole complex is still in shambles, and it looks like people are living in ruins."

"I heard the home minister went to the complex and promised to pay some compensation."

"Nobody has seen a rupee yet. My father distributed some five thousand blankets, and he is planning to distribute more blankets next week. He's also planning to give some more aid in the way of building materials to the slum dwellers, but most of his time has been spent in your search."

"How is his business?"

"What business? He has not attended his office in the last two weeks. In fact, he postponed the opening of his new corporate office in Gurgaon. The new building is ready, the offices are all furnished, he just has to make a decision to do the opening ceremony and move the corporate offices from a building in GK 2 to this new building in Gurgaon."

"How big is the new building?"

"It is a five-story building with close to thirty thousand square feet of office space."

"So is he moving the whole operation there?"

"For now, he's moving the corporate headquarters and part of the software development operation."

Vijay's parents arrived with food; his mother hugged him gently with tears flowing down her cheeks.

"Mommy, I am okay, please stop crying."

She said, "I'm happy now."

His father, Pooja, and Chemeli all had tears in their eyes and said, "We are so glad to see you."

They fed him his favorite stuffed cauliflower paranthas and yogurt.

"Bharti, when will he be discharged from the hospital?" asked his mother.

"Hopefully, in a couple of days."

"Is he coming home to us?" Mr. Shastri asked.

"Well, he will need some looking after and medical care. I was hoping you will allow me to take him to my place in Golf Links. That way, he will be closer to this hospital, and I can always bring him here for dressing changes, etc."

Vijay's father looked at his mother and asked, "What do you think, Mom?"

She said, "Whatever is good for Vijay is good for me. I'm happy with that arrangement as long as he's not too much of a burden on Bharti and her father." She then looked at Bharti with an inquisitive look.

"He will be no trouble for me or my father. In fact, this plan was suggested by my father, and it'll be my pleasure to look after him. If Pooja wants to come and stay for a few days with him, she is most welcome too."

"I will come for a few days," Pooja said.

"You can come and go as you please, Pooja. In fact, everybody can come and go as they please."

After staying in the hospital for a while, Mr. Shastri said, "I think he's in good hands, and we will leave as I have a few things to take care of at the new school construction site."

Vijay asked, "How is that going, Papa?"

"Very well, we have almost finished digging the foundation and will begin construction after the Diwali celebrations."

The Shastri family left. Soon after, Ajay, Ali, Joy, and Nandita arrived.

Vijay was up and sitting in a *chair*.

"How are you feeling, my buddy?" Ajay asked.

"I'm feeling much better and am getting back to my normal routine. I did some yoga exercises this morning."

"That's really great!" said Ali. "Show me your burns. I have a special herbal ointment that my father and I made. It is working wonders with the slum guys burnt in the fire," he continued.

"Show it to me," Bharti asked.

Ali gave the ointment jar to Bharti.

Bharti opened the jar and remarked, "It looks like a cream, only it has a beige color. I am a doctor, and I'm not supposed to believe in herbal medicines, but I believe you, Ali, so we can apply a little bit on his hands, chin, and neck. But I don't want it to react with the other medicine, so we won't apply it on his chest where the nurse had applied the medicinal cream."

Ali said, "It will not react with any antibiotics. It is made from herbs. Still, if you feel happy, you can apply it only on the other areas."

Bharti washed her hands, wore gloves, and then applied the ointment Ali brought.

Nandita was feeling guilty, so she came close to Vijay and whispered, "I'm sorry, Vijay, I should have recognized you earlier."

"Don't worry, Nandita, it was not your fault. My head was in the tent. Anyway, it was written in my fate to be separated from Bharti and you people for two weeks. Lying in bed, I had a lot of time to think about things and problems of the slum, which I don't normally think of. When I get better, I'm going to persuade my father to stand in the election for a member of parliament to change the course of this nation, to help the poor and homeless first. Otherwise, I see a very bleak and dangerous future. I'm scared of things to come, and it is going to be dangerous for everybody. Poor people are going to come out on the streets, grab what they can, and kill without a cause, without caring or knowing about who they are killing."

Joy remarked, "You're right, Vijay, there is some sort of movement in the slum. People are very hush-hush about it. They are very upset about the broken promises. The whole atmosphere in the country is deteriorating. There are problems in Gujarat. The flood victims have not received the compensation promised by the government. In Mumbai, the slum clusters are being replaced by shopping malls, making thousands of men, women, and children homeless. They live on the streets, have no home, and yet go to work. This is our labor force. All of these men still go to factories from the sidewalk. There is *ashanti* [upheaval] all round, how long will it last, and how long will it be before it erupts like a volcano?"

"Lying down in the poor man's ward, I've heard of events to happen. It is scary, but it seems unstoppable. The government should have seen it coming. They have neglected the poor and the labor class for too long. Let us hope that the hardworking middle class doesn't pay for the mistakes of the government," Vijay remarked.

"I hope you guys are not serious!" exclaimed Bharti.

After a long conversation, Nandita and the boys left.

CHAPTER 28

IN THE NEXT two days, Vijay continued to improve; and finally, that day came when the doctor released him from hospital.

Bharti took him to her residence in Golf Links. Mr. Kapoor welcomed him, "Beta, this is your home and feel free to do whatever you like to do."

He called all the house staff and explained, "Vijay is a member of this family, and he needs special attention. So I'll expect the same kind of care as you'll provide to any member of this family."

They said that they were all very happy to have him there and would look after him.

"What is Vijay's condition, Bharti?" Mr. Kapoor asked.

"He has shown tremendous improvement, especially with the ointment that Ali brought. His chest is quite tender and has scabs on it, his hands have healed quite well, and his face and neck are fine. I talked to the doctor today, and he has allowed him to take a shower without putting any water on his chest," Bharti informed.

"Very good, maybe you can pretend to be his nurse and give him a shower."

Bharti smiled and replied, "I can give him a shower anyway."

"Whatever you do is your business, and can I go to the golf club for the evening?"

"Yes, of course, I'm here to look after him."

Bharti instructed the chef to have dinner ready at eight p.m.

The chef asked, "Do you want anything special, madam."

"Make a nice butter chicken and *naan* for Vijay Sir."

"Yes, madam."

Bharti took Vijay upstairs; he was to stay in the guest bedroom next to Bharti's bedroom.

"Do want me to give you a bath or a shower, honey?"

"Actually, I would like a shower, if in some way you could cover my chest."

"Yes, I can tape plastic all round your wound on the chest, but you have to be very careful while taking a shower."

Bharti put some plastic on his wound on the chest and taped it up all around so that it sealed perfectly.

Vijay took a shower while Bharti was watching him.

She wiped him with a towel very gently; Vijay kissed her gently and asked sheepishly, "Is there any way we can make love?"

"You must be feeling better! And yes, where there is a will, there is a way."

Bharti made love to him, being very careful of his wounds.

Vijay continued to improve; his hands and face were completely healed, but he still had a scab on his chest. However, when he put on his shirt, one could hardly tell that he was once badly burnt.

"Do you want to go over to your parents?"

"I would like that."

"Do you want to stay the night there, or do you want to come back here tonight?"

"I think we can spend the night in our condo as I have not been there for a while."

"That's a brilliant idea, that way, we can have our own celebration tonight."

"In that case, we don't need a driver. I will take you in my car as your car was returned to your company."

"I haven't phoned my company at all."

"I did inform them, and as far as they know, you are still missing. We should tell them only when you are fully recovered as I don't want them to impede your recovery."

"I think I should phone them after Diwali and tell them the whole story truthfully."

"Yes, that's a good idea."

Bharti and Vijay went to his parents' house.

Vijay's parents were very pleased to see them. The whole family gathered around conversing with Vijay and Bharti over a cup of tea.

Pooja remarked, "I don't see any marks on Vijay Bhaiya's face or neck!"

Bharti said, "This is a wonder of modern science and cosmetics." And she smiled.

Vijay said, "Didn't you know, she was a theater artist, and she always did her own makeup."

"Well, I must say, you have done a very good job, Bharti Bhabhi."

Mrs. Shastri asked, "Your wedding is next week. Do you want to change the plans, or do you want to go ahead and get married on the planned date, Bharti?"

"I want to go ahead and get married next week. What do you say, Vijay?"

"It's fine with me."

"Very well then, we will inform all the guests."

"Mommy, if it is okay with you, we want to go and see Ajay and all my friends for a while. We'll come back and have dinner at home," Vijay informed.

Vijay and Bharti went to Ajay's house; they were all ever so pleased to see the lovebirds together.

Geeta said, "Welcome, Vijay Bhaiya, we're so pleased to see you, and you are looking good as ever."

Vijay and Bharti hugged everybody; they all remarked about how good he was looking and that there were no scars on him.

"Little bit of makeup doesn't hurt anybody." Bharti smirked.

Ajay said, "Is that what it is?" He paused and went on to say, "Bharti, it is your love for him, which has saved him." He turned his face toward Vijay and remarked, "Do you know, Vijay, while you were missing, Bharti was like a fish out of water."

"I feel very ashamed for passing those remarks in the hospital that nobody cared or looked for me," apologized Vijay in a very humiliated tone.

"It was all a misunderstanding, and anybody in your condition would have thought the same," Bharti said.

"Ajay, I want to go and see Ali and Hakimji [herbal doctor], thank them for the ointment they sent for me, and show them my chest wounds."

"Do you still have wounds on your chest?"

"Yes."

Bharti, Vijay, and Ajay went to Hakimji.

"We will have tea when you come back," Geeta said.

Ali and Hakimji examined his chest.

"It is healing very nicely. Now we have to change the ointment as scabs are forming on your chest."

"Okay, sir, whatever you propose," Vijay said.

Ali said, "I will have to prepare the ointment, and it may take a couple of hours. If you want, I will bring it over to Ajay's house."

"That's fine, we're going over to the slum complex."

"That's a very good idea as they were all asking about your welfare," Ali informed.

"How are they doing anyway?"

"They all come to Baba [father] and me, and we're giving them free treatment."

"You must be having financial hardship."

"We are surviving."

Bharti called her father and said, "Papa, here is something you can do for the people of the slum."

"What is that, beta?"

"You know, Hakimji is treating the slum folks without charging anything. I think you could help by getting the herbs and other raw materials he needs."

"Consider it done, beta."

She discussed the matter with Hakimji and Ali, and they said, "If we can get the raw materials, that would be great."

"You give me a list of what you need, where we can purchase it, and it'll get delivered to you."

"Thank you, Bharti," said Ali.

"You are most welcome, and thank you very much for treating Vijay."

As Vijay, Ajay, Ali, and Bharti entered the slum complex, everybody came out of their shops and homes and started saying, "Long live Vijay Bhaiya and long live Bharti Didi."

People ran behind their car as they had to go slowly through the marketplace into the middle ground. A crowd gathered around the car.

They asked, "Are you all right?" And they started touching Vijay.

Bharti said, "Please, don't touch as he is very badly hurt."

Ali and Ajay pushed people away from Vijay. Bharti requested Vijay to get inside the car to save him.

Some people said, "He looks okay."

"He's not okay. His chest was badly burnt and has large wounds on it," Bharti said.

Mohan and Joy also rushed to the slum on Mohan's two-wheeler scooter, hearing that Vijay had gone to the slum, anticipating that he might be mobbed by the slum dwellers out of love and affection. Mohan got up on the car and spoke in a loud voice, "Please get back and don't hurt the person you love. He is here because he cares for you, so please stay back."

Some of the slum dwellers also joined in to push the people back. When a comfortable distance was created between the car and the people, Vijay came out of the car. He was overwhelmed by the love and affection shown toward him by the slum dwellers. As he started to talk, a couple of slum dwellers brought a table over and told him to stand on it.

Vijay started off and said, "I love you all, my brothers and sisters. What is it that you want to tell me?" And he opened up his shirt buttons to show them his wounds.

Some of the women started crying; others said that they were very sorry to see him suffer, especially given that he was hurt saving the lives of slum dwellers.

A couple of men started shouting the slogans, "Long live Vijay and Bharti." And then they requested, "We want you to represent us in parliament, we want you to help us, we want you to be our leader."

One of them shouted, "These corrupt leaders have to go, and there has to be cleansing of bad blood. We trust you with our heart, mind, and soul, so please help us, and we will do anything for you, we will give our lives for you."

Vijay stood up on the table and said, "I will consider your request to run in an election, but in any case, I will look after you. My first job is to get you compensation and the toilets and showers you need. We must start rebuilding the homes that were burnt, and for that, Bharti's father has also agreed to help you. Please make a list of what you need to put a roof over your heads, and Bharti's father and his friends will send you whatever they can, free of charge to you."

People were gathering as he was talking. There was quite a crowd gathered in the middle ground, and it looked like an election meeting held by a leader.

The whole slum complex was filled with the sound of applause and cheers for Vijay and Bharti.

One woman started shouting, "Our Lord Rama has returned. It is Diwali time, and on that day, Lord Rama returned to his kingdom after defeating the evil king Ravana."

Another said, "He has come back from the jaws of death as a Savior for us!"

Vijay asserted, "I'm not Lord Rama. I'm just an ordinary human being just like you, people. We are all sent to play our role on this stage called life. I will play my part, will try to change the system, and work toward eradicating corruption. Nehruji said, 'The leaders are not born, but they are made during traumatic times.'"

"That's enough, you will hurt yourself. Your chest is quite weak. Let's go," Bharti said.

Vijay said, "I will be back." And he came down from the table. They got in the car and drove away very slowly through the slum complex with people following them all the way.

They reached Ajay's house with Mohan and Joy following them. Ali went home to prepare Vijay's ointment.

Everybody went inside and sat down around the dining table. Geeta brought samosas, sweets, and chai for everybody.

Joy asked, "You were not expecting us, so how come you made chai for us too?"

"Whenever Vijay Bhaiya comes, the whole gang comes over, but at other times, nobody visits us."

"You have become a leader now, Vijay, and the speech you delivered was very impressive. You committed to stand for election, were you serious?" Ajay asked.

"I don't know, Ajay, it just happened on the spur of the moment. Now I will have to think about it seriously."

"I have a solution. Maybe Vijay can ask his father to stand in the election. Maybe we can all persuade Mr. Shastri to do so," suggested Bharti.

"It's a very good idea and a plausible one too. Mr. Shastri is also a very experienced man and is respected by the people of this colony as well as the slum. Leave it in my hands and let Nandita and I work it out. In the meantime, you people try to convince Mr. Shastri," affirmed Joy.

"It's a great idea," Ajay said.

Bharti suggested, "How about your father? Pehalwanji is very well respected in both the colonies too."

"My father is neither a politician nor a diplomat. If somebody spoke nonsense to him, he would probably punch his nose, or at least tell him to get lost. Anyway, he would never agree as he is quite content minding his own business."

With that thought, everybody left, wishing happy Diwali for the next day.

Vijay and Bharti went to Vijay's house, and they sat down with the family for dinner.

"Mommy, is the dinner ready? We would like to have dinner early as we want to go shopping, if we can, after dinner."

"Yes, it is ready. I made all your favorite dishes. Eat to your heart's content."

"I don't really have the same appetite as I used to, but I will give it a try."

They had dinner and then their favorite, *rasmalai*, for dessert.

"Can we go? We have a lot of shopping to do for Diwali," Bharti asked.

"We have opened up the spare bedroom for you, Bharti, and Vijay can sleep in his own room. You might as well stay here as in any case you have to come back here for Diwali *pooja* [prayer] tomorrow."

"Mommy, we have to go for Diwali *pooja* to my house too. Papa wants us to go to his office first to do *pooja*. After that, we were planning to go for *pooja* in the Golf Links house and then come here. Papa wanted to come here too, with us."

"If that's what you want to do, it's fine with me," Mrs. Shastri said.

They reached the condo, and the security guard said, "Welcome back, sir, we heard you were not well."

"I'm fine, and happy Diwali." He took out a five-hundred-rupee note from his pocket and handed it to the guard.

It is customary to give some money to employees at Diwali. Just like in the West where workers are given a Christmas bonus, in India, they are given a Diwali bonus. It is also customary to exchange gifts among family members.

They went into the condo, and Vijay said, "It is quite dusty in here."

After going through all the rooms, Bharti remarked, "It's not too bad in the bedroom, but the living room is worse than the other rooms."

Vijay called the guard and asked, "Is there a maid who can clean our condo, and we will pay her for it?"

"I know you have come back after three weeks. I will see what I can do, and if I can find one, I'll send her up right away."

Bharti said, "If not, I can do it." And she started cleaning the bedroom.

In a few minutes, they got a knock at the door.

Bharti opened the door and asked, "Have you come here to clean the condo?"

"Yes, madam, I work two doors away as a nanny to the children. As I was going out, the guard told me that you need your condo cleaned. Is it very dirty?"

"You can see for yourself."

The woman walked around with Bharti and informed her, "I'll have it cleaned up in no time. Give me a vacuum cleaner, duster, and a mop."

The cleaning woman worked very hard; and within an hour, she had the whole condo, including the kitchen, all cleaned up.

"You are very good," complimented Bharti.

"I like cleanliness. I have a small house, but I keep it clean."

Vijay took out a five-hundred-rupee bill and gave it to her.

"Thank you very much," she said.

However, Bharti was not happy, and she took another one thousand rupees and said, "This is for Diwali for your children."

She said, "So much! I work as a nanny all day for thirty days, and I only make two thousand rupees."

"Have a good time and have a happy Diwali. Thank you for coming in at such a short notice and that too after a whole day's work at night. If you ever need anything, come and see us," Vijay said.

"Thank you very much! You have really made my Diwali a happy one." And she left.

Vijay asked, "Do you want to go shopping now, or do you want to stay home and have a glass of wine? I have an unopened bottle of red wine."

"It is too late to go shopping. Let us celebrate our being together, again."

Vijay went to open the bottle, and Bharti said, "Please, don't put pressure on your chest. I will open the bottle."

She opened the bottle and advised, "You have to be very careful about what you do till the time your chest wounds are completely healed."

"Yes, Doctor Ma'am."

Between sips of wine, she said, "I have been meaning to tell you that I stopped taking birth control pills ten days ago."

"So last time when we made love, you had no protection?"

"I had met you after two weeks, and you wanted to make love. I didn't have the heart to say no to you."

"What if you get pregnant?"

"Nothing, we will have the baby, and there are no two ways about it. So it is imperative that we get married next Saturday as planned."

"Yes, I agree with you, let's not tell anybody."

"Of course not, let us hope everything goes as planned."

"Even if it doesn't, we will get married, and that I promise."

"No more lovemaking, let us not take any more chances as I cannot even start taking birth control pills in case I'm pregnant."

Vijay said, "That's settled. Let us watch the news, and let's see what is happening in the world."

The news anchor started, "Today is Saturday at ten p.m. on the eve of Diwali. We now present a special report on Diwali in which we will show you how different segments of society are celebrating Diwali, highlighting the disparity between the rich and the poor, followed by a special report by Nandita Basu.

"Look at the hustle and bustle in the markets. People are busy shopping, and the markets and the malls are full of shoppers. People are buying whatever they can lay their hands on. The stores are so busy that they have long lineups at the checkouts.

"We are now in a rich neighborhood of Delhi. When we asked the people here how they were celebrating Diwali, most said they were celebrating with their family and had bought gifts, new clothing, sweets, and firecrackers for their children and relatives. Some said they were having an all-night gambling session, and when asked how much they planned to gamble, the answer was up to five hundred thousand rupees.

"Next, we went to a slum complex and asked them the same questions, but their answers were quite different! They said that they didn't have food to eat, so how did we expect them to buy sweets, new clothing, and firecrackers to burn?"

The reporter said, "Every child expects these things at Diwali."

The reply was, "We are at the mercy of our employers and rich people in neighborhoods close by. We will accept, with thanks, whatever they hand out to us, new or old clothing, sweets and fire crackers, or leftover food."

The anchorman said, "It is a shame on us, on our country, and on the society as a whole that there is no minimum standard of living, that there is such a disparity in the country."

The anchorman said, "Now we present to you a special report by Nandita Basu."

"I'm in the slum where there was a devastating fire on the Dushehra day. Whereas the home minister promised compensation within a week, no such promise has been kept. Poor people are suffering and are still waiting for the compensation. I followed up with the home ministry, and I was told that the home minister has sanctioned the compensation, which is now held up with the clerks of the ministry. When I was coming out, I saw a lady with three children sitting outside the office, demanding compensation for her husband and her jhuggie. All her belongings were burnt in that devastating fire. She told me that the clerk is demanding 5 percent of the check upfront before he releases the money. She further said 5 percent of six hundred thousand rupees is thirty thousand rupees, and she did not have even three rupees to her name. They are all corrupt. They said this money was shared from bottom to top. The home minister may not be corrupt, but if his department is, he is responsible for it. He's not looking at the plight of the poor people. He should order his department to release the checks immediately so that poor people can get on with their lives. Here is what the poor woman said. You can hear her for yourself: 'My children and I are starving and have not had a decent meal in two weeks. We are forced to beg whereas when my husband was alive, he had a good job and our children were going to school. It was the hoods of one of the ministers who made us homeless and took away the father of my children.'

"In the meantime, it is all quiet in the slum complex. Diwali will be celebrated here too, but the spirit of Diwali will be missing. It is being celebrated on a low-key basis with sad hearts and old clothes to wear. Please help these poor people, come over here and show your generosity, and see for yourself, in contrast to you, what they have and how they are living. I guarantee you that you will be safe, and God helps those who help others," appealed Nandita Basu.

"That was Nandita Basu, a champion of the poor. It is unusually quiet all around the country. There are no incidences of violence from anywhere in the country. Maybe, it is the calm before the storm," remarked the news anchor.

Vijay and Bharti went to sleep arm in arm as they usually did.

In the morning, Vijay was up and back to his usual routine of yoga exercises.

"Rise and shine, sweetheart," Vijay whispered.

Bharti looked at Vijay's chest wounds and said, "It is healing very nicely, some of the scabs have come off. I will tape on your chest, and you take a shower, then I will clean up your chest wounds and apply ointment on them."

"But Ali did not bring the ointment over as he promised."

"I have his old ointment. Maybe I can put that on."

"Let me call Ali." Vijay called Ali and asked, "Where is the medicine you were going to make for me?"

"We did not have a couple of ingredients. I phoned Mr. Kapoor for help, like Bharti said, and he is sending a driver over in the morning with all that we need."

"I guess it will be about noon by the time you get here."

Bharti took the phone and said, "If my driver is coming to you with the ingredients, can you make him wait for Vijay's medicines? He can then bring them to us here as he knows Vijay's condo."

"Will do, and that will save me a trip as I am very busy making medicines for the slum dwellers."

Bharti called up her father. "Good morning, Papa, happy Diwali."

"Happy Diwali to you both, and what time are you planning to come home?"

"Have you sent the driver to Ali?"

"Yes, he left an hour ago. He had to pick up some herbs and things from old Delhi side, and then he will go to Ali."

"When the driver returns from Ali, he can pick us up on his way back. One more request, I was thinking it'll be great if we can send some sweets over to the slum complex to distribute among the children there."

"I already did that yesterday. I ordered a truck full of sweets to be delivered to the slum complex this morning."

"Oh really!"

"This morning, two of my staff members are going to make sure that the boxes of sweets are distributed to the children living in jhuggies. I also called Ajay this morning and requested him to help with his friends in making sure that this operation goes smoothly."

"Oh, Papa, you're the best, and how did you think of that?"

"I wanted people's blessings for Vijay's recovery."

Bharti's eyes filled up with tears, and she complimented him, "Thank you very much, Papa, you have to be the greatest father on this earth."

"This is not the only thing we're doing for the slum people. My friend owns a factory that manufactures corrugated tin sheets, the kind that goes on temporary roofing. Today, two trucks loaded with sheets are going to reach the slum complex. They will be distributed free of charge to the people who need them the most, and they'll be told that the sheets are sent by Vijay and Bharti and are free of charge."

"That will bring happiness into the slum complex. Do you have the cell number of the driver you sent?"

Mr. Kapoor gave her the cell number of the driver and said, "He will see a missed call and will call you back when it's convenient as while driving, he's not supposed to talk on the phone."

"That's fine. We want him to pick us up and bring us back to Golf Links."

"Very good! That way, we can be together for the whole afternoon, do the *pooja* at home, at the office, and finally at Vijay's house."

The driver brought the ointment, and Bharti applied it on Vijay's chest. They arrived in the afternoon; and in the early evening, Mr. Kapoor, Vijay, Bharti, and the whole house staff sat down to do *pooja*. Bharti sang a *bhajan* (hymn), and everybody joined in.

After the *pooja*, Mr. Kapoor asked Bharti and Vijay to distribute bonuses to his house staff and personal drivers and told them, "You can go home now and have a very happy Diwali."

They all thanked him for his generosity, and one of his old drivers said, "My children have grown as you know. You put them through school and college, and my wife is away to her village. I would like to be with you and will take you wherever you want to go."

"What about Tara, where is she going?"

"She is spending the evening with the other staff members in their quarters at the back as they are all having a get-together."

Mr. Kapoor, Bharti, and Vijay, along with the driver, went to do *pooja* at all the places they were supposed to and ended up at Mr. Shastri's house. After the *pooja*, Chemeli informed them, "Dinner is served."

Mr. Shastri said, "Mr. Kapoor, please join us for dinner, but it is only vegetarian food."

"That's fine, on Diwali day, we eat vegetarian food too," remarked Mr. Kapoor.

They all sat down for dinner, and as they started eating, Vijay got a call on his cell phone, "Hi, Nandita, happy Diwali."

"Happy Diwali to you too. Did you hear the news?"

"No, I didn't, what's special about it?"

"A curfew has been imposed in the Union Territory of Delhi. All the borders have been closed."

"But why?"

"Incidents of shootings have been reported, all over the city."

"Oh really?"

"Reports of assassinations are coming in from Bihar, Lucknow, and Mumbai."

"What has happened? It was all calm this afternoon."

"The president of India has called for an emergency meeting with the prime minister and home minister, and the army has been called in. Just keep watching the news, and I will call you later if there is any new development."

"Thanks, Nandita."

Mr. Kapoor and Mr. Shastri were very inquisitive and asked Vijay, "What happened?"

"Nandita called, and she said that a curfew has been imposed throughout the Union Territory of Delhi. Several people have been shot. We will hear the details in the news."

CHAPTER 29

V IJAY WENT AND switched on the
television.

"Breaking news: We have confirmed that several members of parliament and
bureaucrats holding high positions in the government have been shot. This seems
to be a planned widespread operation throughout the country. The news is coming
in from Lucknow, Mumbai, and various other cities as well. Several members of the
legislative assemblies have also been shot. All we know at this time is that there is a
piece of paper left at the crime scene, marked PPA. A curfew has been imposed in
various cities, including the Union Territory of Delhi. An emergency meeting has
been called by the president to discuss homeland security. We will keep you posted,
and we'll be back with this breaking news."

After a little while, the anchorperson reported, "We interrupt our regular
programming to bring you an update on the recent assassinations. In fact, this news
is of national importance. Therefore, we have suspended our regular programming
and have set up a monitoring panel to bring you updates all the time from now
on. These assassinations were so well organized that they have been planned and
orchestrated on a national level. There have been reports from Haryana, Punjab, UP,
Bihar, Bengal, Gujarat, and Mumbai, not to mention the Union Territory of Delhi.
Several members of local legislature have been shot and taken to various hospitals.
We infer that PPA stands for the Poor People's Army. It is obvious to us that the
poor people in this country have been neglected and the system is so corrupt and
corroded that, even in emergencies, the wheels of the system don't turn without
greasing. But it is incredible to see the poor people organized in such a fashion as to
cause devastation on a national scale. There is talk that it could be orchestrated by
a foreign country. We don't think so, and you will also arrive at that opinion if you
review what has happened in the past four months in this country. There were floods

in Gujarat, which made millions homeless. Promises were made, but to date, people are waiting for those promises to be fulfilled. Bihar is riddled with corruption, and the poor man lives in fear of gangs protected by the corrupt politicians. In Mumbai, we see the trend of demolition of slums. Working people have been made homeless, and grand malls are being built on those sites. Look at the case close to our home where a whole slum was burnt to the ground by arsonists, who supposedly had links with the local minister. The home minister promised them compensation, which is still to be paid.

"Now we present to you a report from a crime scene by our investigative reporter, Nandita Basu."

"It is ten p.m. We are here at the residence of a member of parliament who was shot and has been taken to the hospital. Police have cordoned off the area. From what I understand, a courier van with a driver and a helper arrived here at seven p.m. to deliver a parcel, supposedly from another member of parliament. The van was stopped by the security guards and checked for explosives and guns. After that, it was allowed to enter to deliver the parcel. While the helper carried the parcel, the driver went with him supposedly to get a signature, but instead, he pulled out a gun with a silencer and shot the member of parliament and several other household staff. The driver, along with the helper, quickly got back in the van and drove off. The security guards at the gate thought that firecrackers were being fired by the children, being Diwali evening. It was only after a man came out of the house bleeding that the security guards realized what happened and the police were called. Several members of parliament and other senior staff of the government have been shot with the same modus operandi in all cases. It seems the perpetrators had taken the courier vans from a national courier service with the conveyance of somebody in their van yard. This operation has all the signs of careful planning. We were told by the security guards that the same van with the same driver and helper came here a day before and delivered another parcel of sweets. The remarkable point to note is that all the vans had arrived at exactly seven p.m. at all the crime scenes, which shows that the operation was meticulously planned and implemented on a national scale. Furthermore, the time of their operation was carefully chosen to be when Diwali firecrackers being fired are in full force such that it is hard to differentiate between the sound of gunfire and that of the crackers. We are told by the police that they left a piece of paper with PPA stamped on it. This is Nandita Basu with cameraman Ray Bose reporting from one of the crime scenes on the evening of Diwali."

The Shastri family, along with Mr. Kapoor and Bharti, were sitting in the living room and watching television. Chemeli came and asked, "Would you like some tea?"

Mrs. Shastri said, "Yes, of course, and, Chemeli, please make arrangements for Mr. Kapoor to sleep in the guest room, and Bharti will stay in Pooja's room. Just put a spare bed in Pooja's room."

Pooja went to help Chemeli.

"I'm sure I can get home," Mr. Kapoor said.

"It will not be safe to go back. There is going to be a long lineup at the border, and it is likely that the police will turn you back. Our house is not as comfortable as yours, but we'll try and make you feel as comfortable here. I can give you a new set of *kurta pyjama*," Mr. Shastri said.

"What will happen to my driver?"

"Before we ate, the food was sent to your driver. He can probably sleep in the car. Otherwise, I can get my neighbor to open up his garage which has a washroom and a bed so your driver can sleep there while his driver is away."

"That'll be fine," Mr. Kapoor said.

Bharti had an amazing personality to find pleasure in little things and was fun loving too. She suggested, "It will be fun if we can play cards till midnight like the old times when we use to live in a small house in London."

"Mr. Kapoor can stay in my room as it is more comfortable with the attached bathroom, and I will stay in the guest room," suggested Vijay.

They all played cards till past midnight and went to sleep.

At six a.m., Mr. Shastri got up, and after his morning chores, he put on the television to watch the six thirty morning news before going for a walk.

Vijay and Mr. Kapoor also woke up and came into the living room.

Mr. Shastri asked Mr. Kapoor, "Did you sleep well?"

"Yes, I slept like a lord."

Quietly they listened to the news.

"We bring the news to you as it happens, when it happens. Now the latest on last night's shootings and curfew is that the police and the army have sealed off the city. In fact, curfew has been imposed in Mumbai, Lucknow, Patna, Chandigarh, Calcutta, and various other cities. Delhi Police have seized more than one hundred courier vans and have taken several hundred people in their custody for questioning. Many international flights have been diverted to other cities close by, where there is no curfew. Some flights have landed, and after intense checking, tourists have been sent to the hotels and have been told to stay in their hotels and not to go out. Other passengers have been allowed by police to go with the relatives who had come to receive them. It is the same situation with the trains. All trains have been suspended till further notice. No trains were allowed to leave since nine last night, and many evening trains were held up due to police checking. The president of India is due to deliver a speech at eight a.m. Most probably, he will declare a state of emergency. For now, there is curfew in all parts of the city of Delhi. Police are advising not to travel in or out of Delhi."

Mr. Shastri asked Mr. Kapoor, "Do you want to go for a walk for about an hour?"

Mr. Kapoor said, "I don't have proper shoes to walk, so please go ahead, and I will be fine here with Vijay."

Pooja and Bharti also got up; Pooja went to the kitchen and told Chemeli to make a pot full of masala chai.

"Good morning, Papa, and good morning, Vijay."

"Did you sleep well, Bharti?" Vijay asked.

"Oh yes, Pooja and I were chatting, and I dozed off. The next thing I knew, it was morning and I heard some voices in the living room. So what is happening?"

"They've caught quite a few people, and the president is addressing the nation at eight a.m.," informed Mr. Kapoor.

"The wedding is next Saturday, and we have people coming from abroad starting tomorrow!" Bharti said in an anxious tone.

"The news must have reached abroad too."

"I think everything will be under control within a day or two."

"I think so too," Vijay said.

Mr. Shastri also returned from his walk and said, "My friends think it is a vigilante group formed by the poor in the slums of India. Maybe the government will pay more attention to the poor now. I think the police and the army will have the situation under control within a day or two."

"The government will have to pay more attention to the poor now. But we also need somebody in the government who is totally committed to the cause of the poor, like you, Mr. Shastri," Mr. Kapoor said, pointing at Mr. Shastri.

"Me, no, I'm too straight to be a politician."

"That's exactly what we need – an honest, straight person who is liked and respected by the people. I heard the slum population wants to make Vijay their leader."

"I have no objection to Vijay becoming a politician to help the poor."

"But he will need your support, he's not experienced enough."

"I'm too old for that job."

"No, you're not. You're much younger than the other politicians. I think the father-and-son team will be a great idea, and I, along with my friends, will support you all the way."

"I don't know."

"You can do it, Mr. Shastri. You don't need to be at the school. There are others who can look after that function. For example, Pooja can look after the school very well. Please think about it seriously."

"Yes, Papa, you will make a great leader. You are calm, calculative, and you plan. You have all the qualities of a leader, and Vijay is like you. I'm sure that the slum people would want you, as well as Vijay, to represent them in the parliament," Pooja said.

"What are your thoughts, Vijay?" Mr. Kapoor asked.

"I am seriously thinking about it. I also think it'll be a great idea if Papa stands in the election. Even all my friends and Pehalwanji were of the same opinion too," Vijay said.

"Please think about it seriously, and I will talk to a couple of politicians I know."

"All right, if you insist, I'll think about it and will talk to Mrs. Shastri."

"What was there to talk to me about? I think it is a great idea. You've always tried to help the poor, and you have been frustrated by these politicians many times. This is your chance to be in command and make a difference. Stand in the election, and I'm sure you will win, and you will be a voice for the poor, which you have always wanted to be," Mrs. Shastri said.

"Okay, I will also talk to my friends and promise I will think about it seriously." And he went to his room to get ready.

"Papa, I want to tell you that I don't really want to delay our wedding plans, even if it means having a wedding in our house, on a low-key basis."

"Understood, but sometimes, things are not in your hands. Let's wait and see what happens. Last time, when Vijay was missing, we did not inform anybody because of your intuition that he would be found. This time also, I'm not going to inform anybody for a couple of days. Let's wait and see. In the meantime, I will talk to the hotel manager to find out what instructions they have from the police regarding hosting the wedding parties," Mr. Kapoor said.

"Thank you, Papa."

"It is eight o'clock, let's watch the news."

"We bring live to you this very important president's address to the nation televised on all stations in India.

"Here is the president of India: 'I am saddened to hear that some people have taken the law in their own hands. They have killed several members of parliament and members of local state legislatures. I therefore find it necessary to declare a state of emergency in the country and dissolve the parliament of India as well as local legislatures of Bihar, UP, Haryana, Punjab, and Maharashtra. We will review the situation tomorrow, and my office will issue a statement. In the meantime, curfew has been imposed in many cities. I expect all of you, the citizens of India, to cooperate with the police to catch the culprits who shot and killed some innocent lawmakers and other citizens. I do not believe that this is a religious issue, nor do I believe that there is a hand of a foreign government. Please stay calm, and we will have the situation under control within a day or so. The army has been called to help control the situation in the larger cities. Once again, my humble request is to stay calm and cooperate with the police, Jai Hind.'

"We now bring to you the latest on the shootings. As we reported earlier, many have been shot dead or injured. We do not have the final tally. As it comes in, we will bring it to you on the hour, every hour. In the meantime, we expect the curfew to be lifted for a few hours starting at twelve noon, possibly till four p.m. There will be a four-hour window for trains, buses, and planes to leave and arrive. We are monitoring the situation minute by minute, and we will interrupt our regular programming to bring you the latest news on this very important national issue."

"We will keep the television at low volume. In the meantime, let's get ready and have breakfast," Vijay said.

"Is the water situation okay in this complex?" Bharti asked.

"We don't have any shortage of water in this complex. I have placed fresh towels in everybody's washroom, so please go ahead and take a shower," Pooja informed.

"Do you want anything special for breakfast, Bharti Bhabhi?"

"No, whatever you are making for everybody."

"I'm making stuffed cauliflower paranthas."

"That's lovely, and do you have homemade yogurt to go with it?"

"Yes, of course."

They all got ready and started eating breakfast.

Between mouthfuls, Mr. Kapoor remarked, "This is like the old times. When I was young, the whole family would have breakfast together like this on Sundays. It is really good to be together. I'm having a great time."

"Sure you are, Papa. You can eat all you want without anybody stopping you."

"Sometimes, you should be just my daughter and not my doctor."

"All right, Papa, just think whether you want to play with your grandchildren or not because if you're sick, you won't be able to play with them."

"Okay, I will take care."

They finished breakfast. It was now 10:00 a.m., and the newscaster reported, "Police have arrested several hundred people throughout India under the National Emergency Law. That situation is totally under control in Delhi, Mumbai, and Haryana. The curfew will be relaxed from eleven a.m. to five p.m. There are several police check posts set up in all major cities, and the police have been given powers to arrest, without warrants, any person involved in any kind of suspicious activity."

"What is the plan? Do you want to go with me as I need to go home to change and possibly go to my office?" Mr. Kapoor asked.

Mr. and Mrs. Shastri suggested, "Stay for lunch and then go."

"I'm full with breakfast and will probably skip lunch. Please, there is no formality."

"I would like to go to my condo," Vijay said.

"I need to go there to dress your wounds and to apply medicine."

Mr. Kapoor, Vijay, and Bharti all left after saying bye to the Shastri family.

Mr. Kapoor asked his driver, "How was your night, and did you sleep well?"

"Yes, sir, I slept in the room behind the garage. It was very comfortable."

"Good, let's leave Bharti and Vijay at their condo."

"Very well, sir."

"When will you come home, Bharti?"

"Most probably tomorrow."

Mr. Kapoor dropped off Bharti and Vijay and informed them, "I won't come up as I have many things to do."

"That's fine, Papa, and thank you very much."

"I want to sleep for a while as we were up talking till late," Bharti said.

"That's fine, even I want to rest for a while."

Five hours passed by.

"Oh my god, I slept for five hours."

"So have I," Vijay said.

Bharti looked at Vijay's chest, cleaned his wound, and applied the new ointment that Ali had sent through the driver.

"How does it look?" Vijay asked.

"It is looking very good. I think in a couple of days, you should be able to take a shower without covering it, but you will still have to be careful."

Vijay called Nandita and asked, "What's new, Nandita?"

"Not much except that the minister, whose hoods were killed by Badal, has been shot dead."

"By whom?" Vijay asked.

"We don't know yet, it is too early. Apparently, the police have arrested quite a few people along with a few from the slum complex too."

"I hope it's not Mohan."

"It is not him as he was there this morning."

"Police are very hush-hush being a national emergency."

"What's happening with the curfew?"

"It will probably be lifted for the daytime starting tomorrow."

"You know, our wedding is on Saturday evening."

"You might have to take special permission from the police. No weddings and no gatherings are allowed."

"Thanks, Nandita, please keep me informed."

"I'll call you as soon as I have something new."

"Have you seriously thought about going into politics?" Bharti asked.

"Yes, I want to go into politics because I want to help the poor, but it all depends on you whether you want me to go into politics or not. After all, you are my life partner, and I would need your support, all the way."

"Yes, Vijay, I'll support you till the time you stay honest and don't let the power get to you. Very often, I've seen people change when they come into power or money."

"Did your father change when he came into money?"

"Yes, slightly, but his change was gradual and he's a very balanced man. When you go into politics, you become a leader overnight, you become a celebrity overnight, and you become powerful overnight."

"What you are saying is very true. If I do become a leader, please keep reminding me of that."

Bharti stayed at Vijay's condo for a couple of days to look after him. They kept having discussions about politics and finally decided that Vijay should stand in the next elections to be a member of parliament for India.

Vijay phoned his workplace and told the whole story to his boss.

His boss remarked, "I am so glad that you're okay. You had us worried for a while when your father called and said you were missing."

"I'm much better now and am still getting married on Saturday. Do you remember?"

"Yes, I do, but I wasn't sure given the circumstances."

"Well, it is on, and are you coming, sir?"

"I certainly will, even if it is just to see you. And when are you planning to join the office?"

"We are going away to Australia for our honeymoon. I'll join the office as soon as I'm back, which I expect will be in about three weeks."

"Very good, it'll be nice to see you in the office, and I'll send your car back with the driver right now as you'll need it."

"Thank you very much, sir."

"I must go back now. For all intents and purposes, the curfew has been lifted and you're feeling much better than before except for some scabs on the chest. Just keep in mind that your chest is still very tender, so you must be very careful, which means no lifting or hugging," advised Bharti.

"Yes, Doctor."

"I mean it, no hugging people. Do you want me to drop you at your parents' house?"

"My boss said he's sending my car back with the driver."

"Oh, that's nice of him," Bharti remarked and left for her house.

Bharti reached home and asked her father, "Were you able to talk to the hotel manager?"

"Yes, everything is a go." And he hugged her. "You are going to get married on Saturday as planned, and somebody is here to see you."

Bharti was in the process of asking who, and suddenly, her very excited auntie from Australia said, "Hello, Bharti, congratulations, I am here to attend your wedding."

"I'm very happy to see you." And they hugged each other.

"Now it looks like a wedding house, and I am feeling the excitement of getting married." The very next minute, she turned all sad and remarked, "I wish my mother was here as she always said that she would dress me up for my wedding."

Bharti's auntie whispered, "I cannot replace your mother, but I will dress you up." She hugged Bharti and continued, "Your uncle was telling me not to go as there is a curfew and there are problems in India. I told him if they can have the wedding, I will not miss it for my life as Bharti is the only niece I have."

"Thank you, Auntie." Bharti hugged her with tears flowing from her eyes.

The wedding took place as planned in a grand manner. The only restriction was that the party had to be finished by ten o'clock as the curfew started at eleven. The hall was decorated with flowers again; only this time, there was only one bar on one side and on the other side was the wedding *mundap* where the wedding ceremony took place.

The groom's side, *barat* (entourage), entered the hall at 6:00 p.m. The pundit performed the ceremony of uniting the families by chanting the mantras. Vijay was dressed in a white *sherwani*, and he waited for Bharti to come into the hall. Bharti entered the hall with her bridesmaids, looking stunningly beautiful in a red sari with gold embroidery. They stood facing each other for a *jaimala* (garland ceremony). Amid the guests watching and cameras clicking, the movie camera was rolling and applause resounded in the hall as Vijay and Bharti exchanged fresh flower garlands.

Mr. Kapoor announced on the microphone, "Thank you very much for coming, please enjoy yourself, drinks are being served at the bar, dinner is served, and in a few minutes, we are going to start the wedding ceremony. Because of a shortage of time, please help yourself to drinks and dinner, and the wedding ceremony will be performed simultaneously."

The wedding ceremony started in the wedding *mundap*, and people started eating and drinking concurrently.

This was a Hindu wedding in which a *havana* was performed. Vijay and Bharti performed the *havana* with the help of the pundit. Finally, to complete the wedding, they went around the fire seven times, taking seven vows. Close family, sat closely, witnessed the wedding ceremony. When the wedding was complete, everybody threw flower petals on Vijay and Bharti. Vijay and Bharti then joined the crowd to have dinner and to meet their guests.

Finally, Vijay's family took the *doli* (bride); Bharti's brother, Raju, helped Bharti sit in the car with Vijay and gave her a send-off by kissing her with tears in his eyes. Her father also had tears in his eyes and was feeling very sad that he was losing a daughter and a friend. On the other hand, he was very happy that she had found a life partner and a soul mate.

Bharti was welcomed into the Shastri home. Vijay's room, where Vijay and Bharti spent their *suhag raat* (first night), was decorated with flowers.

CHAPTER 30

THE NEXT DAY, Vijay and Bharti left for their honeymoon to Australia as planned.

They had a fantastic time in Australia. Bharti moved in with Vijay in the condo.

Vijay returned to his job, and his office staff was very happy to see him back.

On a Saturday morning, a month after their wedding, Nandita called and asked, "Can Joy and I come over to see you?"

"Yes, of course, come for lunch."

"No, we'll come in the evening and have tea with you."

Vijay asked Bharti, "Shall I call up Ajay and invite the gang over too for a cup of tea?"

"Sure, they haven't come for a visit ever since we have been married."

Vijay called Ajay.

"Hello, stranger, have you finished your honeymoon, or are you still in bed?" taunted Ajay.

"No, Ajay, we've been very busy with family dinners. What are you doing in the evening?"

"Not much."

"Why don't you, Ali, and Mohan come over and have a cup of tea."

"What's so special about this evening?"

"Nandita and Joy are coming over, so I just thought we'll all get together."

"Sure, I'll go and ask Ali and Mohan if they can come. I'll come for sure around five p.m."

"Try and bring those two with you."

Bharti baked a cake and made some *pakoras* to go with the tea and asked Vijay, "I have some *rasmalai* in the fridge too. Is that enough?"

"Sure, that should be enough."

Joy and Nandita showed up at five, and the security man informed Vijay of them.

Bharti opened the door, hugged Nandita, and said, "Welcome and come on in."

Joy handed a bouquet of flowers to Bharti.

"Thank you very much, but this was not necessary," Bharti softly said.

They sat down, and Vijay asked, "Anything new, Nandita?"

"I've heard that the president of India is calling for elections of the federal parliament as over eighty members of parliament have been assassinated. If you're interested, I can talk to the newly formed labor party president to give you and your father party tickets to stand in the elections."

"When do you expect the elections?"

"Probably in the middle of January 2014."

Bharti said, "Go ahead, and we'll appreciate your help."

"I'm agreeable, but I would like to know the party platform. Why would they sponsor me in the elections as they don't know me from Adam?" Vijay remarked.

"Oh yes, they do know you and your popularity in the slum complex, which is a vote bank of fifty thousand votes. They also know all about you and your father. The party workers keep their eyes and ears open. The fact is, the president of the party asked me if I knew you or your father and if I could arrange a meeting between you and him at the earliest."

"Oh really, that's wonderful news especially since Vijay didn't know where to start and we were talking about it just yesterday," Bharti said.

Vijay said, "Go ahead, Nandita, and arrange a meeting."

The security guard called again. "Three of your friends are here, sir."

"Please let them in."

"That must be Ajay, Ali, and Mohan."

"That's wonderful! I never get a chance to meet these guys," remarked Nandita.

They all hugged each other.

Bharti said, "Gently, don't forget he still has tender skin on his chest."

"I brought another ointment for him," Ali informed.

"That's great because the last one is just finishing."

Bharti went to the kitchen to make tea; Nandita went with her to give a hand.

They brought out the tea. Vijay and Ajay went to help to bring out the snacks Bharti had prepared.

Vijay asked, "Nandita, give us an update on the shootings. Who were the culprits, and how did it all happen?"

"It was a countrywide operation. They have arrested hundreds of people and brought in hundreds more for questioning. The investigation is not finished yet, but the gist of it is that a dismissed senior police officer and a retired lieutenant colonel Patil were responsible for masterminding the whole operation. From what I understand, a police officer named Vir Bahadur Singh was dismissed and jailed on fabricated charges by the corrupt officers. His house was taken away, and his wife left him for a corrupt officer as he could not support the rich lifestyle she was used to leading. Vir Bahadur Singh moved to a slum complex in Mumbai, where he bought a *pukka*, but a small house, and was respected very well as he was always helping the poor."

"What about the colonel?" Bharti asked.

"He was very upset with the army as he did not get his deserved promotions and was surpassed many times for one reason or the other because he refused to pay lip service and refused to obey his senior officer's orders to accept substandard goods for the canteen stores, when he was in charge of the CSD [Canteen Stores Department]. He was finally dismissed on fabricated corruption charges and refusal to accept his senior's orders. He lost his house and bought a house next door to Vir Bahadur Singh in the same slum where they became close friends."

"What triggered the plan of assassinations?" Vijay asked.

"More than three years ago, a process of demolitions started, whereby the slums were removed and shopping malls were built with the connivance of corrupt politicians, city officials, and some corrupt judges, thereby rendering thousands of people homeless. One of those slums was where Colonel Patil and Vir Bahadur Singh were living. That's when they both started planning as they used to meet for drinks anyway. Last year, a shipment of handguns with silencers was hijacked while being transported from the ordinance factory to the government agencies. The guns simply vanished, without a trace, and they did not even reach the underground market. Next, they compiled lists of all the corrupt politicians, officers, and a few judges."

"The list must be a mile long as there are hundreds and thousands of corrupt politicians, police officers, judges, and other senior government officials all over India," remarked Bharti.

"There aren't that many corrupt judges and senior police officers of the police, but the government department officers are really corrupt, and of course, the politicians are mostly corrupt," Nandita said.

"It was a well-planned national operation that required funding. Was there a foreign country involved?" Ajay asked.

"To my knowledge, there was no foreign hand in this operation. Yes, it was a very well-planned operation, which required a lot of travelling, and the colonel did the travelling and the recruiting. The colonel was instrumental in reviving the *shakha*, all over the country. Most of the *shakhas* were instituted in slum all over India, and that's where he recruited the people for this operation," Nandita said.

"It must have taken months of planning, recruiting, and training!" Vijay remarked.

"Yes, the colonel did all that. Then there is one question that remains, and that is where did he get the funding? The answer to that is very simple – that he did not require a lot of funding as most of these people were not paid. They were disgruntled, motivated, and ready psychologically to take revenge. The colonel was very clever in screening and selecting such people. He chose only those who had lost everything and were ready to die to take revenge against one of the politicians or the bureaucrats who had done harm to them or to their family," analyzed Nandita.

"Surely, there must be a team of confidants involved in this kind of operation?" Bharti asked.

"Yes, there was. It was not difficult to build up a team of people who were ready to die for him as he was working against the politicians who caused distress to the poor people. He had to have a few confidants, and they all came from his slum complex. The name of one of his accomplices is Kalu, the driver. Last month, he was involved in kidnapping the son of a rich builder. He was paid the ransom money and is supposedly absconding with the money."

"Was Kalu living in the slum which was partially demolished, Mumbai *bandh* was called, and the whole city was shut down for a couple of days?" Bharti asked.

"Yes, I think so. Why, did you know him?"

"Yes, he was our driver for a couple of days, but we were doubtful of his suspicious activities," Vijay said.

"We didn't trust him from the very start as he was greedy and sounded like a militant. I'm so glad that we didn't trust him."

Nandita said, "Whatever the outcome, the new government will have to change their priorities and focus on the poor people who are the majority in this country."

"I knew something like that would happen. The politicians were busy filling their pockets, and now look at the result!" affirmed Vijay.

"It was inevitable. The corrupt politicians had to go. One way or the other, it is sad that so many innocent poor people had to suffer and so many lives had to be lost to bring about this change," Joy said.

"Why don't you stand in this elections? You are well respected in the slum, and you are dedicated to the cause of the poor," Vijay said.

"I am an introvert, and I only have education in music. I can only serve the people through my music," Joy said.

"The purpose of my visit was to convince you, Vijay, to stand in the election and be a voice of the poor in the next parliament. You may have to sacrifice things in your life, but unless we have honest people like you, this corrupt system will never change," Nandita said.

"All right, I will try, if Bharti is with me."

"It is settled then. I will talk to the party president and will get back to you. We must leave now. Joy has to teach a music class, and I have some important work to do."

Bharti said, "From here on, we have to work hard to get Vijay and his father elected so that they can represent the poor in the parliament to help remove the scourge of poverty from this country and to work toward removing corruption from our system."

Everybody agreed and then left after hugging each other.

Mr. Shastri and Vijay both stood in the election, won with an overwhelming majority, and became members of parliament for India. Vijay was given the portfolio of minister for urban development.

Sitting down alone with Vijay, while celebrating Vijay's victory with champagne, Bharti said, "Here is to your becoming a minister."

"Here's to us," responded Vijay.

"What happened to Colonel Patil who they say masterminded the operation of assassinations, and what happened to all the people who they put on trial for killing the politicians and bureaucrats?"

"Most of the people who were involved with the shootings were either shot on the crime scene or were captured and committed suicide later. A few accomplices were caught who did not know Colonel Patil or the officer, Vir Bahadur Singh. They could not find any substantial evidence except that he was running the *shakha*, and a few people identified them but did not give evidence against them. So the courts found that their direct involvement in the shootings could not be proved, hence they were given light sentences. The courts suggested that there had to be another mastermind behind this organization called the Poor People's Army."

"Do you think there was another mastermind?"

Vijay answered with a naughty smile with dimples on his cheek, "If there was, I'll give him a prize for cleaning up the dirty blood."

"Really, I am shocked to hear that so many people were killed and you'll give him a prize!"

"Look at it this way, when thousands of slum dwellers were burnt, and hundreds killed, no emergency was declared. Perpetrators caught by Ajay and me were let go on bail a few days after, and they are still at large. No charges were laid against the minister despite Nandita showing the proof of his involvement to the police. Every man in India is equal whether he's a poor man, rich man, or a politician. The law applies to everybody, and we have to make sure that everybody is dealt with according to the law in the same manner."

"I'm in full agreement with you, Vijay. However, somehow, I feel that we are not criminals like those corrupt politicians."

"Yes, but sometimes you have to fight guns with guns. Those politicians had become so powerful that it would have taken a hundred years or more to bring about a change, and in the meantime, generations would have been lost."

"Tell me the truth. Did you mastermind that operation?"

"When I was lying in the hospital without a name tag, Colonel Patil came to see me. He'd recognized me and told me of his plan. Later, when I got better, he conversed with me several times on my cell phone. I only helped him to polish his plan, and I swear that's all I did."

Vijay got busy in the parliament, and Bharti worked very hard to improve the life of the slum dwellers with the financial help of Mr. Kapoor and his friends.

The president of India, in his address to the nation on Republic Day, January 26, 2014, said, "We are a prospering nation. It is a shame on us that most of our people are still living below poverty conditions. Thirty percent of our population is living in slums. A new parliament was sworn in a couple of days ago, and it must be our top priority to pay attention to the poor of the nation, to remove the slums and provide proper housing for the poor and the downtrodden, and to provide schools for the children and make sure that they're nourished properly as they are the wealth of our nation. We must do everything in our power to remove corruption from our system, which will ensure that nobody in the future will be that unhappy, so as to take the law in their own hands. We are becoming an economic power, but our foundation is hollow and weak. We have learned our lesson. The only way to stop the violence is to deal with the cause of the problem. Poverty and corruption are the two causes and scourges on our society. We must remove them. On the other hand, nobody should think they can get away with killings and murders. They will be dealt with according to the law. Let us remember the Father of the Nation, Gandhiji, who believed in nonviolence. Let us follow his teachings and deal with our problems in a nonviolent, civil manner.

"Jai Hind."

EPILOGUE

A FEW MONTHS later, Mr. Shastri, member of parliament, along with the minister for urban development Vijay Shastri, was due to deliver a speech at India's Independence Day celebration function taking place in the slum.

"We present to you a special report from the slum, where our honorable minister for urban development is about to inaugurate the function for Independence Day's celebration, and here is Nandita Basu with the report," said the anchorman.

Nandita Basu started off and said, "I have two reports for you. First, an interview with Vijay Shastri, our honorable minister for urban development, and then I will take you live to the slum where the Independence Day celebration is going on." And she went on to the taped interview.

"First of all, congratulations on winning the election and becoming a minister. The only question I have is, did you condone the killings of the so-called corrupt politicians?"

Vijay Shastri, composed and calm with Bharti sitting on his side, replied, "I do not believe in violence, and I did not and do not condone killing as a means to an end for any problem. But I must add that the assassinated corrupt politicians had it coming to them as they aggravated too many poor people. Let us now look forward and make it a priority to remove poverty and the web of corruption."

"It is rumored that you had a hand in planning the operations of the PPA. Did you, or any member of your family, plan the operations, or have any connection to the organization PPA, also known as the Poor People's Army?"

"I didn't even know of their existence until after the assassinations. As you know, I was burnt in the slum fire, and after being in the hospital for two weeks, Bharti was looking after me the whole time."

"But you profited the most from the assassinations."

"No, I did not. If I may remind you, I had become popular because I saved the little boy from the burning jhuggie, risking my own life. I didn't want to be a politician, but I stood for election on the insistence of the slum dwellers."

"The police have evidence that the colonel visited the hospital you were in, several times. Sir, what explanation do you have for those visits?"

"The explanation is very simple. He could have been visiting many of the several hundred burnt slum dwellers admitted to the hospital as they were his *shakha* members."

"Thank you very much, Mr. Shastri. I'm sure now people will have no doubt in their minds and can put aside the rumors of you being the mastermind behind the assassinations by the Poor People's Army. Now I take you to the slum where the Independence Day celebrations will be taking place."

Nandita Basu started her live report from the slum.

"Flowers and colorful decorations – with a background of Indian flag bearing colors orange, white, and green – decorate the stage. The front of the stage is decorated with *rangoli* made from flower petals of marigold, white roses, and green leaves. On the stage, the children are all dressed like flowers! It looks like the stage of a birthday party, and why not? It is the sixty-seventh birthday of India's independence. The stage is placed in the center of the slum, on the ground surrounded by over ten thousand small houses. It was erected and decorated by the people of Shastri Colony, which was once a slum. Now a proper paved road is laid, though it becomes narrower, with small shops on both sides of the road. Further into the colony, there is an open ground, which has been turned into a park with a children's playground in it. It is surrounded by small houses, which once were tin shacks. This is overjoyed Nandita Basu reporting from Shastri Colony, which until last year was a slum."

Nandita continued after a short break, "The show is about to start. Joy and his mother are the main organizers of the show with help from Mohan, Ali, and their friends. I see a large motorcade arriving, but this time, instead of bringing the corrupt minister who exploited the poor, it brings to the colony Vijay and Bharti who are responsible for transforming and reforming the slum with the help of their fathers, Mr. Shastri and Mr. Kapoor, and Mr. Kapoor's generous friends. The members of the colony excitedly await their arrival as they truly deserve to be chief guests of this Independence Day function."

A few years later, Bharti and Vijay had a beautiful daughter; and when he saw her playing in their backyard, he remembered his cuckoo accountant's vision.

ACKNOWLEDGMENTS

I AM INDEBTED to my daughter, Dr. Meera Luthra-Kumar, for her unrelenting support and encouragement and her continuous effort in reading, editing, and polishing my manuscript.

I want to thank my son, Anuj Luthra; my daughter-in-law, Savanh; and my granddaughter, Tia, for providing much-needed encouragement.

I appreciate very much the valuable input provided by my son-in-law, Dr. Rohit Kumar, throughout the course of my writing and thank him for that.

I wish to thank my nephews, Sachin and Raman Grover, in India for providing me with invaluable pictures of slums.

I especially want to thank my book cover designer, Sreenath, who goes by the name Hablema in Kerala, India. He designed an incredible cover, and the part where he shows steam coming out of the teacup in the shape of India's map is particularly impressive.

I must also thank Victoria White of Virtual Writer for her evaluation of my script and constructive guidance.

Finally, I am grateful to my beautiful wife, Popi, for putting up with my whims and wishes and providing the much-needed encouragement and support in pursuing my writing passion. Thank you, my darling, for your relentless effort in reading and editing every draft and providing first-line editing for my novel and for encouraging me to finish my novel, which I could not have done without your help and support.